CLIMATE CHANGE, ASSETS AND FOOD SECURITY IN SOUTHERN AFRICAN CITIES

There is overwhelming evidence that the climate is changing. It is the poorest countries and people who are the most vulnerable to this threat and who will suffer the most. This book shows how increasing urbanization and growing poverty levels mean that it is imperative to ask how climate change might impact on asset accumulation and food security for the urban poor. It demonstrates how these three, often separate foci, can be brought together to frame a holistic urban adaptation approach.

Furthermore, although much has been written about climate change, limited evidence exists in Southern Africa of how climate change has been integrated in urban planning. The authors explore the urban climate change nexus linking asset adaptation, climate change science and food security through several case study cities. These include Cape Town, George and //Khara Hais (South Africa), Lusaka (Zambia), Maputo (Mozambique), Mombasa (Kenya) and Harare (Zimbabwe). The results shed light on how this nexus might be explored from different perspectives, both theoretical and practical, in order to plan for a more resilient future.

The book comprises ten chapters which focus on southern African cities, with each chapter written by highly experienced academics, research-focused practitioners and professional planners. Although the book concentrates on southern African cities, the insights that this book presents can be used to understand other urban centres in low and middle-income countries outside of this region and around the world.

Bruce Frayne is Assistant Professor and Director of the Master of Development Practice (MDP) program in the School of Environment, Enterprise and Development (SEED), University of Waterloo, Canada.

Caroline Moser is Professor of Urban Development and Director of the Global Urban Research Centre (GURC), School of Environment and Development, University of Manchester, UK, and Senior Non-Resident Fellow, Global Economy and Development, Brookings Institution, Washington DC, USA.

Gina Ziervogel is a lecturer in the Department of Environmental and Geographical Science, University of Cape Town, South Africa.

CLIMATE CHANGE, ASSETS AND FOOD SECURITY IN SOUTHERN AFRICAN CITIES

Edited by Bruce Frayne, Caroline Moser and Gina Ziervogel

Routledge
Taylor & Francis Group

LONDON AND NEW YORK

First published 2012 by Earthscan

2 Park Square, Milton Park, Abingdon, Oxfordshire OX14 4RN
711 Third Avenue, New York, NY 10017

Routledge is an imprint of the Taylor & Francis Group, an informa business

First issued in paperback 2017

British Library Cataloguing in Publication Data
A catalogue record for this book is available from the British Library

Library of Congress Cataloging in Publication Data
Climate change, assets, and food security in Southern African cities / edited by
Bruce Frayne, Caroline Moser, and Gina Ziervogel. -- 1st ed.
    p. cm.
    "Simultaneously published in the USA and Canada"--T.p. verso.
    Includes bibliographical references and index.
    1. Climatic changes--Social aspects--Africa, Southern. 2. Urbanization--
Environmental aspects--Africa, Southern. 3. Poverty--Africa, Southern.
4. Food security--Africa, Southern. 5. Africa, Southern--Environmental
conditions. 6. Africa, Southern--Social conditions. 7. Africa, Southern--
Economic conditions. I. Frayne, Bruce. II. Moser, Caroline O. N.
III. Ziervogel, Gina, 1975–
QC903.2.A356C56 2011   363.80968--dc23
2011027109

ISBN: 978-1-84971-418-1 (hbk)
ISBN: 978-0-8153-5744-5 (pbk)

Typeset in Times New Roman by
Bookcraft Limited, Stroud, Gloucestershire

CONTENTS

LIST OF ILLUSTRATIONS

List of figures

List of tables

List of Boxes

CONTRIBUTORS

Jane Battersby is a Lecturer in the Department of Environmental and Geographical Science, University of Cape Town, South Africa.

Belinda Dodson is an Associate Professor in the Department of Geography, University of Western Ontario, Canada.

Willemien Faling is a Lecturer in the Department of Town and Regional Planning, University of Pretoria, South Africa.

Bruce Frayne is Assistant Professor in International Development in the School of Environment, Enterprise and Development (SEED), Faculty of Environment, University of Waterloo, Canada.

Gareth Haysom is a Researcher in the African Centre for Cities, University of Cape Town and a Research Fellow in the Sustainability Institute, Stellenbosch University, South Africa.

Grace Lubaale is Director of Eco-Build Africa Trust, Nairobi, Kenya, and is a PhD candidate at the University of the Witwatersrand, Johannesburg, South Africa.

Collins Miruka is Associate Professor of Management Sciences in the Graduate School of Business and Government Leadership, North West University, Mafikeng Campus, Mmabatho, South Africa.

Caroline Moser is Professor of Urban Development and Director of the Global Urban Research Centre, School of Environment and Development, University of Manchester, United Kingdom.

Alfred Omenya is Senior Lecturer in the School of the Built Environment, University of Nairobi, and Director of Eco-Build Africa Trust, Nairobi, Kenya.

Inês Raimundo is Director of the Centre for Policy Analysis, Department of Population Studies, Faculty of Arts and Social Sciences, Eduardo Mondlane University, Mozambique.

Danny Simatele is a Teaching Fellow in Sustainable Development in the School of Geography and Geosciences, St Andrews University, United Kingdom.

Godfrey Tawodzera is a Post-Doctoral Fellow in the African Centre for Cities (ACC) and Department of Environmental and Geographical Science, University of Cape Town, South Africa.

Gina Ziervogel is a Lecturer in the Department of Environmental and Geographical Science, University of Cape Town, South Africa.

ACKNOWLEDGEMENTS

This project has been funded by the Ford Foundation, New York City and is a collaboration between the African Centre for Cities (ACC) at University of Cape Town, the Global Urban Research Centre (GURC) at University of Manchester and the African Food Security Urban Network (AFSUN). The editors would like to thank the Ford Foundation for their generous support that brought researchers and other experts together in a workshop held at the University of Cape Town in February 2010. The aim of the workshop was to explore the idea of a climate change, asset adaptation and food security nexus in Southern African cities. The Ford Foundation grant also made possible the production of this edited book, which is gratefully acknowledged.

1

UNDERSTANDING THE TERRAIN

the climate change, assets and food security
nexus in Southern African cities

*Bruce Frayne, Caroline Moser
and Gina Ziervogel*

Introduction

Framed by the complexities of climate change and population growth, there is no
question that human society faces considerable risks and challenges as the 21st
century unfolds. The United Nations Environment Programme (UNEP) recognizes that 'climate change is one of the major challenges of our time [and is]
threatening food security' and that it is a 'serious risk to poverty reduction and
could undo decades of development efforts' (UNEP, 2010: 1). All this is happening
at a time when the world's population is considered to be the most economically
prosperous in human history.

The World Bank's data for the last 28 years show that gross national income
(GNI) per capita has risen more than threefold from US$2,756 in 1980 to
US$10,357 in 2008 (at parity purchasing power; World Bank, 2009). However,
if we dig below these numbers, we find that these benefits of 'development' are
not evenly distributed. Using the same World Development Indicator data, the
gains in GNI per capita in sub-Saharan Africa are much more modest and still
very low, rising from US$825 to only US$1,991 (1980–2008). There are major
differences within countries in the region. For example, while the income trend
in South Africa has largely mirrored the global trend, income in some countries
has actually declined over the past three decades. Similarly, while urbanization
is associated with improvements in prosperity, these economic benefits are not
uniformly distributed. In Asia levels of urban poverty have decreased, while the
cities and towns of sub-Saharan Africa are experiencing a 'transfer' of poverty
from rural areas.

We argue that the current urban transition should be centre-stage in the global
relationship between climate change, poverty and food security. By mid-century,
an additional 2–3 billion people will inhabit the planet, and almost all of this
increase will be absorbed by cities in the global South. In sub-Saharan Africa,

where climate variability and change are expected to be the most acute, and where poverty and food insecurity are already intensifying, rates of urbanization are twice the global average (UN-HABITAT, 2008; UNESA, 2010). By 2050, it is estimated that about 77 per cent of Southern Africa's population will be living in towns and cities; a proportion comparable to the projected 2050 figure of 82 per cent for developed countries (UNESA, 2010). Meeting the rising demand for food within the context of exponential population growth, persistent poverty, sustained urbanization and climate change constitutes a defining challenge of this century.

In 2008, the Food and Agriculture Organization of the United Nations (FAO) stated that the phenomenon of urbanization 'will be one of the strongest social forces in the coming years', bringing severe challenges to household food security in the context of high rates of unemployment, increasing growth of the informal sector, deteriorating infrastructure, overcrowding and environmental degradation (FAO, 2008; SACN, 2011). One major challenge will be 'how to provide adequate quantities of nutritious and affordable food for more urban inhabitants, with less water, land and labour' (FAO, 2008). A recent review of the impacts of climate change on food security in sub-Saharan Africa agrees that all four dimensions of food security will be affected: availability, access, stability and utilization (Schmidhuber and Tubiello, 2007). The same study also concludes that climate change will negatively accentuate existing levels of food insecurity and that these adverse impacts will fall disproportionately on the poor (Schmidhuber and Tubiello, 2007: 19708).

Within this context – which characterizes the accelerating urban transition for the majority of the world's population – multidimensional poverty is at the centre of urban development challenge. Unlike the rural development focus of the past century, the Millennium Development Goals (MDGs) will largely be achieved in the urban context. Indeed, it is the urban poor that carry the greatest burden in all respects: underemployment, hunger and malnutrition, illiteracy, gender inequality, infant and maternal mortality, disease and low life expectancy, exposure to negative environmental conditions, and political and social marginalization (UN, 2011). Climate change will also be felt acutely within cities and, again, it is the urban poor that will likely shoulder the greatest costs in this regard. The C40 Cities Climate Leadership Group emphasize this point when they state that 'many of the world's major cities are at risk of flooding from rising sea levels. ... In cities of the developing world, one out of every three people lives in a slum, making them particularly vulnerable to the health and environmental risks posed by climate change' (C40, 2011).

Researchers, planners and policy makers in Southern African cities are already focusing on the impacts of increasingly severe changes in weather associated with climate change. Key issues include how climate science knowledge is used at the level of the city and how the impacts of climate change might affect city functioning at the metropolitan and household scales. What has not been addressed in any detail is the extent to which climate change will affect the food security of the city and its inhabitants, especially within the context of high levels of poverty and widespread food and nutrition insecurity (Ziervogel and Ericksen, 2010). This book is therefore about bringing to the attention of researchers, urban planners and managers the dynamic convergence of climate change, poverty (assets) and food security within the context of rapid urbanization, and exploring approaches to proactively minimize the impacts of climate change on the poorest and most vulnerable citizens. Although these themes are of direct relevance to all regions, the focus of the book is on Southern Africa where rates of urbanization are highest, poverty is greatest, food insecurity is widespread and where the impacts of climate change will be significant. This approach to development that brings together climate change, assets and food security as a nexus of research and analysis does so in recognition of the need to link actors at all levels, including the urban poor themselves.

The conceptualization of this 'development nexus' between climate change, assets and food security is a novel one. It is represented in this book as the first concrete step towards building a collaborative framework that can enhance locally appropriate steps towards improving the resilience of urban communities to the convergence of climate change impacts on assets and food security, while also providing support and tools for enhancing the mitigation of these impacts. The case studies that are presented in Chapters 2–9 review aspects of this climate change, assets and food security nexus; their findings and conclusions form the basis on which the nexus framework is discussed in Chapter 10.

In addressing key elements of the climate change, assets and food security nexus in Southern African cities, the case studies complement each other in a number of important ways. In Chapter 2, Jane Battersby examines in detail the links between food (in)security in Cape Town and how this links to current and expected climate change impacts at different points in time and at a variety of geographic scales. In this chapter, she tackles the complex challenge of linking the macro-scale outcomes of climate science modelling with the complexity of food insecurity that is experienced at the level of the household and the individual. Importantly, Battersby recognizes that there are factors that influence food security outcomes for urban residents that may have origins far from the city, and these factors may include climate change. In Chapter 3, it is at this level of household food security that Godfrey Tawodzera focuses his analysis. Tawodzera uses survey data and key informant interviews from Harare and elsewhere in Zimbabwe to identify ways in which asset adaptation might be used to strengthen the poor's resilience to climate change impacts on food security at the local scale.

Explicit in the climate change, assets and food security nexus are migration and urbanization, and this dimension is examined in both Chapter 4 and Chapter 5. Belinda Dodson (Chapter 4) argues that migration is a 'missing link' in both the climate change and asset adaptation work in Southern Africa. By placing the migrants at the centre of the discussion, she makes the case for linking climate change to asset adaptation in urban and rural areas, and highlights the interconnectedness of urban and rural livelihoods that is characteristic of the social economy of households in Southern Africa, and to think beyond 'climate refugees'. This discussion is followed by an empirical study in Chapter 5 of the impacts of climate change on migration and food security in Maputo, the capital city of Mozambique. Importantly, extreme weather events are on the increase in Maputo (and the country), and Inês Raimundo and Bruce Frayne demonstrate the clear links between climate related impacts on both migration to the city and food security within the city. Raimundo and Frayne show how the increases in the frequency of cyclones, floods and drought are factors that together cause migration to the city, and which in turn adversely impact urban agriculture, fishing and housing conditions – all of which are major household assets – for the urban poor in Maputo.

In Chapter 6, Danny Simatele demonstrates that recent changes in weather patterns in Lusaka, Zambia, are affecting the urban poor in terms of both their assets and their food security. Within this context of a changing climate, Simatele draws on recent field research in two informal settlements in Lusaka in his analysis of the ways in which the different asset adaptation strategies used by poor households and communities contribute to or take away from their food security.

Although still very much focused on community responses, both Chapter 7 and Chapter 8 offer valuable insights into the relationship between communities and broader urban management processes and institutions. In Chapter 7, Gareth Haysom looks in detail at the case study of a group of urban farmers in Cape Town, South Africa, and how the city's government has attempted to remove them to build houses, under the guise of protecting this community from potential extreme weather events. Haysom argues that adaptation that takes place at a community level is very different from adaptation that is driven through official governance structures (top down). This disconnect between local and adaptive strategies and government action therefore has to be bridged in ways that support asset building in poor urban communities, rather than leaving the likes of the Ithemba community with the stark choice between housing or food. This discussion is followed in Chapter 8 by Alfred Omenya, Grace Lubaale and Collins Miruka who consider similar institutional issues in their research on climate change, asset adaptation and food security amongst the urban poor in Mombasa, Kenya. Based on 50 years of data, their research shows that Mombasa's climate is changing, with more extreme weather events having significant impacts on the assets of the poor in the city. While the urban managers of Mombasa are cognizant of climate change as a development challenge, the authors argue that current policies and programmes are incapable of addressing the impacts of climate change on local communities. Omenya et al. propose a community-centred approach by the city's managers to asset adaptation in Mombasa, one that is by definition pro-poor and developmental in orientation.

Moving away from local community perspectives, the final case study in this book comes at the issue of climate change, asset adaptation and food security from a spatial planning perspective. Willemien Faling uses two different and instructive case studies from South Africa to demonstrate the importance of how spatial planning at a city-wide level can reduce the consequences of climate change and contribute to asset adaptation and food security. The two case studies are of George and //Khara Hais, which are similar to other municipalities in developing countries, and which have to confront the dual challenge of protecting the natural environment whilst pursuing economic growth in a sustainable manner – this in the face of multiple social, economic, political and environmental stressors occurring at various levels. Faling concludes her chapter by exploring how spatial planning can intervene at a local level to address the convergence of climate change, asset adaptation and food security, with the objective of building resilience.

The final chapter draws on the lessons learned from these case studies, and returns to the conceptual question of the climate change, asset adaptation and food security nexus, and assesses the utility of this approach in coordinating pro-poor development strategies in Southern African cities. The book concludes by constructing a framework for this 'development nexus' between climate change, assets and food security that can be built on by future researchers and can be used to frame development approaches and strategies by urban planners and managers that better serve the needs of the urban poor.

The discussion now turns to the thematic material and context of Southern African cities. Here an overview of the areas of climate change, asset adaptation and urban food security is presented, which provides the context for the case studies and the concluding chapter in which the nexus framework is developed.

Climate change in the urban context

There is overwhelming evidence that the global climate is changing, observed directly through increasing average air and ocean temperatures, changes in the frequency and severity of storms, changes in precipitation patterns and other extreme weather events (IPPC, 2007). In addition to observed changes, climate change scenarios, based on global circulation models (GCMs), project changes in the future climate including increases in temperature, changes in precipitation patterns, with some areas expected to receive more rain and others less, and an increase in extreme events. These changes are expected to happen more rapidly in some areas than others, but the general consensus is that society needs to find new ways to manage the growing climate risk.

These changes in the climate impact on many different aspects of the socio-ecological system including disease coverage, biodiversity, land degradation and changes in water availability, to name a few. These changes have significant implications for social systems, although the way in which change is actually experienced will depend on location, exposure, sensitivity and the ability of a society to respond (Eakin and Luers, 2006). In particular, urban areas experience these changes in climate in unique ways (Satterthwaite *et al.*, 2007).

The fact that populations, economic activities and built environments are concentrated in urban environments increases exposure to floods, heat waves, and other climate and weather hazards that climate change is expected to aggravate (Romero-Lankao, 2008). Some of the potential climate impacts expected in cities include increased intensity of heat waves and a decrease in cold spells, increased urban flooding, more air and water pollution incidences and increased coastal flooding and storm surges (Huq et al., 2007; Wilby, 2007). The interlinked nature of rural and urban economies suggests that urban economies may feel the impacts of climate change associated with decreasing possibilities for agriculture in the surrounds (Huq et al., 2007). The dependency between urban and rural house-holds and vice versa means that urban areas should not be considered in isolation as many of the impacts from climate in one area are likely to ripple through to other areas, both spatially and across sectors.

Cities already experiencing frequent extreme weather events are most at risk of experiencing more intense or frequent events in the future (Huq et al., 2007). Linked to these events is the increased potential for disasters to occur, which are often because of inadequate planning and governance (Satterthwaite et al., 2007). For this reason, understanding climate impacts and the associated planning and governance in place that might facilitate processes to reduce vulnerability to climate impacts, is key to preparing for climate change.

Much previous research has focused on the impacts of climate change for rural areas, with urban areas having been neglected in terms of how climate change has impacted and might impact, although this is changing rapidly (Wilby, 2007). Yet, the implications of climate change and extreme weather events for urban areas are critical to understand, particularly in the context of increasing urbanization inter-nationally and in Africa. In addition, the characteristics of urban settlements are very different from rural areas and so need to be understood in order to determine the nature of the climate impacts (Ziervogel and Ericksen, 2010).

Understanding urban climate change

Much of the existing research on the implications of climate change for urban areas focuses on broad processes such as changes in precipitation, temperature, extreme events and sea level rise (McGranahan et al., 2007; World Bank, 2009; McCarthy et al., 2010). There is also scientific research emerging that looks more closely at urban climate change dynamics including how aerosols can change the nature of urban precipitation and how temperature inversions might shift with changing synoptic states (Anderson et. al., 2001; Mickley et al., 2004; Jacobson et al., 2007). This applied urban climatology is generally not in a form that can be easily integrated into sustainable urban planning (Mills, 2006) and tends to neglect the intersection with social impacts and the potential for adaptation (McCarney, 2009).

The limited consideration of local climate change dynamics can in part be attributed to the fact that, until recently, broad climate change scenarios had not been sufficiently downscaled. Downscaling processes involve taking the output from GCMs and interpreting them (via statistical techniques or more complex methods like those available in neural networks), in relation to local climate dynamics. Empirical downscaling makes use of quantitative relationships between the larger-scale climatic environment and local variations sourced from historical data (Ziervogel and Zermoglio, 2009). At the urban scale, GCM data are too coarse to be of use and so downscaled information is necessary for projecting future changes in climate. However, downscaled data seldom explicitly focus on urban climate dynamics resulting in limited information about urban climate change.

It is important to understanding how the built environment and society interact with climate in the urban context. The concentration of populations, and the type of economic activity and built environments in urban areas can change exposure to floods, heat waves, and other climate and weather events. For example, heavy precipitation might fall equally over neighbouring urban and rural areas. However, hard impermeable surfaces within the urban landscape could lead to increased surface run-off and cause flooding that might not be experienced in the adjacent rural area (Hollis, 1988). Similarly, the impact of a general increase in temperature can differ between neighbouring urban and rural areas. The heat generated by the city (known as the urban heat island effect) results in higher temperatures than vegetated areas because building materials retain heat during the day, there are lower wind speeds in urban areas and less evapotranspiration, in addition to urban processes such as heating, cooling, transport and industry that emit additional heat (Wilby, 2007).

Climate change is expected to aggravate these different phenomena. Understanding the nature of climate change impacts on different variables is slowly evolving, with some climate projections being relevant to understanding both urban and rural areas in a region. While for some variables the specific context of the urban landscape is needed in order to consider the feedback impacts. Importantly it is the interaction of these different components of climate vulnerability that is the biggest risk (Parnell et al., 2007).

Although our understanding of potential links between future climate change and the urban landscape is limited, there is a better understanding of how past climate events have impacted on urban areas, particularly within the literature on urban disasters (Pelling, 2003; de Sherbinin et al., 2007; Satterthwaite et al., 2007). This has enabled the Intergovernmental Panel on Climate Change (IPCC) to produce a typology of how changes in climate are likely to impact on urban areas (Table 1.1; Wilbanks et al., 2007). Despite such efforts to unravel the probable impacts of future climate variability and extremes on urban areas, there has been little consideration of the implications for urban policy and practice. This is likely to rapidly change as local government and civil society start to engage with the realities of urban climate change. However, climate scientists need to tailor information to the urban scale and potential users need to learn to ask for appropriate information and find ways to integrate this information into daily planning, policy and adaptation responses at the city and neighbourhood scales (Ziervogel, 2009).

Table 1.1 Projected impacts on urban areas of changes in extreme weather and climate events

Climate phenomena and their likelihood	Major projected impacts
Warmer and fewer cold days and nights Warmer and more frequent hot days and nights over most land areas *Virtually certain*	Reduced energy demand for heating Increased demand for cooling Declining air quality in cities Reduced disruption to transport due to snow, ice Effects on winter tourism
Warm spells/heat waves: frequency increases over most land areas *Very likely*	Reduction in quality of life for people in warm areas without air conditioning Impacts on elderly, very young and poor
Heavy precipitation events: frequency increases over most areas *Very likely*	Disruption of settlements, commerce, transport and societies due to flooding Pressures on infrastructure, potentials for use of rain in hydropower generation Loss of property
Areas affected by drought increases *Likely*	Water shortages for households, industries and services Reduced hydropower generation potentials Potential for population migration
Intense tropical cyclone activity increases *Likely*	Disruption by flood and high winds Disruption of public water supply Withdrawal of risk coverage in vulnerable areas by private insurers (at least in high-income countries) Potential for population migration
Increased incidence of extreme high sea level (excludes tsunamis) *Likely*	Costs of coastal protection versus costs of land-use relocation Decreased freshwater availability due to salt-water intrusion Potential for movement of population and infrastructure (also see tropical cyclones)

Source: Wilbanks *et al.*, 2007 in Romero-Lankao, 2008

Responding to climate change in urban areas

Cities are major contributors to the problem of climate change, as they have high emissions linked to transport, infrastructure, industry and residential electricity use. Linked to this has been the call for more efficient infrastructure and transport systems along with the decoupling of resource use from economic development (Mills, 2006) to mitigate or reduce cities' emissions. This aspect of mitigation is not expanded in detail in this book.

Cities are also highly vulnerable to the impacts of climate change, which has stimulated thinking and action on how to respond. In the field of climate change, adaptation to the impacts is defined as 'initiatives and measures to reduce the vulnerability of natural and human systems against actual or expected climate change effects' (IPCC, 2007). Adaptation can be *anticipatory* or *reactive*, *private* or *public*. Establishing coastal setback lines that limit the extent of coastal development is an example of a public response, managed by local government, in anticipation of expected storm surges linked to sea level rise.

Adaptation can be implemented at different spatial scales, including the micro level such as local protection of endangered species or raising flood-prone areas, or at the meso level, which might include land-use strategies or new urban policies implemented across the city. The macro level, relating to national policy, might be beyond the control of city actors; however, it can directly inform city responses through regulations such as changing flood insurance requirements or enforcing building regulations to reduce exposure to heat.

Within the urban context, McEvoy *et al.* (2006) and Shaw *et al.* (2007) suggest that adaptation could also be broken down into levels that recognize different urban forms, where conurbation would be addressed through strategic planning, neighbourhoods would require a combination of planning and urban design, and at the individual building scale urban design could be used.

Implementation of adaptation strategies has started to occur at both the local level and at the city scale. At the local level, examples of green buildings are growing rapidly, with green roofs becoming popular and helping to reduce surface temperatures, reduce run-off, filter air pollutants and increase the uptake of carbon dioxide (Gill *et al.*, 2007; Foster *et al.*, 2011). Sustainable urban drainage (SUD) techniques, such as improving infiltration of water, and increasing detention and retention ponds, can reduce flood impacts and can be used to store excess water during times of drought (Gill *et al.*, 2007).

At the meso scale, cities are starting to develop policies and plans to adapt to the impacts of climate change, including the likelihood of an increase in extreme events (Corburn, 2009; Birkmann *et al.*, 2010; Horton *et al.*, 2010). This response has been driven in part by the international scientific community that is encouraging adaptation as an important and urgent way to complement ongoing mitigation efforts that have formerly tended to dominate policies and finance (Pielke *et al.*, 2007; Romero-Lankao, 2008). It has also been driven by a bottom-up response that reflects an awareness of the need to better plan for climate variability, including extreme events, in order to increase the resilience of cities and protect its inhabitants (Ziervogel and Parnell, 2011).

The London Climate Change Partnership was one of the earliest groups to recognize the need to understand urban climate change and conducted a study for the city detailing what the key climate change impacts might be on different issues such as water resources, health, biodiversity, transport, and business and finance. This has been used to develop guidance material for assisting developers in increasing the climate resilience of designs and to inform the scrutinization of applications (Wilby, 2007). Specifically they focus on ways to improve ventilation and cooling, urban drainage and flood risk, water resources and outdoor spaces.

9

In Southern Africa, the City of Durban in eThekwini municipality has a Municipal Climate Protection Programme (MCPP). This was initiated in 2004 when the Environmental Planning and Climate Protection Department started an impact analysis to inform a climate change response strategy that formed Phase 1 of the work. Out of this Phase 2 emerged with a Headline Climate Change Adaptation Strategy project, followed by Phase 3 with an Urban Integrated Assessment Framework that highlights the need to incorporate climate change into planning processes (Roberts, 2010) and considers food security as an important component.

Although urban planning has been slow to integrate climate change issues, it has embraced sustainability concepts and attempted to integrate concern for environmental issues along with economic and social issues (Mills, 2006). The challenge of addressing climate change in urban settlements is clearly one to which architects and planners can contribute significantly. For example, they can look at developing settlements and constructing houses that are more energy and water efficient while also looking at ways to reduce risks to human and environmental health (Mills, 2006).

Access to and utilization of food within urban areas is a key challenge, yet there is little evidence of this being integrated into thinking about responding to urban climate change. Climate change can impact the assets of the urban poor in many complex ways, not least through damage and loss of infrastructure such as housing and roads. While adaptation to these threats to assets may already be taking place in affected communities, the impact of asset damage and loss to household food security had not been adequately examined. For example, a flood may impact a home business, resulting in a loss of income and therefore a reduced ability of that household to purchase food. Similarly, extreme weather events may reduce agricultural yields in urban areas where households grow food to supplement their food needs and/or sell on the market. Urban climate change responses must therefore realize the significance of extreme weather events on household-level food security as yet another important dimension of building resilience and promoting adaptation and mitigation.

Responding to urban climate change in the context of Southern Africa

In Southern Africa there has been a warming trend consistent with global temperature rises, along with below-normal rainfall years becoming more frequent, with a high number of drought events being reported in the last few decades. However, the biophysical impacts from climate change need to be understood within the socio-economic context, if adaptation responses are to be successful. This requires adaptation in Southern African cities to be contextualized in the broader development challenges. This is important in order to ensure buy-in from a range of actors who have heavy demands on their time and resources (Ziervogel and Ericksen, 2010) and are facing the pressure of service delivery and growing urban poverty.

Many large cities of the global South are highly exposed to extreme events as well as 'insidious' events (Parnell *et al.*, 2007). Within these cities, growing levels of informality create conditions conducive to flooding, poor sanitation and housing tensions, making these populations at risk to many climate impacts. Unfortunately many urban policies do not favour the poor so it is important to explore how their voice might be heard and their vulnerability to climate hazards reduced (Huq *et al.*, 2007). Huq *et al.* (2007) also highlight that local adaptation measures for climate change can support development goals through improved housing protected from storms and flood, for example. These are the kinds of changes needed in urban planning and governance to make cities climate resilient. Parnell *et al.* (2007) stress the need to address both the structural and chronic vulnerability to global environmental change as a starting place for action.

Much of the knowledge on climate change comes from the global North, although the global South is starting to contribute local knowledge to the field of climate change that is critical in building adaptive capacity relevant to the local context (Huq *et al.*, 2007; Leary *et al.*, 2008). Unfortunately in many developing countries, applying scientific knowledge is challenging because of existing resources and capacity constraints (Moser and Satterthwaite, 2008; Ziervogel and Zermoglio, 2009).

In Southern Africa, planners responsible for the provision and management of bulk infrastructure, a key aspect of urban vulnerability to climate variability, have engaged little in addressing climate change risk (Muller, 2007). This was highlighted in a case study of the City of Cape Town (CoCT), where one of the key challenges in climate adaptation planning has been the lack of integration across government departments and a limited understanding of how to access and interpret climate change information (Miller *et al.*, 2010). Out of this research, Miller *et al.* (2010) suggest a number of steps in order to build adaptive capacity and implement adaptation actions at the municipal level, starting by increasing awareness of climate change impacts and improving access to information, followed by defining adaptation priorities that link to development priorities and are contextualized in the socio-economic history. Following this, departments need to work together to strengthen technical capacity and implement projects collaboratively where appropriate.

The experience of developing and implementing a climate programme in the municipality of eThekwini, South Africa, has highlighted some of the challenges and opportunities in undertaking adaptation work in the region. Climate change was initially seen as an environmental issue, which limited buy-in from political actors who feel the pressure of addressing development challenges, with the environment not being something that wins votes. However, there were a series of coastal disasters beginning in 2007 and continuing in 2008 and 2009 that hit local communities and resulted in a number of deaths and loss of houses. These events led to the mayor taking a stronger leadership role around climate change born out of his experience of the importance of reducing risk to these events. Because of the pressure to ensure development-linked co-benefits adaptation, responses have received more support than mitigation (Roberts, 2010).

Despite the clear link between changes in future climate variability and extremes and urban impacts, there is limited exploration of how this might impact on policies and practice. This is rapidly changing as local government and civil society start to engage with urban climate change. However, there is limited experience on the integration of climate science for society and so progress is slow as climate scientists learn to tailor information relevant to the urban scale and to the user-needs, and as potential users learn to ask for appropriate information and find ways to integrate this information into daily planning, policy and adaptation responses at the city and neighbourhood scale. It is clear this is necessary and requires support from a range of actors, all of which are likely to experience the challenges of changes in the frequency and intensity of extreme climate events as well as gradual shifts in the climate means.

Although engagement with climate science is important in order to understand what changes might occur, it is as important to explore the linkages between current climate variability and food security. In many cases, current variability is not well managed. Focusing on current challenges helps to ensure that climate change is not seen as a distraction that is only valuable for those with time to plan. For example, understanding how to reduce the current impacts of flood risk on food security is an important starting point if flood risk is expected to increase in future. Reducing vulnerability to current variability should therefore be a priority as it helps to address many current development challenges.

The discussion now turns to the question of asset adaptation within the context of climate change.

Asset adaptation to climate change in urban areas[1]

Conceptual background: the asset accumulation framework

Asset-based approaches to development are an outcome of the poverty alleviation/ reduction debate of the 1990s. This dialogue contested income and consumption measurements of poverty, identified its multidimensional nature, and elaborated on the relationship between inequality, economic growth and poverty reduction in the South. In so doing it redefined the meaning of poverty itself, and elaborated new poverty-reduction strategies. It *defined concepts* such as assets, vulnerabilities, capabilities and endowments, and *developed policies* to address the impacts of shocks by focusing on the assets and entitlements of the poor. At the core were issues of risk and insecurity, with vulnerability the outcome (Moser, 1998).

Defining an asset

An asset is a 'stock of financial, human, natural or social resources that can be acquired, developed, improved and transferred across generations. It generates flows or consumptions as well as additional stock' (Ford Foundation, 2004). Assets are not simply resources that people use to build livelihoods. As Bebbington (1999) argues, assets give people the capability to be and act. Thus the acquisition of assets is not a passive act but one that creates agency and is linked to the empowerment of individuals and communities (Sen, 1997). The concept of asset accumulation draws on theoretical and policy-focused literature on asset-based development approaches (see for instance Sherraden, 1991; Carter and Barrett, 2006).

The concept of asset or capital endowments includes both tangible and intangible assets. The most widely recognized assets are natural, physical, social, financial and human capital (see Box 1.1). Recently researchers and practitioners have expanded the notion of assets to include a broader range of particular intangible assets such as aspirational, psychological, civic and political assets. Assets can be both individual and collective in nature. This means they can be possessed by individuals, households, communities or entire societies, depending on the asset type.

Box 1.1 Definition of most important capital assets

Physical capital: the stock of plant, equipment, infrastructure, and other productive resources owned by individuals, the business sector or the country itself.

Financial capital: the financial resources available to people, such as savings and supplies of credit.

Human capital: investments in education, health and the nutrition of individuals. Labour is linked to investments in human capital; health status determines people's capacity to work; and skills and education determine the returns from their labour.

Social capital: an intangible asset, defined as the rules, norms, obligations, reciprocity, and trust embedded in social relations, social structures, and societies' institutional arrangements. It is embedded at the micro-institutional level (communities and households) as well as in rules and regulations governing formalized institutions in the marketplace, the political system, and civil society.

Natural capital: the stock of environmentally provided assets such as soil, atmosphere, forests, minerals, water, and wetlands. In rural communities land is a critical productive asset for the poor; in urban areas land for shelter is also a critical productive asset.

Moser, 2009

Defining an asset accumulation framework

An asset accumulation framework has the following two components:

- An *asset index*: This is an analytical and diagnostic tool for understanding poverty dynamics and mobility. It quantitatively, or qualitatively, measures the accumulation or erosion of different assets over time and clarifies the interrelationship between different assets. This may, or may not, mirror changes in income or consumption poverty.
- An *asset accumulation policy*: This is an associated operational approach that focuses directly on creating opportunities for poor people to accumulate and sustain complex asset portfolios.

Asset accumulation policy is not a set of top-down interventions. Though it may include interventions that focus on strengthening individual assets, it is essentially a framework that provides an enabling environment with clear rules, norms, regulations and support structures to allow households and communities to identify and take advantage of opportunities to accumulate assets.

The components of an asset accumulation policy

To facilitate asset accumulation it is necessary simultaneously to address components at the following three interrelated levels:

1 *Structural level*: The fact that structural factors can have direct and indirect impacts on assets at the local level demonstrates that development is not just a technocratic process but a structural one. The process of accumulating assets involves complex political contestation, as well as the negotiation of social power relations as much as technocratic solutions. Asset accumulation does not occur in a vacuum. Opportunities are influenced by *complex causal relationships* between both external and internal structural factors and internal social processes – both of which need to be addressed.

2 *Institutional level*: International, national and local; public, private and civil society organizations are critical in providing an 'enabling environment' for the accumulation of assets. While the state establishes the normative and legal frameworks that can either block initiatives or provide incentives, private sector entities, including banks and microfinance institutions, support opportunities and facilitate access to promote asset accumulation.

3 *Operational level*: Assets are not static. In a changing global political, socioeconomic and environmental situation it is important to recognize constant revalorization, transformation and renegotiation. In addition, the accumulation of one asset often results in the accumulation of others, while insecurity

in one can also affect other assets. This means that at the operational level, an asset accumulation policy framework recognizes prioritization, sequencing, trade-offs and negotiation potential, and combines a range of context-specific strategy options.

The stages or 'generations' of asset accumulation strategies

Finally, it is important to distinguish different stages or 'generations' of asset accumulation strategies (see Table 1.2). First-generation asset accumulation strategies are by far the most widespread, and aim at accessing assets. Such strategies frequently focus on the provision of 'basic needs' including water, roads, electricity, housing plots, better health care and education, and microfinance. Essential for getting out of poverty is this primary emphasis on human, physical and financial capital.

Once assets are provided it is assumed that individual well-being improves and 'development' occurs. However, the conditions for accessing assets do not necessarily bring the expected development outcomes. Second-generation asset accumulation strategies, therefore, are intended to ensure their further consolidation and prevent erosion – including the intergenerational transfer of assets. Such strategies go beyond the provision of basic services to embrace a range of concerns relating to citizen rights and security, governance and the accountability of institutions. Third-generation asset accumulation strategies, still very nascent, need to explore interventions that can maximize the linkages between different types of interdependent asset, thereby ensuring 'added value' and long-term sustainability.

Table 1.2 Aims and programmes of different asset generation strategies

	First generation	*Second generation*	*Third generation*
Policy aims	Accessing an asset portfolio	Consolidating assets and preventing erosion	Maximizing linkages between interdependent assets
Type of programme	Provision of land, housing, basic services and infrastructure, and microfinance	Citizen rights and security, good governance and accountability, including intergenerational transfer of assets	Securing long-term financial and institutional sustainability of agencies, economic growth, permanent employment and income

Source: Adapted from Moser, 2009

From asset accumulation to asset adaptation

In order to better understand the opportunities the urban poor have to build long-term resilience to the impact of climate change, Moser *et al.* (2010) highlight the importance of shifting from an asset accumulation to an asset adaptation framework.[2] This has two core objectives:

- At the analytical level, to understand the sources of *asset vulnerability* of poor households, businesses and community organizations in terms of the mechanisms through which variability associated with climate change impacts leads to the erosion of assets.
- At the operational level to classify the types of *asset adaptation strategies* and sources of reliance that enable households and communities to protect themselves, or to recover, from the negative effects of severe weather associated with climate change.

Linked to these objectives, the framework comprises two associated components.

An asset vulnerability analytical framework

This identifies the links between different vulnerabilities and the poor's capital assets. These relate both to external shocks and stresses, as well as to internal capacities to resist or withstand them. While vulnerability has long been recognized as an important constraint for asset accumulation, climate change also requires a consideration of the uncertainty of future risk, and associated with this an insecurity concerning the bundle of assets that will enable adaptation and greater resilience, or lead to increased vulnerability. In the case of climate change it can be identified in terms of two specific dimensions: first, an external dimension that comprises the potential damage caused by shocks (such as sudden climatic events like hurricanes), trends (such as environmental degradation over time) or stresses to which people are subjected; and second, an internal dimension that encompasses their capacity and associated means to withstand, or adjust, to damaging losses.

The social dimensions of vulnerability to climate change predominantly focus on the internal dimension – namely how assets, institutions and people's relationships are affected by such external threats. Climate change vulnerability, therefore, is closely linked to assets. The more and diverse assets people have, the less vulnerable they are, and the greater the erosion of people's assets, the greater their insecurity (Moser, 1998). Poor populations are particularly vulnerable to climate change not only in terms of individual assets such as human and social capital, but also in terms of household, small business and community assets such as financial and productive assets. The capacity of individuals, households and communities to deal with such impacts in turn determines their resilience to weather stress.

An asset adaptation operational framework

This explores and categorizes the asset adaptation strategies as households, small businesses and communities exploit opportunities to develop resilience, cope and resist, or to recover from, the negative effects of climate extremes. Three closely interrelated phases of asset-based adaptation comprise:

• asset adaptation to build long-term resilience
• asset damage limitation and protection during severe weather events
• asset rebuilding after extreme weather and disasters.

Complementing this is an appraisal of the current climate change institutional policy domain at both national and local level. Together both sources of information provide the basis for local-level policy makers and other local stakeholders (civil and community organizations) to propose concrete climate change adaptation policies and to provide specific strategies and programmatic interventions that can be adopted and implemented by local authorities and institutions, with positive impacts on poor households and their local communities. Obviously, the greater the success in building long-term resilience, the less is the need for intervention in the later phases.

The remaining part of this section highlights a few of the most important asset adaptation interventions in the three phases identified above, prioritizing those focusing on local communities.

Asset adaptation to build long-term resilience to extreme weather

The most effective adaptation in terms of avoiding disasters is establishing the infrastructure and institutions that reduce the risk of storms or floods becoming disasters. This is also the most difficult to implement, most frequently because of the lack of funding and government capacity and the large deficits in infrastructure provision that need to be remedied. This can relate to the retention of power, resources and fund-raising capacities by higher levels of government, which are needed by urban-level governments. At the same time it is important to recognize that most low-income urban groups already have a range of measures by which they adapt to risk and to changing circumstances. Nevertheless their survival needs and economic priorities often conflict with building resilience.

Since housing is often the first and most important asset that poor urban households seek to acquire (Moser, 2007), the relocation of existing houses and settlements away from areas that cannot be protected from floods and storms, coupled with land-use management strategies to prevent new settlements in such areas, is an important component of any asset-based strategy. But homeowners and renters alike will often resist relocation, because it can result in a decline in financial capital and social networks, as well as the loss of the physical asset itself. Thus those owning houses are more likely to opt for housing improvements rather than relocation. But climate change can decrease the availability of safe, residential sites as it increases the sites at risk of subsidence, mudslides, wind damage, flooding and (for coastal cities) sea level rise.

Most current existing adaptation measures are local bottom-up community-based initiatives. In order that community-level action can build more resilience to extreme weather events, representative, inclusive community-based organizations (CBOs) are required. Yet many interventions to ensure long-term resilience require large-scale, expensive infrastructure that is part of city-wide systems. These include storm and surface drains (and measures to keep them free of silt and solid waste), and effective piped water and sewerage systems. Most sites at high risk from extreme weather can have risks reduced if building quality is improved and infrastructure and services provided. But this often requires government agencies to reach agreements with residents over the transfer of land tenure. Conflicts can develop with forced relocation, including stand-offs, physical resistance and even personal injury to those trying to defend informal property and associated livelihoods. This is exacerbated when alternative sites are inadequate or not provided at all.

Asset damage limitation and protection during extreme weather events

Although households and communities often have well-developed immediate measures to cope during storms and flooding, climate change can alter the frequency, timing, and severity and intensity of such events. A range of interventions occur, not only by households but also by local government, CBOs and non-governmental organizations during severe weather. For instance, one of the foundations of asset damage limitation is an early warning system that not only identifies the risk but also communicates the information to all neighbourhoods at risk. Many low-income countries do not have adequate weather monitoring or extreme event early warning systems, and even if they do exist they do not necessarily generate the required response, if the information is not disseminated in an appropriate manner and if local communities do not trust the information provided.

Growing awareness of the assets and capabilities of women, men, youth and children affected by a disaster, and their importance in immediate post-disaster response, has resulted in more community-focused approaches that include maternal and child health care and nutritional supplementation set up in the immediate aftermath. In addition, many of the problems experienced during disasters relate to delivery systems for emergency and transitional assistance. Local people frequently feel little or no control of their lives, and no role in decisions that affect them. So, where people are displaced, shelter should be organized with the aim of keeping family members and communities together; adults, including women, as well as men and adolescents should participate in concrete, emergency relief activities; and as soon as resources permit, school-aged children should have access to schooling and to recreational activities.

Asset rebuilding after extreme weather

While the reconstruction process can be an opportunity for transformation for long-term development, it frequently fails to do this, simply replacing old problems with new ones or reinforcing old ones. There tends to be limited understanding of how reconstruction rebuilds social as well as physical assets. For poor households the most urgent issue is their housing – whether they can get back their previous home or the site in order to rebuild. But lack of land title, and government decisions that prevent rebuilding in affected areas, can both act as constraints. Gender analysis should be included in rebuilding. Often, individual reconstruction does not work well, while community-led development works better. The location of rebuilt settlements has obvious implications for livelihoods as well as for access to such amenities as schools, markets and health facilities. Recovering the household and local economy is a cornerstone of progressive adaptation post-disaster. The recovery of the local economy and land ownership are interdependent. Loss of rights over land and forced resettlement during reconstruction, under the guise of 'adaptation' or 'risk reduction', can serve to transfer land rights from the poor to the rich.

In sum, climate change asset adaptation strategies are based on a number of basic principles, which include the following:

- Adaptation does not take place in a vacuum and is constantly shaped by government policy, political institutions and non-governmental actors. Laws, norms and regulatory and legal frameworks either block or enable access, or indeed positively facilitate asset adaptation, in a variety of ways (Moser and Satterthwaite, 2008).
- Assets are highly interrelated and facilitating the adaptation of one may affect others and vice versa – the erosion of one may impact others.
- Household asset portfolios are not stable and may change – either over time or abruptly – in response to external shocks or internal changes, for example death, marriage, etc. It focuses, on the one hand, on local government adaptation policy, and on the other on community, small business and household responses, their ability to negotiate and be active in decision making. Clearly the asset portfolios of individuals, households and communities are a key determinant of their adaptive capacity, not only to reduce risk and to cope with and adapt to increased risk levels, but also to influence, make demands on, and work with, local governments. An asset adaptation framework recognizes and aims to strengthen the capabilities of poor individuals and households to protect and adapt their assets.
- The outcome of this climate change asset adaptation framework is a solution-oriented approach based on the adaptive capacity and the asset portfolio that households, small business and communities command and control (Moser and Stein, 2011).

Perhaps one the most vital assets a person, household or community can have is appropriate access to food. Without adequate food – or without means to access food – the full range of capital assets described earlier in this chapter have the potential to be negatively impacted, so eroding the very entitlements that may help to improve the multigenerational development prospects of poor communities. The discussion that follows outlines the key issues that relate to food security for poor, urban communities.

Urban food security

Defining urban food security

The most common definition of food security is that used by the FAO, which states that food security exists 'when all people, at all times have physical and economic access to sufficient, safe and nutritious food to meet their dietary needs and food preferences for an active and healthy life' (FAO, 1996). Missing from this definition, however, is the notion of sustainable food production. In its 2020 Vision, the International Food Policy Research Institute (IFPRI) accommodates the principle of sustainability in its definition of food security as 'a world where every person has access to sufficient food to sustain a healthy and productive life, where malnutrition is absent, and where food originates from efficient, effective, and low-cost food systems that are compatible with sustainable use of natural resources' (2011).

Although qualitatively different, these two definitions agree that the components of food security extend beyond food production to encompass broader socio-economic issues surrounding food availability and the ability to effectively translate hunger into an economic demand for food. This broader perspective is encapsulated by the food system as a whole. Ericksen (2008a) builds a very useful conceptual framework comprising the various components of the food system (Figure 1.1). In this framework, she describes the key actors and activities involved in food systems, as well the social and environmental outcomes that are part of any given food system. Four primary food system activities are identified, which are food production, processing and packaging, distributing and retailing, and consumption. In turn, these activities result in three important food system outcomes, which are social welfare, food security and environmental security/natural capital (Figure 1.2).

The stability of any food system is important both on the supply side (in terms of production) and the demand side (in terms of people being able to trade for food). The complexity of the links between food systems and food security have been described as 'dynamic interactions between and within the bio-geophysical and human environments lead[ing] to the production, processing, preparation and consumption of food, resulting in food systems that underpin food security' (Gregory *et al.*, 2005: 2139). These food systems contribute to four food

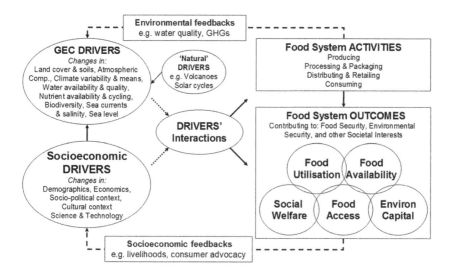

Figure 1.1 Food systems and their drivers (Source: Ericksen, 2008a)

Figure 1.2 Components of food systems and food security outcomes (Source: Ericksen, 2008a)

security outcomes, namely availability, accessibility, stability and utilization of food (Ziervogel, 2009).

Food availability depends on the production, distribution and exchange of food and includes the production of adequate crop, livestock and fisheries as well as the collection of wild foods and resources for migratory and indigenous communities. While the components of food availability are contextual, domestic production, reliable import capacity, presence of food stocks and, when necessary, access to food aid are the major elements of a secure food supply (Maxwell and Slater, 2003).

Food accessibility refers to the affordability, allocation and preference that enable people to effectively translate their hunger into demand. Poverty and vulnerability play a central role in food accessibility, as this component is centrally concerned with the purchasing power of households and individuals and the social dynamics governing access to food. The growth of urban areas has been accompanied by a greater emphasis on the incomes and social networks that are used in accessing food (Ruel *et al.*, 1998). National economic security is also a factor in accessibility, as reflected in the presence of adequate food transportation venues and market infrastructure. Food distribution systems in cities also impact on food accessibility (Maxwell and Slater, 2003).

Food stability involves continuity in the urban food supply and access to food. Factors affecting food stability include seasonal variations in food supply or income that can be impacted by climate variability, price fluctuations, and political and economic factors.

Food utilization refers to how a person is able to utilize food and nutrients (depending on age, health and disease) as well as the quality of food intake (Pelletier, 2002; World Bank, 2006). In countries plagued by poor health, poor sanitation and inadequate safety standards, chronic illness may compromise a person's digestion and undermine nutrient intake.

Although the first MDG aims to eradicate extreme poverty and hunger by ensuring that the criteria for a food secure society are met, various factors threaten this goal. They include population growth, rising demand for food, the non-sustainable industrial agricultural system and the dominance of fossil fuels as the primary energy source, and the current climate change trajectory.

The urban food security challenge

Urban food security is a defining development challenge in the 21st century. In 2007, the global proportion of people living in urban areas passed 50 per cent, marking the first time in human history that more people lived in urban than in rural areas (UN-HABITAT, 2007). As the global population continues to grow toward a mid-century estimate of 9–10 billion, the majority of this demographic increase will be in cities; and approximately 95 per cent of that growth will be concentrated in the cities of the developing world (UNESA, 2010). Future urban growth will be most intense in Asia and Africa, and these two regions will have the largest populations on the planet by 2030: 2.66 billion and 748 million respectively (UN-HABITAT, 2007: viii, 4). At twice the global average, the pace of urbanization is already highest in sub-Saharan Africa. The average rate of urban growth for sub-Saharan Africa is close to four per cent and this positive trend is expected to persist for decades to come (UN-HABITAT, 2008).

Turning to Southern Africa, the regional population is approximately 210 million, of which at least 100 million already live in urban and peri-urban areas. By 2020, this figure is estimated to rise to 150 million and to exceed 200 million by 2030. However, rapid urbanization is not associated with increased incomes and better standards of living in Southern Africa as it is in some other developing regions (Ravallion *et al.*, 2007). Moreover, poor urban households are facing significant pressures as a direct result of the current global economic crisis and the high price of food staples. Consequently, urban food security is an emerging area of development concern that is fundamentally different from questions of food security within the rural and agricultural sectors (Crush and Frayne, 2009).

A food security lens is useful in conceptualizing the urban poverty dynamic that is unfolding in cities of the global South, and in Southern Africa in particular. In 1996 the World Food Summit made a commitment to halve the number of undernourished people in the world by 2015. By 2006, little progress had been made. In sub-Saharan Africa the number of undernourished people grew from 1990 to 2002 by 37 million. In 2009, the FAO estimated that the number of undernourished passed one billion for the first time (FAO, 2009).[3] Each year, 10 million children under the age of five die in the world, with the majority in developing countries. Malnutrition is often cited as the 'silent emergency', and is the outcome of chronic food insecurity and hunger. In urban areas, food *availability* is seldom the constraint, but rather *access* to food for the urban poor, especially for children (Crush *et al.*, 2011). In a report highlighting the urgency of the matter, the World Bank (2006) argues that despite decades of interventions, malnutrition still affects at least one third of the developing world's population. Micronutrient deficiencies and stunting associated with poor levels of food security are considered an 'extremely serious development issue' by the Bank, with the highest prevalence concentrated in South Asia and sub-Saharan Africa. Furthermore, the report makes the salient point that the scale of malnutrition is such that it may prevent many countries form attaining the MDGs (World Bank, 2006).

The United Nations Children's Fund (UNICEF) reports that the urban–rural gap is closing with respect to malnutrition (UN-ESCWA, 2010). This is the consequence of rising urban poverty associated with urbanization in developing countries. Also, malnutrition rates are generally reported at the city level rather than the neighbourhood level; yet it would be expected that malnutrition levels would be disproportionately higher in low-income and slum areas, and possibly greatly exceeding levels in rural areas (von Braun *et al.*, 1993; Frayne, 2010). Urban areas will inevitably become the focus of hunger and malnutrition as the world's urban population doubles in the coming decades; by 2019 the majority of developing countries' populations will be urban (UNFPA, 2008).

Recent research undertaken by the African Food Security Urban Network (AFSUN) in eleven Southern African cities demonstrates the strong links between urban poverty and high levels of food insecurity at the household level, with 77 per cent of poor urban households surveyed reporting conditions of food insecurity.[4, 5] The study revealed the following main points about urban food insecurity:

- three out of four households sampled in all eleven cities are food insecure
- dietary diversity is poor
- poverty and food insecurity are directly correlated
- food price increases have negatively impacted four out of five households surveyed
- there is a temporal dimension to urban food security
- urban food security has a gender dimension to it, with female-centred households the most food insecure
- health and urban food insecurity are related, with food insecure households having higher levels of all cause morbidity and mortality (including HIV/AIDS and TB)
- urban–urban and rural–urban inter-household food transfers are important, especially for food insecure urban households
- the contribution of urban agriculture as a food source for poor urban households is highly variable between cities.

While urban food security is often characterized as being 'invisible' to policy makers (Maxwell, 1999), the AFSUN findings demonstrate that chronic food insecurity is pervasive in urban centres throughout Southern Africa. Dealing with urban food poverty will therefore be a major policy and development challenge to city and national governments across the Southern African Development Community (SADC) region over the coming decades. Persistent urbanization and poverty mean that governments, urban managers and civil society have a significant challenge ahead in relation to improving food security for the poor while also addressing the currently unsustainable functioning and growth trajectory of the country's resource-hungry cities. While this is a daunting challenge, it is also a major opportunity. Tackling ecological sustainability from the food security vantage point provides a direct and tangible approach to creating wealthier, healthier and less environmentally consumptive cities.

Although food supply is generally adequate at the city level in Southern Africa, there is compelling evidence that the majority of the urban poor do not have equal or universal access to sufficient food, and that the food that is consumed is often highly processed and devoid of good nutrition. This demands a new focus on urban food security at the city scale. From an urban management perspective, supporting local food production is important in promoting livelihoods and health within the city, reducing costly food imports, using local waste productively and contributing to sustainable urban development. An increase in local food production necessitates the development and support of local-level, neighbourhood-accessible marketing systems to distribute produce throughout the city, to wealthy and poor alike.

Links to higher order production systems and retail value chains are also required. To realize the goals of creating a healthy, vibrant and prosperous city around the basic need of food requires an enabling and supportive environment – food (in all its complexity) must be fully integrated into the planning and management systems of the city, further enabled and supported by provincial- and national-level line ministries. An important characteristic of the food sector in developing country cities is its dualistic nature. Although there are strong formal components, there are many informal components that are just as critical. Box 1.2 outlines some of these elements. This duality needs to be considered when supporting adaptation to climate change.

In addition to these local-level characteristics of urban food security, it is important to understand how the processes that impact on food security operate at different scales (Table 1.3). The range of processes listed is certainly not exhaustive, but it does illustrate that their impacts on food security can be disaggregated by scale. The ability of local groups to secure food, resources and livelihoods is at least partially affected by national-scale determinants. The table also suggests that it is necessary to tackle food insecurity at the local, provincial and national scales.

What is missing from this table is the role of climate change in the food system, and how this translates into food security at global, regional, national and local scales. The discussion now turns to the question of climate change, and how this relates to urban food security.

Box 1.2 Characteristics of the informal food sector

- The absence of specialization: informal trade develops more by diversifying products sold.
- Very low capital investment.
- Interlinkage between production and consumption: the informal food trade can be both producer and consumer of food products and services.
- The absence of accounts and the non-payment of all or some taxation.
- The possibility of dovetailing with the formal food sector to satisfy a differing demand and customer base. The informal sector overwhelmingly addresses households and micro-enterprises with varying and limited purchasing power.
- Innovation is often more social than technical. Because of the relations it often maintains with the rural sector, the informal food trade can provide raw materials at lower cost. The social networks can also provide low cost or 'free' labour in the form of apprentice help or family members who are fed but receive no or little pay.

Table 1.3 Processes that impact food security at different scales

Local scale (e.g. household)	National/provincial scale
Loss of customary rights and change to modern 'tenure' systems	Urbanization
Loss of access to communal resources	Changing legislation and tenure systems
Increasing need for cash	Population growth
Monetization of resources and services/ increasing health and education costs	Increasing penetration of global markets/ reorientation of production away from local circulation and reciprocity
Privatization of land and resources	Increasing HIV/AIDS prevalence
Deagrarianization (diversification out of agricultural-based livelihoods)	Declining biodiversity and forests, and expansion of agriculture

Source: Adapted from Adger *et al.,* 2004

Climate change and urban food security

It is well understood that not only does climate change influence the vulnerability and/or resilience of the food system, but that the food system in turn contributes to climate change (Ericksen, 2008b). However, making the link between climate change and urban food security is challenging, not least because climate change is a long-term event whereas urban food security – particularly for poor households – is an immediate and daily concern. We argue here that the dynamics of both climate change and urbanization are in fact converging spatially and temporally. On the one hand, the pace of research on potential impacts of climate change on society is increasing rapidly as our growing understanding of this change underscores the need for urgent action. On the other hand, the unavoidable demographic growth and urbanization of humanity – concentrated in the cities of the developing world – mean that the face of poverty will increasingly be urban. These two dynamic global forces are converging to create an ecologically unsustainable pathway, and at an exponential rate. Already cities occupy only some 2 per cent of the planet's land area, yet they consume 75 per cent of the world's resources (Girardet, 2009).

Looking at this sustainability challenge of climate change and urbanization through the food and nutrition security lens is a useful way to highlight the linkages between cities and climate change. For example, agriculture is resource intensive and generates about 30 per cent of greenhouse gas emissions; this ignores the additional and serious ecological impacts of current systems of processing, marketing and consumption, as well as the costly waste of food (Met Office Hadley Centre Observations Datasets, 2009). In her paper on food systems and environmental change, Ericksen, (2008a: 40) writes that 'in addition to food security, food system activities contribute to environmental outcomes, and food security itself is determined in part by environmental factors independent of the food system activities'. Food security, climate change and sustainable development are intimately connected in a web of feedback process and outcomes – the extent to which these are positive or negative depends on how these relationships are conceptualized and managed. Given that the urban poor constitute the increasing majority of those vulnerable to food insecurity, urban growth and development programmes to address the problem must include this constituency in their design.

To understand the impacts of climate change on food security it is necessary to understand the general linkages between climate change, food security and its direct and indirect drivers, as shown in Figure 1.3. Climate change impacts both on the direct and indirect drivers. The indirect drivers include elements such as global economics, demography and environmental trends, whereas the direct drivers centre on the biophysical system and its management as well as some key socio-political and economic variables.

The impacts of climate change on food security are generally considered in relation to agricultural production, which is characteristically viewed as geographically remote from urban consumers (Adger, 2006; Ericksen, 2008b). However, significant food production takes place in cities and is often used as a livelihood strategy by the poor (Mougeot, 2006; Crush *et al.*, 2010). The impacts of climate

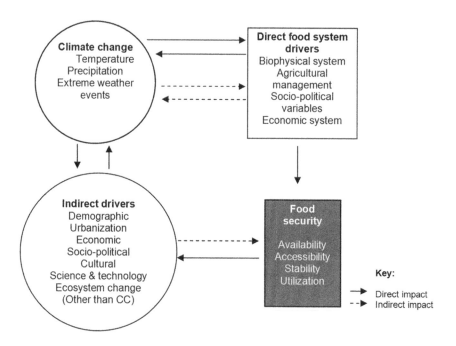

Figure 1.3 Linkages between climate change and food security

27

change and consequent extreme weather events on urban food security are therefore threefold:

1   Reduction in farm yields that may increase food prices and market volatility (affecting food availability, accessibility and stability).
2   Urban and peri-urban food production losses that may result in direct household food supply shocks and local price increases (affecting food availability, accessibility, stability and utilization).
3   Damage to capital assets that promote food security (affecting accessibility and utilization).

Within this context, food security, and increasingly *urban* food security, is therefore both a *poverty* and an *ecological* challenge. While the poverty dimension is encapsulated in the MDGs highlighted in our earlier discussion, the ecological dimension is captured in the United Nations' five sustainable development priority areas, identified as water and sanitation, energy, health, agriculture and biodiversity. These areas encompass physical and social systems, recognizing the complex relationships between each major priority area. Once again, in applying a food and nutrition security lens to these five development areas, the cross-scale and intersectoral linkages that impinge on the climate change–food security–society nexus are highlighted. Figure 1.4 makes some of the more obvious links from a food security perspective, which are consistent with the literature that focuses on the environment–food security (ecological) connections (Wood *et al.*, 2005; O'Brien, 2006; Easterling *et al.*, 2007; Ericksen, 2008a) as well as authors who emphasize societal processes (poverty) in determining food security (Devereux and Edwards, 2004; Misselhorn, 2004; Adger, 2006; Ericksen *et al.*, 2009).

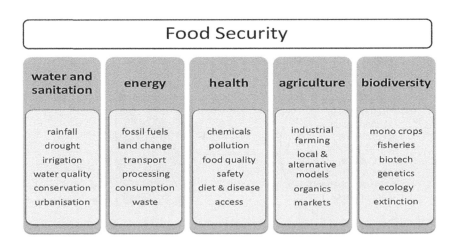

Figure 1.4 Links between food security and the United Nations' five sustainable priority areas

Conclusions

This chapter has provided an introduction to a potential urban climate change nexus linking climate change science, asset adaptation and food security. Researchers, planners and policy makers working in Southern African cities are already focusing on the impacts of increasingly severe changes in weather associated with climate change from a number of perspectives linked to different academic and planning disciplines. These include:

- climate science knowledge at the level of the city
- urban asset vulnerability and associated adaptation strategies to address increasingly severe weather at household, small enterprise and community levels in poor areas
- impacts of climate change on poor households' food security in both rural and urban areas.

The challenge presented by this book is to focus on the interrelationships between all three areas of climate change, poverty and food security. The intention, therefore, is to raise interest in exploring the added value of addressing the nexus between these three related issues, thereby developing an approach to more appropriate long-term responses and solutions to the impacts of climate change on poor households in cities. The case studies in the following chapters represent various elements and dimensions of this nexus, and provide the building blocks for constructing the climate change–asset adaptation–food security nexus framework, which is developed in the final chapter.

Notes

1   This section draws on Moser (1998, 2007, 2009) and Moser and Stein (2011).
2   This is the result of recent conceptual and empirical research on climate change and assets with fieldwork in Mombasa, Kenya, and Estelí, Nicaragua (see Moser and Satterthwaite, 2008; Moser and Stein, 2010; Moser *et al.*, 2010).
3   Full discussion available in Crush and Frayne, 2009.
4   Full discussion available in Frayne *et al.*, 2009
5   AFSUN is supported by funding from the Canadian International Development Agency (CIDA) under its University Partners in Cooperation and Development (UPCD) Tier One Program.

References

Adger, W. N. (2006) 'Vulnerability', *Global Environmental Change*, 16: 268–281.
Adger, W. N., Brooks, N., Bentham, G. and Agnew, M. (2004) *New Indicators of Vulnerability and Adaptive Capacity*, Norwich: Tyndall Centre for Climate Change Research, http://www.tyndall.ac.uk/ (accessed April 2011).
Anderson, H. R., Derwent, R. G. and Stedman, J. (2001) *Air Pollution and Climate Change: The Health Effects of Climate Change in the UK*, London: DEFRA.

Bebbington, A. (1999) 'Capitals and capabilities: a framework for analyzing peasant viability, rural livelihoods and poverty', *World Development*, 27, 12: 2021–2044.

Birkmann, J., Garschagen, M. A., Kraas, F. and Quang, N. (2010) 'Adaptive urban governance – new challenges for the second generation of urban adaptation strategies to climate change', *Sustainability Science*, 5, 2: 185–206.

C40 (2011) C40 Cities Climate Leadership Group, http://www.c40cities.org/ (accessed April 2011).

Carter, M .R. and Barrett, C. B. (2006) 'The economics of poverty traps and persistent poverty: an asset-based approach', *Journal of Development Studies*, 42, 2: 178–199.

Corburn, J. (2009) 'Cities, climate change and urban heat island mitigation: localising global environmental science', *Urban Studies*, 46, 2: 413–427.

Crush, J. and Frayne, B. (2009) 'The invisible crisis: urban food security in Southern Africa', *Urban Food Security Series, 1*, Cape Town: IDASA Publishing.

Crush, J., Hovorka, A. and Tevera, D. (2010) 'Urban food production and household food security in Southern African cities', *Urban Food Security Series, 4*, Cape Town: IDASA Publishing.

Crush, J., Frayne, B. and McLachlan, M. (2011) 'Rapid urbanization and the nutrition transition in Southern Africa', *Urban Food Security Series, 7*, Cape Town: IDASA Publishing.

de Sherbinin, A., Schiller, A. and Pulsipher, A. (2007) 'The vulnerability of global cities to climate hazards', *Environment and Urbanization*, 19, 1: 39–64.

Devereux, S. and Edwards, J. (2004) 'Climate change and food security', *IDS Bulletin*, 35, 3: 22–30.

Eakin, H. and Luers, A. L. (2006) 'Assessing the vulnerability of social-environmental systems', *Annual Review of Environment and Resources*, 31: 365–394.

Easterling, W. E., Aggarwal, P. K., Batima, P., Brander, K. M., Erda, L., Howden, S. M., Kirlenko, J. M. A., Morton, J., Soussana, J.-F., Schmidhuber, S. and Tubiello, F. N. (2007) 'Food, fibre and forest products', in Parry, M. L., Canziani, O. F., Palutikof, J. P., van der Linden, P. J. and Hanson, C. E. (eds) *Climate Change 2007: Impacts, Adaptation and Vulnerability. Contribution of Working Group II to the Fourth Assessment Report of the Intergovernmental Panel on Climate Change*, Cambridge: Cambridge University Press.

Ericksen, P. J. (2008a) 'Conceptualizing food systems for global environmental change research', *Global Environmental Change*, 18, 1: 234–245.

Ericksen, P. J. (2008b) 'What is the vulnerability of a food system to global environmental change?', *Ecology and Society*, 13, 2: 14.

Ericksen, P. J., Ingram, J. S. I. and Liverman, D. M. (2009) 'Editorial introduction', *Environmental Science and Policy*, 12, 4: 373–542.

FAO (Food and Agricultural Organization) (1996) *Rome Declaration on World Food Security*, Rome: FAO.

FAO (Food and Agricultural Organization) (2008) 2008 *The State of Food Insecurity in the World: Eradicating Hunger – Taking Stock Ten Years After the World Food Summit*, Rome: FAO.

FAO (Food and Agricultural Organization) (2009) *The State of Food Insecurity in the World 2009: Economic Crises – Impacts and Lessons Learned*, Rome: FAO.

Ford Foundation (2004) *Building Assets to Reduce Poverty and Injustice*, New York: Ford Foundation.

Foster, J., Lowe, A. and Winkelman, S. (2011) *The Value of Green Infrastructure for Urban Climate Adaptation*, Washington, DC: Center for Clean Air Policy.

Frayne, B. (2010) 'Pathways of food: migration and food security in Southern African cities', *International Development Planning Review*, 32, 3–4: 291–310.

Frayne, B., Pendleton, W., Crush, J., Acquah, B., Battersby-Lennard, J., Bras, E., Chiweza, A., Dlamini, T., Fincham, R., Kroll, F., Leduka, C., Mosha, A., Mulenga, C., Mvula, P., Pomuti, A., Raimundo, I., Rudolph, M., Ruysenaar, S., Simelane, N., Tevera, D., Tsoka, M., Tawodzera, G. and Zanamwe, L. (2010) *The State of Urban Food Insecurity in Southern Africa*, Urban Food Security Series, 2, African Urban Food Security Network (AFSUN), Cape Town: Idasa Publishing.

Gill, S. E., Handley, J. F., Ennos, A. R. and Pauleit, S. (2007) 'Adapting cities for climate change: the role of green infrastructure', *Built Environment*, 33,1: 115–133.

Girardet, H. (2009) 'Giant Footprints', in Global Development Research Centre, http://www.gdrc.org/uem/footprints/girardet.html (accessed April 2011).

Gregory, P. J., Ingram, S. I. and Brklacich, M. (2005) 'Climate change and food security', *Philosophical Transactions of the Royal Society B*, 36: 2139–2148.

Hollis, G. E. (1988) 'Rain, roads, roofs and runoff: hydrology in cities', *Geography*, 73: 9–18.

Horton, R., Rosenzweig, C., Gornitz, V., Bader, D. and O'Grady, M. (2010) 'Climate risk information: climate change scenarios and implications for NYC infrastructure, New York City Panel on Climate Change', *Annals of the New York Academy of Sciences*, 1196, 1: 147–228.

Huq, S., Kovats, S., Reid, H. and Satterthwaite, D. (2007) 'Editorial: reducing risks to cities from disasters and climate change', *Environment and Urbanization*, 19, 1: 3–15.

IFPRI (International Food Policy Research Institute). (2011) *2020 Vision for Food, Agriculture and the Environment*, Washington, DC: International Food Policy Research Institute.

IPCC (2007) *Summary for Policymakers, Working Group I Report The Physical Science Basis, Contribution of Working Group I to the Fourth Assessment Report of the IPCC*, S. Salomon, Q., Dahe, M. Manne (eds). Cambridge and NY: Cambridge University Press.

Jacobson, M. Z, Kaufman, Y. J. and Rudich, Y. (2007) 'Examining feedbacks of aerosols to urban climate with a model that treats 3-D clouds with aerosol inclusions', *Journal of Geophysical Research*, 112.

Leary, N., Adejuwon, J., Barros, V., Burton, I., Kulkarni, J. and Lasco, R. (2008) *Climate Change and Adaptation*, Oxford: Earthscan Publications.

McCarney, P. (2009) 'City Indicators on Climate Change: Implications for Policy Leverage and Governance', World Bank's 5th Urban Research Symposium Cities and Climate Change: Responding to an Urgent Agenda, Marseille, France, 28–30 June 2009.

McCarthy, M. P., Best, M. J. and Betts, R. A. (2010) 'Climate change in cities due to global warming and urban effects', *Geophysical Research Letters*, 37.

McEvoy D., Matczak, P., Banaszak, I. and Chorynski, A. (2006) 'Framing adaptation to climate-related extreme events', *Mitigation and Adaptation Strategies for Global Change*, 15, 7: 779–795.

McGranahan G., Balk, D. and Anderson, B. (2007) 'The rising tide: assessing the risks of climate change and human settlements in low elevation coastal zones', *Environment and Urbanization*, 19, 1: 17–37.

Maxwell, D. (1999) 'Urban food security in Sub-Saharan Africa', in Koc, M., MacRae, R., Mougeot, L. and Welsh, J. (eds) *For Hunger-Proof Cities: Sustainable Urban Food Systems*, Ottawa: IDRC.

Maxwell, S. and Slater, R. (2003) 'Food policy old and new', *Development Policy Review*, 21, 5–6: 531–553.

Met Office Hadley Centre Observations Datasets. (2009) General Information, http://www. metoffice.gov.uk/about/what/parliamentary/ (accessed April 2011).

Mickley, L. J., Jacob, D. J. and Field, B. D. (2004) 'Effects of future climate change on regional air pollution episodes in the United States', *Geophysical Research Letters*, 31.

Miller, F., Osbahr, H., Boyd, E., Thomalla, F., Sukaina, B., Ziervogel, G., Walker, B., Burkmann, J., van der Leeuw, S., Rockstrom, J., Hinkel, J., Downing, T., Folke, C. and Nelson, D. (2010) 'Resilience and vulnerability: complementary or conflicting concepts', *Ecology and Society*, 15, 3.

Mills, G. (2006) 'Progress towards sustainable settlements: a role for urban climatology', *Theoretical and Applied Climatology*, 84: 69–76.

Misselhorn, A. (2004) 'What drives food insecurity in Southern Africa? A meta-analysis of household economy studies', *Global Environmental Change*, 15: 33–53.

Moser, C. (1998) 'The asset vulnerability framework: reassessing urban poverty reduction strategies', *World Development*, 26, 1: 1–19.

Moser, C. (2007) 'Asset accumulation policy and poverty reduction', in Moser, C. (ed.) *Reducing Global Poverty: The Case for Asset Accumulation*, Washington DC: Brookings Press.

Moser, C. O. N. (2009) *Ordinary Families, Extraordinary Lives: Assets and Poverty Reduction in Guayaquil, 1978–2004*, Washington, DC: Brookings Press.

Moser, C. and Satterthwaite, D. (2008) 'Towards pro-poor adaptation to climate change in the urban centres of low- and middle-income countries', Human Settlements Discussion Paper Series, *Climate Change and Cities, 3, IIED / GURC Working Paper, 1*, Manchester: Global Urban Research Centre, University of Manchester.

Moser, C. O. N. and Stein, A. (2010) 'Implementing urban participatory climate change adaptation appraisals: a methodological guideline', *Global Urban Research Centre Working Paper, 5*, Manchester: Global Urban Research Centre, University of Manchester.

Moser, C. O. N. and Stein, A. (2011) 'The importance of assets in current development debates: Millennium Development Goals, social protection and climate change', *Global Urban Research Centre Working Paper, 7*, Manchester: Global Urban Research Centre, University of Manchester.

Moser, C. O. N., Norton, A., Stein, A. and Georgieva. S. (2010) *Pro-Poor Adaptation to Climate Change in Urban Centres: Case Study of Vulnerability and Resilience in Kenya and Nicaragua*, Washington, DC: World Bank.

Mougeot, L. (2006) *Growing Better Cities: Urban Agriculture for Sustainable Development*, Ottawa: IDRC.

Muller, M. (2007) 'Adapting to climate change water management for urban resilience', *Environment and Urbanization*, 19, 1: 99–113.

O'Brien, K. (2006) 'Are we missing the point? Global environmental change as an issue of human security', *Global Environmental Change*, 16, 1: 1–3.

Parnell, S., Simon, D. and Vogel, C. (2007) 'Global environmental change: conceptualising the growing challenge for cities in poor countries', *Area*, 39: 1–13.

Pelletier, D. L. (2002) 'Toward a common understanding of malnutrition. Assessing the contribution of the UNICEF framework', in *World Bank/UNICEF Nutrition Assessment*, Washington, DC: World Bank and UNICEF.

Pelling, M. (2003) *The Vulnerability of Cities: Social Resilience and Natural Disaster*, London: Earthscan Publications.

Pielke, R. A., Prins, G., Rayner, S. and Sarewitz, D. (2007) 'Climate change 2007: lifting the taboo on adaptation', *Nature*, 445: 597–598.

Ravallion, M., Chen, S. and Sangraula, P. (2007) 'New evidence on urbanization of global poverty', *Population and Development Review*, 33, 4: 667–701.

Roberts, D. (2010) 'Prioritizing climate change adaptation and local level resilience in Durban, South Africa', *Environment and Urbanization*, 22, 2: 1–17.

Romero-Lankao, P. (2008) 'Urban areas and climate change: review of current issues and trends', Issues Paper for the 2011 Global Report on Human Settlements, unpublished paper.

Ruel, M. T., Garrett, J., Morris, S., Maxwell, D., Oshaug, A., Engele, P., Menon, P., Slack, A. and Haddad, L. (1998) 'Urban challenges to food and nutrition security: a review of food security, health and caregiving in the cities', *FCND Discussion Papers*, 51, Washington, DC: Institute for Food Policy Research, Food Consumption and Nutrition Division.

SACN (South African Cities Network) (2011) *State of the Cities Report*, Johannesburg: South African Cities Network.

Satterthwaite, D., Huq, S., Pelling, M., Reid, A. and Romero-Lankao, P. (2007) 'Building climate change resilience in urban areas and among urban populations in low- and middle-income countries', *International Institute for Environment and Development (IIED) Research Report*, 112.

Schmidhuber, J. and Tubiello, F. N. (2007) 'Global food security under climate change', *Proceedings of the National Academy of Science of the United States of America (PNAS)*, 104: 19703–19708.

Sen, A. (1997) 'Editorial: human capital and human capability', *World Development*, 25, 12: 1959–1961.

Shaw, R., Colley, M. and Connell, R. (2007) *Climate Change Adaptation by Design: A Guide for Sustainable Communities*, London: TCPA.

Sherraden, M. W. (1991) *Assets and the Poor: A New American Welfare Policy*, Armonk, NY: M.E. Sharpe.

UNEP (2010) Six Priority Areas Factsheets on Climate Change, http://www.unep.org/pdf/Overview_folder.pdf (accessed April 2011).

UNESA (2010) World Population Prospects: The 2010 Revision, New York: United Nations, Population Division of Department of Economic and Social Affairs, http://esa.un.org (accessed April 2011).

UN-ESCWA (2010) Health and Millennium Development Goals in the ESCWA Region, http://www.escwa.un.org/divisions/scu/healthMDG/statistical_annex.pdf (accessed April 2011).

UNFPA (2008) *State of World Population 2008: Reaching Common Ground: Culture, Gender and Human Rights*, New York: UNFPA.

UN-HABITAT (2007) *State of the World's Cities Report 2006–2007*, Nairobi: UN-HABITAT.

UN-HABITAT (2008) *The State of African Cities, 2008: A Framework for Addressing Urban Challenges in Africa*, Nairobi: UN-HABITAT.

United Nations (2011) 'Millenium Development Goals', http://www.un.org\millenium-goals (accessed March 2011).

Von Braun, J., McComb, J., Fred-Mensah, B. and Pandya-Lorch, R. (1993) *Urban Food Insecurity and Malnutrition in Developing Countries: Trends, Policies, and Research Implications*, Washington, DC: International Food Policy Research Institute.

Wilbanks, T., Romero-Lankao, P., Bao, M., Berkhout, F., Cairncross, S., Ceron, J., Kapshe, M., Muir-Wood, R. and Zapata-Marti, R. (2007) 'Industry, settlement and society', in

Parry, M., Canziani, O., Palutikof, J., van der Linden, P. and Hanson, C. (eds) *Climate Change 2007: Impacts, Adaptation and Vulnerability. Contribution of Working Group II to the Fourth Assessment Report of the Intergovernmental Panel on Climate Change*, Cambridge and New York: Cambridge University Press.

Wilby, R. L. (2007) 'A review of climate change impacts on the built environment', *Built Environment Journal*, 33: 31–45.

Wood, S. and Ehui, S. *et al.* (lead authors) (2005) 'Food ecosystem services', in *Millennium Ecosystem Assessment; Ecosystems and Human Well-being: Current State and Trends*, Washington, DC: Island Press.

World Bank (2006) *Repositioning Nutrition as Central to Development: A Strategy for Large-Scale Action*, Washington, DC: World Bank.

World Bank (2009) *World Development Indicators*, Washington, DC: World Bank, http://data.worldbank.org/products/data-books/WDI-2009 (accessed March 2011).

Ziervogel, G. (2009) 'Climate change and food security in the Western Cape', unpublished paper.

Ziervogel, G. and Ericksen, P. (2010) 'Adapting to climate change to sustain food security', *Wiley Interdisciplinary Reviews: Climate Change*, 1, 4: 525–540.

Ziervogel, G. and Parnell, S. (2011) 'South African coastal cities' response to climate change adaptation', in Glovovic, B. *et al.* (eds) *Adapting to Climate Change: Lessons from Natural Hazards Planning*, New York: Springer.

Ziervogel, G. and Zermoglio, F. (2009) 'Climate-change scenarios and the development of adaptation strategies in Africa: challenges and opportunities', *Climate Research*, 40: 133–146, http://www.int-res.com/abstracts/cr/v40/n2-3/p133-146/ (accessed March 2011).

2

URBAN FOOD SECURITY AND CLIMATE CHANGE

A system of flows

Jane Battersby

Introduction

Whilst the connections between food security and climate change have been examined extensively at the national and regional scales, the urban scale has been largely neglected in both fields as have the connections between the two. As will be discussed further in the chapter, urban food security has been neglected due to the perception that poverty and food security are still predominantly rural challenges in the global South. Climate change models tend to operate at the global or regional scales, resulting in downscaling to the urban scale requiring additional work. As a result very few city-scale climate models exist as they require an understanding of the regional climate dynamics as well as the nuances of urban climate feedbacks that are often not well understood. The challenge of scale mismatches potentially hinders the development of models that connect urban food security and climate change, as it is difficult to connect processes occupying different spatial and temporal frames. The timescale on which climate change is unfolding is long and the time line has considerable uncertainty in the short term (10–30 years). The drivers of vulnerability to food insecurity (such as changes in food systems, relationships of trade, economic development trends, etc.) also operate over longer time periods, but the actual experience of food insecurity in urban areas is often triggered by single events, such as a food price increase or a loss of a household income. In order for meaningful connections to be drawn between climate change and urban food security it will be necessary to find ways to make cross-scale linkages.

This chapter addresses food security and climate change at the spatial and temporal scales appropriate to the processes connecting the two. In doing so, it acknowledges that urban food security is affected by events that may be far from the urban area itself. Urban food security needs to be viewed as being impacted by climate change in multiple locations and at various scales, and not simply *in situ* (as highlighted in the chapter by Dodson on "Mobility and migration"). This chapter therefore proposes a model to assess the connections between urban food security and climate change and suggests that this model may be useful as a means to develop greater resilience of urban areas to the impacts of climate change. The model is based on viewing urban food security as the connection of a series of resource flows each with their own sets of vulnerabilities and resiliences. Through this model, it may be possible to evade the scale-mismatch challenge and identify priority areas to protect urban food security from climate change risks. The chapter draws on the findings of the 2008 African Food Security Urban Network's (AFSUN) urban food security survey conducted in Cape Town to identify key elements of urban food security (Battersby 2011).

The chapter begins by highlighting the need to consider urban food security as a different development challenge from rural food security with a different set of relationships to climate change. It then identifies key elements of urban food security through analysis of the strategies households employ to access food and of the dynamics of the urban food system in terms of food sources. From this empirical basis, it then proposes the model and draws conclusions based on the application of the model to key flows.

Placing urban food security on the development agenda

Urban food insecurity is increasingly recognised as a key developmental challenge in sub-Saharan Africa (see Cohen and Garrett 2009 and Crush and Frayne 2010b for overviews of the challenge). However, because food insecurity has traditionally been conceptualised as a rural development problem, the existing conceptual tools used to understand the challenge and frame the responses are inadequate to address food security in urban areas. The focus remains largely on issues of availability and therefore finds solutions in increased food production, whereas the challenge of urban food insecurity is primarily one of access (Atkinson 1995; Crush and Frayne 2010a). Where issues of access have been considered, the supply chains have tended to be short and simple in comparison to the urban food system, which ultimately draws its food from a wide range of sources that have complex and diverse supply chains.

Maxwell (1999) suggests that urban food security has remained relatively invisible for three main reasons. Firstly, urban policy makers and practitioners do not address food insecurity because limited budget and capacity mean that "more urgently visible problems" (Maxwell 1999: 1940), such as housing and sanitation, take priority. Although historically the growth and form of cities was determined by their food system (Steele 2008), this is no longer the case. Food is rarely on the urban planning agenda. Secondly, he argues that urban food insecurity is rendered invisible by how it manifests. Food insecurity in rural areas is often linked to times of famine, in which entire communities experience food insecurity at the same time. Food insecurity in urban areas is not triggered by absolute food shortages, but by failures of households to be able to access food. Urban food security is therefore more an idiosyncratic than covariate shock than rural food security, though covariate shocks, such as food price increases, are also significant. Food insecurity is therefore experienced primarily at the household scale and households employ a range of localised coping strategies, which render the struggle invisible. Finally, he argues that the long established perceptions of food security and poverty being rural problems make policy makers less likely to see urban food insecurity. Urban food security is thus politically invisible and has been largely neglected by researchers. It is out of this paucity of research that the connections between urban food security and climate change have been left largely un-interrogated.

While the challenge of urban food security has historically been considered as secondary to rural food security, demographic and economic realities in the developing world are forcing a reappraisal. In 2008, the world became predominantly urban, with sub-Saharan Africa being the most rapidly urbanising region (UN-HABITAT 2009: 25). While poverty and food insecurity have been viewed as predominantly rural, this reality is shifting as not only do urban areas become more significant in terms of absolute population, but also in terms of proportion of the population living in poverty. Ravallion notes that the poor urbanise faster than the non-poor (Ravallion 2007: 442). In addition, conditions in many urban areas in terms of access to shelter, security of tenure, lack of basic services and increasing inequality are driving many urban residents into poverty (Mehta 2000). The face of poverty is increasingly urban and the urban can be considered the new development frontier.

It is not enough, however, simply to note that poverty and food security are increasingly urban and hope to employ the same means of analysis and attempt the same solutions that are applied to rural areas. The ways in which poverty and food security manifest in urban areas and their drivers need to be examined independently of prior rural assumptions. This section therefore uses the findings of the African Food Security Urban Network's Cape Town household food baseline survey to highlight some key issues pertaining to food security in urban areas.

The food security baseline survey was conducted between August and October 2008 in three locations in Cape Town: Ocean View, Ward 34 (Brown's Farm, Philippi) and Ward 95 (Enkanini and Kuyasa, Khayelitsha). Within this survey 1060 households were sampled and the survey was part of a wider 11-city survey across Southern Africa sampling over 6500 households.[1]

Across the region as a whole, 77 per cent of households were either severely or moderately food insecure (Frayne et al. 2010).[2] In Cape Town this proportion was marginally greater at 80 per cent. Therefore, whilst food insecurity has been considered to be a predominantly rural problem, the data from the AFSUN survey indicates very high levels of urban food insecurity, comparable to those in rural areas.

A recent study in rural Eastern Cape using the same food security measurement tool found 100 per cent of participant households to be severely or moderately food insecure (Ballantine et al. 2008). However, while food insecurity appears to be more extensive in rural areas than urban areas, the AFSUN survey found that the severity of food insecurity in poor areas of Cape Town was greater than that in the rural area sampled (see Figure 2.1 for a comparison of food security in Cape Town and Klipplaat). This is largely due to the dependence on the cash economy in urban areas, and, as will be demonstrated within this chapter, a limited range of livelihood strategies and therefore greater vulnerability to shocks, including climate change and increased climate variability.

Urban food insecurity manifests differently from rural food insecurity in a number of important ways, most notably its temporality. Figure 2.2 illustrates the months in which households in Cape Town experienced food shortages. Unlike rural areas, these months do not correlate to particular periods in the agricultural cycle, but are determined by annual periods of low casual labour availability, high expenditures (for example heating in winter) and other non-food related factors.

The drivers of food insecurity in urban areas are more complex and less directly related to food availability than those in rural areas. In urban areas the need to consider food accessibility, stability and utilisation is ultimately as great as the need to consider food availability. In addition, the food system in urban areas tends to be complex and diverse. As the following sections will demonstrate, households access food through a number of formal and informal sources and have multiple means by which they secure and employ assets to secure this food. Each of these sources and strategies has the potential to be impacted by climate change, both directly and indirectly. It is therefore vital to understand the dynamics of the urban food system in order to consider the connections between urban food security and climate change.

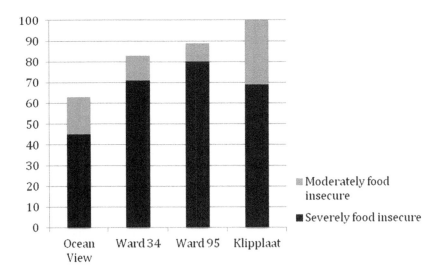

Figure 2.1 Comparison of food security in Cape Town and Klipplaat

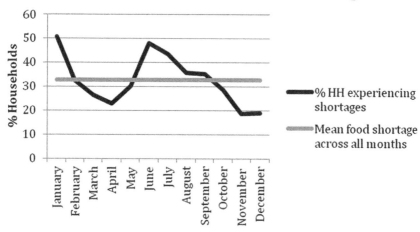

Figure 2.2 Months of adequate household provisioning

Household strategies for accessing food in Cape Town

Given the high levels of food insecurity within the Cape Town sample population it may be expected that households would have diversified livelihood strategies in order to maximise potential food security and increase resilience. However, livelihoods in Cape Town were relatively un-diverse. Half of the sampled population indicated that they had no alternative livelihood strategies, and were entirely dependent on their main source of income, and 31 per cent had just one other strategy. This makes households extremely vulnerable, should their existing source of income be lost, which is a very real threat in the context of the current economic circumstances.

At the time of the survey 45.6 per cent of respondents classified themselves as not working, but looking. Just 585 of the 4177 individuals (14.0 per cent) included in the survey were in formal waged work, with an additional 292 (7.0 per cent) employed in casual labour. Just less than half of the households (42.5 per cent) were in receipt of some form of state grant (pension, child support and disability). Those employed in the formal wage sector earned a median income of South African Rand 2000 per month. The median income of a casually employed worker was just half that amount, and the median amount received by a grant-receiving household was South African Rand 620.

Households that had members employed in the formal wage sector were the least likely to have alternative strategies. There is a sense of security that comes with formal employment; however, these households are extremely vulnerable to food insecurity should the source of income fail, or food prices rise rapidly, as they did in 2008 and are again in 2010/2011.

The alternative strategies that were being employed were dominated by casual labour (in addition to that listed by the main source of income of the household). This was an alternative strategy of 16.2 per cent of households; a further 8.2 per cent were self-employed at home. Other significant livelihood strategies were marketing (4.8 per cent) and renting space to lodgers (4.5 per cent). The oft-advocated strategy of urban agriculture was listed by only 10 out of 1060 house-holds. The urban population of Cape Town, as in many developing world cities, is highly dependent on the cash economy to secure food, rather than growing their own food source, which makes them vulnerable to the impacts of climate change across a far broader geographical range than is assumed in rural food security and climate change research.

As will be discussed further in the following section, urban households were also highly dependent on informal safety nets, when their ability to source food through purchase fails. Almost half of the sampled households (44.5 per cent) had acquired food through sharing with neighbours in the last year, through eating food provided by others (34.1 per cent) and through borrowing food (29.2 per cent).

Households also ensured some form of food security through manipula-tion of their diet and volumes of food consumed. It was common practice for households to reduce the variety of foods they were eating due to lack of resources (49.0 per cent reported they did this sometimes or often) or even to eat food that they would prefer not to have to eat due a lack of resources to obtain other types of food (48.0 per cent). In addition households were reducing meal sizes (46.4 per cent), eating fewer meals per day (43.4 per cent) and even finding no food of any kind in the household because of lack of resources (36.3 per cent). These reductions in dietary diversity and overall food intake will have long-term health and development impacts on the house-holds. Within our survey we found a median dietary diversity of 6 out of 12 food types but, as Figure 2.3 shows, this seemingly high figure masks the fact that three of the most common food types consumed are largely non-nutritive ("other" was usually tea and coffee). Limited dietary diversity is a part of the struggle for food access linked to food prices and the food geography of the city. Prices are ultimately linked to fluctuations in availability and manage-ment of the wider food system. These fluctuations in availability are often attributed to climate variability, thus connecting household dietary choices and climate change.

A final household survival strategy related to food is that households may defer consumption of food to meet other immediate pressing needs (de Waal 1990). This may be evidenced by Figure 2.2, which illustrates months of adequate nutri-tion. The supply of food to the city was constant throughout the year, so the chal-lenge was not one of availability, but of a failure of access. This may be due to

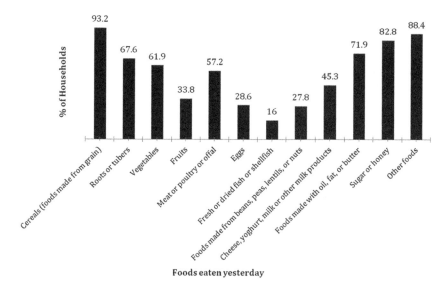

Figure 2.3 Dietary diversity of sampled households

a reduction in income, as happens in January in the city when many sources of formal and casual labour close for the holidays, but it is also likely to be due to demands for increased expenditure for other goods. During the winter months there are higher fuel costs as well as other expenses. Households may defer income that would have been spent on food at these periods pushing them into food insecurity as a livelihood strategy.

The strategies that households are able to employ are both endogenous, but also shaped by wider spatial and economic circumstances of the city. This was evident when the spatial variation in livelihood strategies was considered across the three study sites. For example, casual labour, the most common alternative strategy, was far most frequently utilised in Ocean View due to its proximity to wealthy areas of the city and therefore sites of potential employment. The extremely peripheral Khayelitsha site had the lowest proportion of casual labour. The urban form and relations between places play a significant role in determining possible livelihood strategies, and also the ability to access food. In considering strategies to address food insecurity it is vital to engage with the spatial nature of the urban food system and access to food in urban areas. The following section on sources of food will highlight these issues.

The sources of food in Cape Town:
a justification for the new model

Within the Cape Town survey, households accessed food from a wide range of sources (Figure 2.4). This chapter proposes that the evidence of this diversity of sources necessitates a more systematic assessment of the impacts of climate change on urban food security. Each source of food and each food type will have its own path from source to site of consumption and is dependent on a different set on economic, social and political relations, and therefore each will be differently impacted by climate change. This diversity of sources of food provides the starting point for the model proposed in this chapter.

As is evident from Figure 2.4 the vast majority of survey respondents accessed food most frequently through purchase, either in the formal or the informal sector. Virtually every household sampled (99.3 per cent) had purchased food at a supermarket at some point in the previous year. However, just 26.8 per cent went to supermarkets once a week or more. Households were far more likely to purchase their daily or weekly supplies of food from small shops/restaurants/take-aways (mainly spaza shops) or from informal markets/street foods (61.5 per

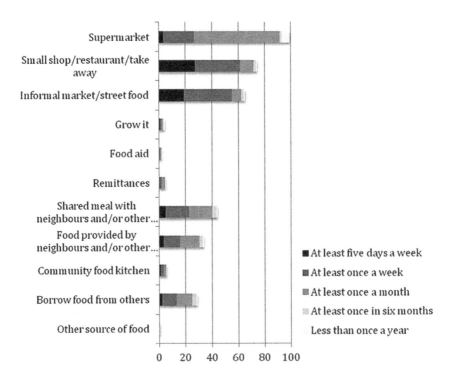

Figure 2.4 Sources of food of sampled households

cent and 55.1 per cent respectively). Supermarkets are generally cheaper per unit purchased than small independent formal shops and spazas. For example, in 1995 the markup on brown bread in a national supermarket was less than 13 per cent, whereas it was 20 per cent in an independent supermarket and 20–26 per cent in urban cafés and spazas (Benyon 1995 in Watkinson and Makgetla 2002: 6). While South African supermarkets are currently being taken to court over price fixing (Harrison 2009), prices in spaza shops are consistently higher. Not only are prices higher, but local politics in Cape Town is ensuring that prices remain high. In June 2009 spaza shop owners in Gugulethu made local Somali traders raise their prices so that the South African-owned spaza shops could remain competitive on price, thus removing access to cheaper food from the urban poor (Underhill 2009).

Supermarkets are generally cheaper per unit than spazas and have higher quality food and far greater diversity of goods. Given the apparent benefits of supermarkets over spazas, why do the urban poor continue to shop at the spaza shops? The first reason is one of geography. Supermarkets are a recent addition to townships and their penetration is only partial. Many areas, like Ocean View, are not serviced by a supermarket at all and other areas have only one supermarket servicing a large spatial extent. Residents tend to be dependent on public transport. Lack of proximity coupled with limited mobility of residents makes spaza shops the only viable daily source of food. In addition, supermarkets may be cheaper per unit, but they tend to sell in larger packages than spazas, who then break these bulk supplies into smaller units before resale. Poor urban residents cannot afford to buy in bulk and therefore buy in smaller amounts at spazas, which are more expensive per unit of weight. And finally, many spazas extend credit to customers, a service that supermarkets cannot offer (Ligthelm 2005: 210).

Supermarkets are increasingly penetrating township markets though. South African supermarkets are increasingly entering the Southern African market too, and changing the food-retailing sector (Abrahams 2010). Supermarkets now account for 60 per cent of all food sales in South Africa, but account for less than 2 per cent of all food retail outlets, and a far smaller minority of all food retailer outlets in township areas (Weatherspoon and Reardon 2003: 337). The recent surge in supermarket entry into township areas can be attributed both to growing disposable income among African consumers, which has effectively opened new markets to the supermarkets and their subsidiaries (such as Boxer owned by Pick N Pay and Sentra owned by Shoprite) (van Wyk 2004). In addition, the improved infrastructure in many townships has made the presence of large retail businesses feasible (Tustin and Strydom 2006: 56). This movement of the larger formal retailers into township areas will clearly impact the informal food markets, which have been valued at between R20bn and R30bn per year (Apps 2004). The African Co-operative for Hawkers and Informal Businesses (ACHIB) has stated that about 150 informal retail stores (spazas) in Soweto alone have been forced out of business in part due to the entry of large retail chains into the township (Bissiker 2006).This shifting dynamic within the food retail sector in South African cities in general and townships in particular raises some interesting questions around urban food security with reference to climate change. Supermarkets and spazas differ in both the diversity of foods on offer and the source of foods on offer. While spazas sell many highly processed foods that are also available in supermarkets (bread, potato chips, carbonated drinks, sweets), many spazas and street traders also sell locally sourced and locally produced foods. For example, it is estimated that some 30 per cent of produce grown in the Philippi Horticultural Area (a commercial agricultural area within the city of Cape Town) finds its way into the local informal food sector. Research recently undertaken by a Master's student at the University of Cape Town suggests that this figure may be higher (Jackson 2011). The fresh produce sold in supermarkets is far less likely to be locally sourced, coming from elsewhere within South Africa or from beyond national borders. Climate change and climate variability will affect supplies of fresh fruit and vegetables differently according to the region of origin. The supply chains in place within the formal and informal sectors are also different and are therefore not affected by economic and political processes in the same ways.

It therefore appears that a blend of formal and informal food systems within the city may bring resilience to food access for the urban populations. However, this blend itself may not be sustainable, as evidenced by the data on spazas going out of business because of the presence of supermarkets. Cities need to consider the value of the informal sector for urban residents in future development planning. Informality may be viewed as an indicator of poverty, but it is also an important source of insurance for the poor against hunger. In addition, it provides an opportunity for the enhancement of a localised food system that acts in parallel with the more commercially viable linear food system operated by the supermarkets.

While this section has thus far focused on the market, formal and informal, Figure 2.4 clearly indicates that the market does not work adequately for the urban poor. Not only are people often buying lower quality foods for higher prices, but many people are also dependent on alternative sources of food. A large proportion of the sample population acquired food from neighbours and other households through sharing meals (44.5 per cent in the last year), eating food provided by others (34.1 per cent) and borrowing food (29.2 per cent). A smaller amount received food as remittances (5.5 per cent in the last year). As Figure 2.4 illustrates, those households receiving food in this manner tend to receive it from these sources at least once a month. Furthermore, the more food insecure a household is, the more likely it is to be dependent on these informal sources of food. The importance of these social networks to ensure food security will be returned to in the following section.

A final point to be addressed with regard to sources of food is the relative absence of urban agriculture (UA) in the Cape Town data. Less than 5 per cent of sampled households stated that they sourced food by growing it. The city of Cape Town is the only city in Africa to have an urban agriculture policy and has dedicated much attention to the encouragement of UA (City of Cape Town 2007). The benefits of UA in providing an alternative means of accessing food for households has been acknowledged by many authors (e.g. May and Rogerson 1995;

Mougeot 2006), and yet it is not significant in poor areas of Cape Town. Barriers to the take up of UA include access to land, skills and local attitudes to farming. Given resistance to UA by residents and local climate change projections coupled with increasing pressure on land and water supplies, it does not appear prudent to advocate for significant extension of UA in Cape Town. However, it is potentially an important source of food in other cities and provides a source of food from local areas (as opposed to the more distant sourcing of food from supermarkets for example). If simply as a means of providing an alternative path for food to flow into the urban food system, it should be considered as a means of increasing the resilience of food supply.

This section has already begun to consider multiple means of supplying food as a means to bring resilience into the urban food system. This introduces the theme of flows, which will be discussed more extensively in the following section.

A new model to understand the impacts of climate change on urban food security

One of the challenges associated with conceptualising connections between urban food security and climate has been a concern about scale mismatches, both temporally and spatially. Many of the problems, with particular reference to the spatial scale mismatch, can be associated with the attempt to look at climate change and food security *in situ*. However, as the material presented above indicates, much of household and broader city-scale food security is determined by processes and relationships only indirectly connected to the urban area itself. For example, food prices are shaped by climate variability in growing areas, oil prices, currency fluctuations, commodity speculation and food policy failures, to name a few (Wiggins 2005; Cohen and Garrett 2009; Minot 2011). These factors are largely external to the cities, but fundamentally affect urban food security. In addition, because the urban food system and the factors shaping access to food are so diverse and operating at so many different scales, attempting to draw a single local model is inappropriate.

As a result of the findings presented, this chapter proposes a model for understanding the connections between urban food security and climate change, and perhaps for developing strategies to enhance food security, which views food security as a series of flows to and within cities. For the purposes of this chapter, the focus will be on flows of food, cash, people and social networks, although it is acknowledged that in other contexts other flows may be important.

The ability of households to ensure their food security is dependent on their ability to navigate and manipulate these flows. Households may depend on each of these flows in different ways at different times. Each of these flows is potentially impacted by climate change.[3] Should this occur, the model hypothesises that households will use their adaptive capacity to modify how they engage with the flows in question and use alternative paths to attempt to meet their food security needs.

It is important to look at each of these flow types in some detail to consider how they operate and the likely impact of climate change upon their operation. In this model all flows have common features (see Figure 2.5). In each there is a site of consumption (the household) and a source of flow. The path that a good or service takes is subject to points of friction (indicated by the symbol ⩗ in Figures 2.5–2.7), which make the flow less efficient and reduces the volume of the flow. These may be points that are particularly vulnerable to climate change, for example a limited germination season or a vulnerable cold chain. Each path may also have points of divergence where the good or service takes alternative paths, only to reconnect to reform a single flow (indicated by the symbol ⟡ in Figures 2.5–2.7, where the thickness of the line represents the strength of the flow on the alternative paths). An example of this may be the sale of food to different types of distributors (such as a supermarket and an informal trader), which allows different paths to the site of consumption. There may also be absolute barriers to the flow (indicated by the symbol ⊠ in Figures 2.5–2.7), such as a tariff barrier, a pricing mechanism or a weather event that makes it impossible for the good or service to reach the site of consumption. Another form may be the loss of an important source of household income. In cases where this occurs, it is anticipated that alternative pathways may emerge, but these will be much more limited than the original path. Different points along the flow will be impacted by climate change in different ways.

There is rarely just one source of each kind of flow entering an urban area, and therefore a site of consumption. As Figure 2.6 illustrates, there will be a number of different sources leading to the same site of consumption. Given the differences in the sources, and perhaps also the substance of the good or service (for example, maize not wheat), the flows will be resilient or vulnerable to different conditions of change through the presence of redundancies. If one flow is weakened by climate change, it is likely that another emanating from a geographical source, operating along different paths, may be less impacted.

Through understanding the dynamics of the flows in operation and potential additional sources, it is possible to use this model to think of ways to enhance

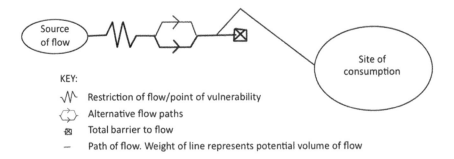

Figure 2.5 Factors shaping the flow of resource from source to site of consumption

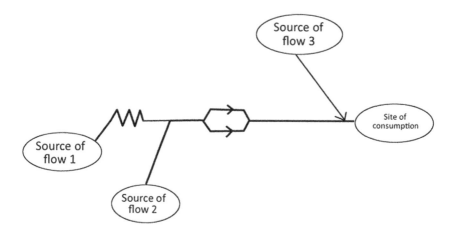

Figure 2.6 The connections between different sources of the same flow type to the site of consumption

urban food security and reduce vulnerability to climate change. Using this model, it may be important for national governments to encourage production of a range of staples and to have a wide import base. It may also be important to put in place policies to support informal traders and to facilitate the diversification of livelihoods of the urban poor.

Households access food through drawing on multiple types of flows, not simply food, but also cash, people and social networks. These types of flow are drawn on concurrently by households to ensure food security (see Figure 2.7), and each is potentially impacted by climate change in different ways at different times. It is essential to understand the connections between these diverse flows and the capabilities of households to draw on these flows to access food. The model as

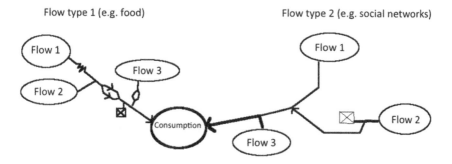

Figure 2.7 The connection between different flow types and the site of consumption

proposed therefore argues that it is important to understand not just the dynamics of the food system, but also how households are able to use their asset base to optimise navigation of these diverse flows.

Flows and climate change

This chapter has identified four key sets of flows households draw upon to ensure food security. These are all potentially impacted by climate change. The following section highlights some critical points in each form of flow.

Food

The diet of the urban poor is based largely on cereals, with 93.2 per cent of sampled households eating products made from grains within the past 24 hours. In Cape Town there is a high dependency on bread and maize products as the staple of the diet. It is therefore most important to examine the potential impacts of climate change on this aspect of the food flow system.

There are four key sources that feed into how the urban poor in Cape Town access grain and associated grain-based products. They are either bought in the formal sector, or bought in the informal sector, through social networks or sourced directly from relatives and friends. This last option was not very important in the Cape Town context with very few households obtaining food in this manner, but it is included in this chapter because it was an important source of food in a number of the other cities within the AFSUN survey. Remittances of food have been recognised as an increasingly important feature of urban life, particularly in times of economic hardship. This will be examined further in the cash, people and social networks sub-sections.

As noted, the formal sector tends to source food from beyond the local food context. In the case of wheat and maize products, the informal sector is also largely dependent on big national companies. The important spatial scales to be considered are therefore the national and regional projections for climate change. These projections suggest either a decline or a collapse of the wheat sector in the Western Cape and a reduction in maize production (Gbetibouo and Hassan 2005; Akpalu *et al.* 2008). There are suggestions in the literature that farmers could shift to other crop types more adapted to projected climate regimes.

Climate change is not the only factor likely to shape the ongoing trends of availability of grain production. In a presentation in February 2010, Theo de Jager of Agri-SA stated that climate change was just one threat amongst many that were issuing a challenge to national food sovereignty. He highlighted uncertainty in the agricultural sector with regard to land reform as already impacting productivity and spoke extensively about pricing structures. The prices that farmers are currently receiving from the local market for wheat are making local agriculture commercially unviable. It makes better economic sense for retailers to purchase from Latin America (de Jager 2010). The position that Agri-SA has taken is that ensuring national food sovereignty is vitally important, should a circumstance like the food price increases of 2008 occur again.[4] In 2008, exporting countries like Argentina blocked the export of grain to ensure national food supply, therefore forcing up global prices. Given that South Africa became a net importer of food in 2008, this makes the country more vulnerable to international pricing trends, which may be driven by climate impacts amongst other things (Agri-SA 2009).

The major climate related impacts upon the flows of food are likely to be those at the regional and national scales, but local, city-scale climate change and variability may also impact the food flow, particularly within the informal sector. The projected increase in temperature in Cape Town will reduce the shelf life of many foodstuffs (Bentham and Langford 1995; Hall *et al.* 2002). Given the limited cooling and temperature regulation capacity of most informal traders, this will impact the availability and therefore the prices of food. In addition, extreme weather events, which are projected to increase in frequency, may lead to the widespread loss of stock, which will lead to short term shortages and extended periods of recovery through increased prices.

It is vital to recognise that similar foods, even food emanating from the same source but taking different paths to the site of consumption, may be impacted by climate change in different ways. Supermarket wholesalers may raise prices in anticipation of shortages using seasonal forecasts, but traders buying directly from farmers and selling to smaller traders may not shift their pricing structures through lack of information. Thus the same food from the same source may enter the market at different prices.[5]

The question is therefore how to make the flows of food more resilient to ensure urban food security. Some authors suggest that farmers will diversify or even completely shift their crop type in light of projected climate change (Gbetibouo and Hassan 2005). This wholesale shift is unlikely given that farmers (both commercial and small scale) are notoriously risk averse (Thornton *et al.* 2004). However, there may be some shifts in production. It has been suggested that urban populations are more open to including new foods in their diets than traditional rural communities, so these shifts may be accepted by urban populations. Increased diversity of foodstuffs and food sources would incorporate various redundancies into the food flow, which would help to ensure urban food security.

Cash

While the flow of food is vital to ensuring food security, it is also essential to recognise that access to cash to purchase food is also integral. Cash flows into households through formal waged work, casual labour, through social grants and through remittances. As with flows of food, there are different points of vulnerability within these flows, impacted by events in a range of locations. As discussed earlier, household livelihoods are not particularly diverse in the Cape Town survey and this makes them vulnerable to external shocks, as they are dependent on one source of flow to enable them to purchase food.

It is difficult to make generalisations about the potential impacts of climate change on the flow of cash to ensure food security, given the diversity of sources of employment and therefore sources of income. However, it is useful to note that while the direct causes of employment loss may be locally generated (firm closures, work ceasing due to seasonal fluctuations), the indirect causes may be generated from processes occurring at a regional or international scale. The flows model calls for these direct and indirect factors to be considered in understanding the points of restriction of flow and vulnerability and barriers to flows. While it is difficult to identify potential impacts of climate change on the flow of cash, what the flow model does highlight is the possibility of food security being ensured through the navigation and manipulation of multiple sources of flow within a particular flow type. The cash from casual labour flow may be impacted by short-term climate variability (storms, floods, seasonality) but the formal wage sector is likely to be more resilient to this. Likewise, the alternative livelihood strategies in the informal wage sector may be more resilient to economic shocks, such as recessions, than the formal wage sector. Flows of cash through remittances from rural areas can be drawn upon in times of climate related or other crises in the urban area. It is clear that being able to draw upon multiple sources of flows of cash, vulnerable and resilient in different circumstances and points in the flow, is an important means of ensuring food security and insuring against climate related risk.

People

The flow of people is a slightly different kind of flow. Migrancy itself can be a food security strategy. A household may relocate members in order to increase potential earnings or to reduce expenditure. This may be a relatively short-term strategy or a long-term strategy, in which households maintain a rural and an urban base to spread risk. These "stretched households",[6] like all things elastic, have a snapping point when too much pressure is exerted on the flow. Under conditions of increased climate variability and climate change there is likely to be increased marginality of smallholder farming in rural South and Southern Africa. Given this, there may be less benefit to having these stretched households as the stability of an agricultural income declines. It is likely that there will therefore be increased rural to urban migration as households consolidate in urban areas. In addition, with the pressures from climate change and other factors discussed in the food flow section, the commercial agriculture section is likely to displace more farm workers from residence on farms as profit margins fall and job security will be lost (Agri-SA 2009). This will place strain on the remittances that feed into the cash flow, and ultimately lead to a reduction in existing stretched households[7] and increased urbanisation. However, while the in-country rural–urban stretched household may be in decline, some cities, most notably Harare in Zimbabwe, are seeing evidence that cross-border stretched households are becoming increasingly important (Tawodzera 2010). This new source of flow of people introduces a more resilient form as it enables households to source finance and resources from places with different political and economic circumstances, and, particularly in the case of Zimbabwe, to navigate differences in currency to the households' benefit.

Social networks

The final type of flow is the flow of social relations. This refers to the ways in which households negotiate access to food through drawing on existing relationships in their community. This flow is largely independent from the wider flows of food, flows of cash and even flows of people. It is the flow that operates when the other flows are weak. As was evident in Figure 2.4, many households, particularly the more food insecure households, depend on frequently borrowing food and sharing food with neighbours. This practice is widely accepted as culturally appropriate, but it does place responsibility for forming a social safety net in the event of market failure on residents in poor areas of cities. This can ultimately lead to reduced resilience of these households. In the event of the other flows being negatively impacted by climate change (increased prices, limited employment, limited rural to urban flows) these supporting households may find that they are no longer able to provide food to food insecure households, thus greatly weakening or even blocking this flow. In Cape Town there was very limited evidence of non-governmental organisations (NGOs) working to ensure food security in the sampled communities. The need for social safety nets will increase as a result of climate change, at the same time as the ability of communities to provide these informal safety nets declines. There is therefore a need to reconfigure the functioning of this flow to introduce new forms of safety nets that can respond to needs of households when access to food through other flows fails.

Non-access related climate change impacts

Moving beyond the focus on flows, it is also important to consider the possible impact of climate change on households' ability to utilise the food they are able to access, which in turn may shape the foods that households access. As in the case of the flows these are both direct and indirectly impacted by climate change and extreme weather events. Many poor households have limited capacity to store goods, particularly foods that require refrigeration. This clearly shapes the quantities and types of foods purchased. As noted earlier, in buying in smaller quantities households incur higher costs per unit. In addition, with limited storage and cooking capacity, many households may be dependent on purchasing processed foods for home preparation or depend on street foods, both of which are more expensive than unprocessed foods and are often nutritionally deficient. Should the long-term projections of increased temperatures in the city occur, the shelf life of foods will be reduced, increasing the chance of spoilage for households with limited refrigeration capacity. Bentham and Langford (1995) argue that in the UK context, projected climate change is likely to increase incidences of food poisoning by 179,000 cases per year. In the Southern context where the cold chain is less secure, and poor households lack adequate refrigeration, this figure can only be higher. This is likely to reinforce the practices of buying relatively highly processed foods in small unit sizes, with attendant knock-on effects for food and nutrition security.

It is also likely that Cape Town will experience more extreme weather events (Mukheibir and Ziervogel 2007). As was seen in the data on months of adequate household provisioning, households may choose to experience food insecurity in an attempt to meet urgent household needs. Damage to housing through storms and flooding means that resources that would have been spent on food and food preparation will be deferred to repair and to attempts to mitigate against future events.

The impacts of climate change across a wide range of locations, from the household and the city, to the nation, the region and beyond, all potentially impact household food security.

Conclusions

This chapter has attempted to develop a new model for understanding the dynamics of food security in urban areas through the use of a flow based model. Thus far food security and climate research has tended to focus on the vulnerability of the agricultural sector with little engagement of the wider food system in which agriculture operates or the questions of access and utilisation that drive household food security. Where there has been work on urban impacts of climate change, the focus has tended to be on city-scale impacts. This neglects the dependency of urban areas on resources flowing from many locations beyond the city itself. Both of these approaches fail to grasp the complex, inter-scale interactions that impact urban food security.

The data from the Cape Town survey highlight the range of sources households utilise and the multiple means they use to ensure food supply. This is the basis of the model proposed, which stresses that urban food security is based on the integration of a range of flow types (and individual sources of flows within these broad flow types) in household survival strategies. Urban food security is not just about food, but about the ability of households to mobilise their asset base to draw on existing flows. Given that these flows emanate in different locations and take a range of paths, they are subject to a range of potential climate related impacts.

The model proposed in this chapter is designed not just to be illustrative, but to provide a means to develop food security strategies. A number of new starting points for policy formulation emerge from the model. The first is that food security needs to look beyond the agricultural (and household) scales and engage with the whole food system. Food production, processing, transport, storage and retail are all potentially impacted by climate change. Ways to address the vulnerabilities of each of these stages need to be factored into food security models, and alternative pathways need to be configured to build in redundancies.

The second key point is that the food reaches the household through both formal and informal networks that are vulnerable and resilient in different ways. Thus far the informal has been largely neglected, but it is a vital source of food security for the urban poor and therefore needs to be considered in food security strategies.

The final key point is that food security is not simply about the flows of food, but also other flows that ensure adequate access and utilisation. In the model cash, people and social networks were highlighted. Food security policies need to be informed both by flows of food and by the capability set that households have and the ways in which they utilise available assets. Governments (local and national) and NGOs therefore need to work to ensure the survival of flow types that have been largely neglected thus far, including the informal food system, rural–urban connections and social networks.

There are at present vast knowledge gaps about the vulnerability of each of the identified flows to climate change. Further research is therefore necessary on which particular flows are most important for the urban poor, which should then be followed by a second phase of research that investigates the vulnerability of that flow to climate change.

In conclusion, this chapter uses the model to argue that by encouraging dependence on a wider range of flow types and specific flows within each flow type (by increasing the number of redundancies), household food security can be enhanced. Given the current formulation of food security policies and functioning of governments and NGOs it may be that the advocated approach is not viable; however, it is hoped that this model provides a means for integrated cross-scale systems thinking to develop more robust connections between climate change and urban food security.

Notes

1   The African Food Security Urban Network (AFSUN) is supported by funding from the Canadian International Development Agency (CIDA) under its University Partners in Cooperation and Development (UPCD) Tier One Program.
2   Levels of food insecurity were calculated using the Food and Technical Assistance Project's (FANTA's) Household Food Insecurity Access Scale measurement tool (Coates *et al.* 2007).
3   These flows will be impacted by many external pressures, but for the purposes of this chapter, the focus is on climate change.
4   As is currently occurring in 2011.
5   There are of course many other non-climate related reasons for this, but for the purpose of this chapter the climate related issues are highlighted.
6   Stretched households are defined by Moultrie and Timaeus as "domestic units that are connected across time by kinship and remittances of income" (2001: 211).
7   This displacement of commercial farm labour households may, however, lead to the stretching of previously nuclear households as households negotiate their new residential and economic realities.

References

Abrahams, C. (2010) Transforming the region: Supermarkets and the local food economy, *African Affairs*, 109: 115–134.

Agri-SA (2009) Agricultural policy statements, http://www.agrisa.co.za/agri_eng1.htm (accessed 5 February 2009).

Akpalu, W., Hassan, R. H. and Ringler, C. (2008) Climate variability and maize yield in South Africa: Results from GME and MELE methods, *International Food Policy Research Institute Discussion Paper Series*, 00843.

Apps, P. (2004) Supermarket chains set sights on lucrative township locations, business report, http://www.eprop.co.za/news/article.aspx?idArticle=4646 (accessed 4 October 2004).

Atkinson, S. J. (1995) Approaches and actors in urban food security in developing countries, *Habitat International*, 19, 2: 151–163.

Ballantine, N., Rousseau, G. G. and Venter, D. J. L. (2008) Purchasing behaviour as a determinant of food insecurity in Klipplaat, *Journal of Family Economy and Consumer Science*, 36: 1–8.

Battersby, J. (2011) The state of urban food insecurity in Cape Town, *Urban Food Security Series*, 8, African Urban Food Security Network (AFSUN), Idasa Publishing, Cape Town.

Bentham, G. and Langford, I. H. (1995) Climate change and the incidence of food poisoning in England and Wales, *International Journal of Biometeorology*, 39, 2: 81–86.

Bissiker, C. (2006) Retailers' drive into the township market threatens spaza shops, http://www.eprop.co.za/news/article.aspx?idArticle=7908 (accessed 28 September 2006).

City of Cape Town (2007) *Urban Agriculture Policy for the City of Cape Town*, Cape Town: City of Cape Town.

Coates, J., Swindale, A. and Bilinsky, P. (2007) *Household Food Insecurity Access Scale (HFIAS) for Measurement of Food Access: Indicator Guide Volume 3*, Washington D.C: Food and Technical Assistance Project (FANTA), Academy for Educational Development.

Cohen, M. J. and Garrett, J. L. (2009) The food price crisis and urban food (in)security, *International Institute for Environment and Development Human Settlements Working Paper Series, Urbanization and Emerging Population Issues*, 2.

Crush, J. and Frayne, B. (2010a) Pathways to insecurity: Urban food supply and access in southern African cities, *African Food Security Urban Network Urban Food Security Series*, 3.

Crush, J. and Frayne, B. (2010b) The invisible crisis: Urban food security in Southern Africa, *African Food Security Urban Network Urban Food Security Series*, 1.

de Jager, T. (2010) Agricultural factors influencing food and nutrition security in South Africa today, *Food and Nutrition Security Workshop,* North West University, Potchefstroom, 9–10 February

de Waal, A. (1989) *Famine That Kills*, Oxford: Clarendon Press.

Frayne, B., Pendleton, W., Battersby, J., Bras, E., Chiweza, A., Dlamini, T., Fincham, R., Kroll, F., Leduka, C., Mosha, A., Mulenga, C., Pomuti, A., Raimundo, I., Rudolph, M., Ruysenaar, A., Simelane, N., Tevera, D., Tsoka, M., Tawodzera, G. and Zanamwe, L. (2010) The state of urban food security in Southern Africa, *Urban Food Security Series*, 2, African Food Security Urban Network (AFSUN), Idasa Publishing, Cape Town

Gbetibouo, G. E. and Hassan, R. M. (2005) Measuring the economic impact of climate change on major South African field crops: A Ricardian approach, *Global and Planetary Change,* 47: 143–152.

Hall, G. V., d'Souza, R. M. and Kirk, M. D. (2002) Foodborne disease in the new millennium: Out of the frying pan and into the fire?, *Medical Journal of Australia,* 177: 614–618.

Harrison, S. (2009) SA retailers under investigation, *Moneyweb,* http://www.moneyweb. co.za/mw/view/mw/en/page91?oid=301185&sn=Detail (accessed 29 June 2009).

Jackson, A. L. (2011) Informal and formal linkages: A case study of the vegetable production in the Philippi Horticultural Area in Cape Town's local food system, unpublished thesis, Department of Environmental and Geographical Science, University of Cape Town.

Ligthelm, A. A. (2005) Informal retailing through home-based micro-enterprises: The role of spaza shops, *Development Southern Africa,* 22, 2: 199–214.

Maxwell, D. (1999) The political economy of urban food security in Sub-Saharan Africa, *World Development,* 27, 11: 1939–1953.

May, J. and Rogerson, C. (1995) Poverty and sustainable cities in South Africa: The role of urban cultivation, *Habitat International,* 19, 2: 165–181.

Mehta, D. (2000) Urbanization of poverty, *Habitat Debate,* 6, 4.

Minot, N. (2011) Transmission of world food price changes to markets in sub-Saharan Africa, *International Food Policy Research Institute Discussion Paper,* 01059.

Mougeot, L. (2006) *Growing Better Cities: Urban Agriculture for Sustainable Development,* Ottawa: IDRC.

Moultrie, T. A. and Timaeus, I. M. (2001) Fertility and living arrangements in South Africa, *Journal of Southern African Studies,* 27, 2: 207–223.

Mukheibir, P. and Ziervogel, G. (2007) Developing a Municipal Adaptation Plan (MAP) for climate change: The city of Cape Town, *Environment and Urbanization,* 19, 1: 143–158.

Ravallion, M. (2007) On the urbanization of poverty, *Journal of Development Economics,* 68, 2: 435–442.

Steel, C. (2008) *Hungry City: How Food Shapes Our Lives,* London: Chatto & Windus.

Tawodzera, G. (2010) Vulnerability and resilience in crisis: Household food insecurity in Harare, Zimbabwe, unpublished PhD thesis, Department of Environmental and Geographical Science, University of Cape Town.

Thornton, P. K., Fawcett, R. H. Galvin, K. A., Hudson, J. W. and Vogel, C. H. (2004) Evaluating management options that use climate forecasts: Modelling livestock production systems in the semi-arid zones of South Africa, *Climate Research,* 26: 33–42.

Tustin, D. H. and Strydom, J. W. (2006) The potential impacts of the formal retail chains' expansion strategies on retail township development in South Africa, *South African Business Review,* 10, 3: 48–66.

Underhill, G. (2009) Cape Town fears xenophobic flare up, *Mail and Guardian,* http:// www.mg.co.za/article/2009-07-26-cape-town-fears-xenophobic-flareup (accessed 26 July 2009).

UN-HABITAT (2009) *Planning for Sustainable Cities: Global Report on Human Settlements 2009,* London: Earthscan.

van Wyk, H. de J. (2004) National Personal Income of South Africans by Population Group, Income Group, Life Stage and Lifeplane, *Research Report No. 333,* Pretoria: Bureau of Market Research, University of South Africa.

Watkinson, E. and Makgetla, N. (2002) *South Africa's Food Security Crisis*, report compiled for National Labour and Economic Development Institute (NALEDI), http://www.sarpn.org.za/documents/d0000077/P93_safscrisis.pdf (accessed 9 August 2011).

Weatherspoon, D. D. and Reardon, T. (2003) The rise of supermarkets in Africa: Implications for agrifood systems and the rural poor, *Development Policy Review*, 21, 3: 333–355.

Wiggins, S. (2005) Southern Africa's food and humanitarian crisis of 2001–2004: Causes and lessons, *Discussion Paper for Agricultural Economics Society Conference*, Nottingham, UK, 4–6 April.

3

URBAN HOUSEHOLD VULNERABILITY TO FOOD SECURITY AND CLIMATE CHANGE

Experiences from urban areas of Zimbabwe

Godfrey Tawodzera

Introduction

The world population has more than doubled in the last 50 years, from 3 billion to the current estimate of around 6.7 billion people (WFP *et al.*, 2009). Over half of these are third world urban dwellers living in deplorable conditions where they face an uncertain future characterized by myriad challenges ranging from inadequate urban infrastructure to shortages of basic food necessities. Urban poverty is at the centre of this vulnerability in Southern Africa, leading the United Nations (2007) to conclude that the target of halving the number of people living in poverty in this region by 2015 (as encapsulated in the Millennium Development Goals; MDGs) will not be met. There are indications that in some countries such as Angola and Zimbabwe, the poor account for over 50 per cent of the urban population and they live daily with the persistent threat of hunger and food insecurity. The severity of these problems is likely to increase in the foreseeable future, given the large-scale urbanization process currently underway in the region.

While urban poverty and food insecurity are undoubtedly major development problems facing humanity in the 21st century, the situation is compounded by the addition of another challenge: that of climate change. Climate change is not only bringing in new challenges but, in the current context of immense global poverty, is undermining efforts to increase food production and availability required to protect livelihoods and reduce the suffering of thousands of urbanites who are currently food insecure. In a developing country such as Zimbabwe, climate change is therefore aggravating hunger, increasing nutrition problems and compounding health issues among the deprived urban populations.

These urbanites live in conditions of extreme deprivation: unable to confront the challenges or effectively adapt to the new demands placed upon them by an uncertain future. Thus, while in the past global attention focused more on mitigation measures than on other aspects of the climate change regime, recent efforts have shifted more to adaptation measures, realizing that climate change is already occurring with unexpected risks, and that society needs to adapt if it is to survive the negative consequences. For urban food security, the implications are enormous as the already ominous food and service burden in cities assumes even greater significance. Poor urban populations are therefore facing even greater challenges as they battle to adapt to changing needs and challenges. While this chapter seeks to highlight the vulnerability of the urban poor to food insecurity in Zimbabwe in the context of climate change, it also endeavours to showcase the ways in which some poor urban households in the city are using their assets to adapt to climate change and in the process protect themselves from food insecurity. The chapter concludes by suggesting a range of potential options and opportunities for supporting the poor's adaptation efforts to building resilient adaptive capacity.

Urbanization, poverty and food security in Zimbabwe

More than half of the world's population currently lives in urban areas and a greater proportion of the growth expected to occur between 2000 and 2030 will be concentrated in cities (UNFP, 2007). The urbanization rates in sub-Saharan Africa are historically unprecedented, averaging around four per cent per annum, and are likely to result in over 300 million new urban residents being added to the subcontinent between 2000 and 2030 (Kessides, 2005). The Southern African region is no exception to these urbanization trends. Its population is growing three times faster than its rural counterpart and predictions are that over half of its population will live in urban areas by 2015 (Crush et al., 2007). The sheer magnitude of these population increases makes it almost impossible for urban authorities to provide adequate infrastructure and guarantee sufficiency in most urban services. Given the evidence that "the poor are urbanizing faster than the population as a whole" (Ravallion et al., 2007: 693), the ability of these underprivileged people in the cities of the region to provision themselves in challenging urban environments becomes uncertain.

Exacerbating Southern Africa's situation is the fact that the urbanization process in the region appears to be taking place without the complementary industrialization and economic growth that seems to have characterized the growth of urban areas in other regions of the world. There is enough evidence to suggest that the urbanization process of the region has often taken place independent from industrialization. As Watson (2007: 208) observes, development in this region seems to have been decoupled from the urbanization process. Worsening this scenario is the fact that economic growth, job opportunities, real wages and per capita incomes have taken a consistently downward trajectory since the 1970s (Bryceson, 2006). Moreover, the sheer numerical population increases in the urban areas has resulted in most urban dwellers being unemployed or underemployed, resulting in the solidification of a large body of the urban poor who have little or no income to meet their daily needs.

In Zimbabwe, as is the case in most of the countries of the region, the negative impacts of the Economic Structural Adjustment Programme (ESAP) of the 1990s precipitated the closure of many factories, triggered massive retrenchments and stalled wages in an environment of persistent skyrocketing consumer prices (Potts, 2006). Although the 2003 Poverty Assessment Study Survey (PASS) indicated that poverty levels were still higher in rural than in urban areas, it also unequivocally showed that the highest increase in poverty levels between 1995 and 2003 was recorded in urban areas (65 per cent) in comparison to rural areas (42 per cent) (Government of Zimbabwe, 2006: 20). Added to this already precarious situation, a decade-long socio-political crisis in the country has created severe hardships for urbanites whose standards of living have deteriorated drastically. Some of these hardships include housing shortages, insufficient water supplies, inadequate refuse collection, health problems, hunger, food shortages and the consequent food insecurity.

The problems of hunger and food shortages in Zimbabwe in the past decade have been extensively debated (e.g. FEWSNET, 2009; USAID, 2009; Mutonhodzo, 2005; ZimVac, 2003, 2004, 2009). Wide-scale disruptions of large-scale commercial farming activities, a controversial fast-track land redistribution programme and frequent droughts in the past few years have combined to negatively affect food production in the country and served to turn the country from being the bread basket of the region to 'a basket case' perennially banking on humanitarian aid for the survival of the population. Since 2002, the country has been experiencing average national food deficits of cereal staple crops of over 500,000 metric tonnes per annum (FEWSNET, 2009). By the end of 2009, with about 7 million people in need of food aid, the country had become the third largest food aid operation in the world after Afghanistan (8.82 million) and Ethiopia (8.67 million) (IFRC, 2009).

Although food security assessments in urban areas of Zimbabwe have been too few and far apart, there is no doubt that the precipitous deterioration of the Zimbabwean economy since 2000 worsened the food security situation in the urban areas of the country. This insecurity was further aggravated by the implementation of Operation Murambatsvina. Launched in Harare in May 2005, this was an operation in which the government destroyed backyard houses, vending stalls, flea markets and informal businesses in the urban areas of the country. They argued that they were enforcing urban by-laws to stop "illegal" activities, and to prevent the "chaotic" manifestations of rapid urbanization that are usually characteristic of African cities (Government of Zimbabwe, 2005). Critics of the government, however, argue that the essence of the operation was to disperse a restive urban population that could have provided a breeding ground for a revolutionary protest against the government for the increasing cost of living and declining urban conditions (International Crisis Group, 2005).

The operation caused massive destruction of livelihoods in the urban areas and affected more than 700,000 urbanites who lost either their homes, livelihoods or both (Mugara, 2007). Thousands more were made homeless without access to food, water, sanitation or health care (Tibaijuka, 2005). The displacement also exacerbated an already precarious housing situation as many families ended up staying in the open, in already overcrowded informal settlements, or living in squalid conditions in transit camps such as Caledonia, on the outskirts of Harare. Besides causing widespread environmental destruction through the cutting down of trees for shelter and fuel, these transit camps also represented a health hazard as outbreaks of cholera, diarrhoea and dysentery increased.

Deteriorating urban health conditions have become more pronounced generally in the urban environment where municipal authorities battle to provide adequate health facilities. A cholera outbreak in the country in August 2008, for example, continued well into 2009, affecting 98,114 people and claiming over 4,274 lives by May 2009 (IFRC, 2009). The disease was concentrated in urban areas, particularly in the cities of Harare, Mutare and Bulawayo where water supply, sanitary and health services had virtually collapsed and most homes were without a source of clean water for over a year. Without access to clean, adequate and safe water, food security for most households in the urban areas thus hangs in the balance as water is essential for proper preparation, consumption and utilization of food.

Besides being rendered homeless by Operation Murambatsvina, people also lost their jobs as informal businesses were demolished; homeowners lost income as properties they used to rent were destroyed; small-scale operators lost business because of the disruption of the supply chain; and many people who were formally employed lost income as they were forced to leave their jobs as a result of the loss of shelter (Tibaijuka, 2005). The livelihoods of the poor were therefore destroyed and food insecurity increased in the declining economic environment. An Urban Household Baseline Survey conducted by the African Food Security Urban Network (AFSUN) in 2008 in Harare, for example, indicated that 95 per cent of the surveyed urban households were food insecure (Frayne et al., 2010). This was a significant increase from the 64 per cent of Harare's urban population that had been classified as food insecure in 2003 (ZimVac, 2004). Although methodological differences between the 2008 and the 2003 surveys present some comparative challenges and the 2008 survey was, admittedly, a pro-poor survey, these statistics nevertheless paint a bleak picture of the food security situation in the urban areas of the country.

Results from other cities in the country have not been different as Bulawayo and Masvingo urban areas were posited to have 71 per cent and 54 per cent respectively of their urban population being food insecure (ZimVac, 2004). The 2009 Zimbabwe Vulnerability Assessment Committee Urban Food Security Assessment (ZimVac, 2009) shows that that between 500,000 and 900,000 of Zimbabwe's urban population were, by the end of 2009, regarded as food insecure. The vulnerability of these urbanites was more pronounced as the country was meeting most of its food requirements through imports rather than domestic production. This made domestic markets captive to the global increases, fuelling domestic prices that had already skyrocketed in the country's hyperinflationary environment. Thus while food imports have, on the one hand served to ease food insecurity by improving the availability of food on the market, they have, on the other, also made basic commodities unaffordable as prices remain higher than regional levels. Although the political situation in the country has improved significantly since the formation of the Government of National Unity in February 2009, and the economic decline has been arrested, the urbanites are still vulnerable to shocks that include: high utility bills, high food prices, high rentals as well as high unemployment rates that forestall the possibility of a stable income in this cash demanding environment (ZimVac, 2009). While these challenging conditions in the city are already daunting for the majority of the urban poor, the additional challenge of climate change is making them even more overwhelming, and calls for measures to be put in place to enable the poor to adapt to the demands of climate change have been made.

Climate change: multiplying urban food security vulnerabilities

The United Nations Framework Convention on Climate Change (UNFCCC, 2011), Article 1, defines climate change as "a change of climate that is attributed directly or indirectly to human activity that alters the composition of the global atmosphere and which is in addition to natural climate variability observed over comparable time periods". This change results from the increased concentration in the atmosphere of gases such as carbon dioxide, methane, nitrous oxide and halocarbons, which are gases that contain fluorine, chlorine and bromine. Evidence of climate change is indisputable, as increases in global air and ocean temperatures; changes in precipitation amounts, ocean salinity and frequency of droughts; increasing intensity of heat waves and tropical cyclones; changing wind patterns; widespread melting of snow and ice as well as rising global average sea levels have been observed (IPCC, 2007a; Hulme, 2009). According to the IPCC (2007a) there is clear evidence that there was a 0.75°C rise in global temperature and a 22 centimetre rise in sea level in the 20th century. Predictions are that the temperature may increase by about 1.1–6.4°C while the sea level may rise by between 28cm and 79cm by the year 2100 (Maslin, 2009). Climate change has moved beyond being an environmental challenge to one that threatens development around the world (Hammill *et al.*, 2008).

Like the rest of the world, Zimbabwe is also experiencing significant climate change. An analysis of the country's climatic history by Unganai (1996) indicates that the country's daytime temperatures increased by about 0.1°C per decade between 1933 and 1993 while precipitation declined by an average of about of 1 per cent per decade between 1900 and 1993. Using these trends, Unganai (1996) argued that it is reasonable to assume that another 1–2°C rise in the next 100 years will be equalled or surpassed given the increase being observed in greenhouse gas emissions.

The impact of climate change in the country is already being felt. Six of the warmest years on record for the country, for example, have been recorded since 1987 (Chasi, 2009). It has been observed that the monthly highest daily maximum temperature for most of the country is on the increase, by about 2°C per century (Climate Change Office, 2004). Furthermore, the frequency of droughts has increased with 10 drought years being recorded between 1990 and 2007. A meteorological report compiled using data from the Belvedere (Harare), Goetz (Bulawayo) and Beitbridge weather stations indicate the lack of consistent rainfall patterns over the past 30 years, demonstrating that changes in temperature and weather patterns are affecting the frequency and severity of rainfall, droughts and floods (Chasi, 2009). Declining rainfall and increasing temperature are already having a significant negative impact on agricultural production and on food security (IPCC, 2007b). Most farmers in Zimbabwe, whether rural or urban, rely on natural rainfall, with as much as 90 per cent of crops in the country being grown under rain-fed conditions (Chetsanga, 2000; Chikozho, 2010). Thus farming activities are being affected significantly by climate change (Nyambara, 2003). Additionally, it has been noted through research on the past rainfall seasons that the onset of rains in the country, as in some other Southern African countries, is delaying significantly (Shongwe et al., 2009). Where the rainfall season used to begin in late October, for example, it is now common for the onset to be in late November (Zimbabwe Red Cross Society, 2007), hence negatively affecting crop production and yields.

On the other hand, the number of cold days in the country has also been noted to be decreasing at a rate of 14–17 days per century (Climate Change Office, 2004). Because of these noticeable changes in the country's climate, the Government of Zimbabwe has been quick to recognize global climate change as a serious issue by signing and ratifying the United Nations Framework Convention on Climate Change (UNFCCC) in 1992 after the Rio Earth Summit (Climate Change Office, 2004). Besides the negative impacts of climate change that are currently being experienced, it is expected that further increases in temperature will exacerbate droughts and wreak havoc in both the rural and the urban areas through the disruption of livelihoods as productivity decreases due to scarcer rainfall (Chasi, 2009).

In the midst of this gloomy scenario of negative impacts of climate change, the urban areas are already facing some enormous challenges, particularly among the poor households in terms of food supply. This is because the majority of the urban poor in the country directly access food from rural production through rural–urban household food transfers. Studies by Potts (1997) and Potts and Mutambirwa (1991) in the country indicate food remittances from the rural areas play a critical role in ensuring food security of the urban households. In a survey carried out by Tawodzera (2010) in Harare's residential area of Epworth, 61.5 per cent of the households indicated that they normally receive food from the rural areas every year and that such food was either important or critical to the survival of the household. Therefore any disruptions to the rural production system negatively and significantly impacts on the food security situation of most households, particularly among the poor segments of the urban society.

Besides impacting on urban food security through remittances, climate change has a direct impact on those households engaged in urban agriculture, for an increasing number of urbanites are now resorting to growing part of their food in the city. A regional baseline survey on urban food security in Southern Africa conducted by the AFSUN in 2008, for example, reveals that approximately 60 per cent of the surveyed households in Harare were participating in urban agriculture (Frayne *et al.*, 2010). Several other studies in the country (e.g. Tshuma and Mashoko, 2010; Gumbo, 2000; Drakakis-Smith *et al.*, 1995; Mazambani, 1982) have highlighted the importance of urban agriculture to the food security situation of the urban households in the country. This is even more critical for most of the nation's towns and cities that are located in the Highveld, where good soils and moderate temperatures make urban production viable. By growing part of their own food, urban households minimize their spending towards food expenses (Mbiba, 1995), leaving them with more money to allocate to other competing urban demands.

Under Zimbabwe's economic crisis, the recourse by urban households to urban farming seems to have enabled the poor to deflect the full impact of the economic crisis and made it possible for them to survive in the harsh conditions of the city (Kutiwa *et al.*, 2010). Any conceivable open spaces in the cities were cultivated as most urban authorities turned a blind eye to the activity, which their by-laws consider to be illegal (Kutiwa *et al.*, 2010). Given the increasing role of urban farming in the livelihoods and food security situation of the urban poor, the challenge brought about by climate change is likely to increase vulnerability of the urban population not only to food issues, but also to other expenses that compete with food.

A very important aspect in the climate change–food security debate is that of water supply. Most urban areas in Zimbabwe rely on dams for their water supply. The urban areas of Harare, Chitungwiza, Norton and Ruwa, for example, rely on water harvested from the Manyame catchment area and stored in Lake Chivero (Nhapi, 2009; Gumbo, 2006). This catchment is serviced by rivers that include: Manyame, Mukuvisi and Marimba (Nhapi, 2009). Even using conservative climate change scenarios, predictions are that the current well-watered and perennial rivers within the catchment will develop flow regimes similar to those currently being experienced in the drier parts of the country in the south and the south-west (Gumbo, 2006). Rivers within the catchment will therefore only be able to supply water to the dams seasonally and only erratically for that matter. For cities such as Bulawayo, the impacts could be devastating as well, given that the city already experiences significant water problems (*The Standard*, 2005; Gwebu, 2002). Efforts to supply the city with water from the Zambezi River (through the Zambezi Water Project), some 450 kilometres away, have been in the pipeline for close to five decades now, but nothing substantial has so far been done to ease the city's water problems (Nyoni, 2007; Gwebu, 2002). This is partly because of the shortage of financial capital as well as there being little or no political will on the part of government to see the project succeed.

Water shortages in urban areas of Zimbabwe will aggravate food insecurity in a number of ways. First, the scarcity of water poses dangers in terms of food processing and food safety (Murinda and Kraemer, 2008). Without adequate water supply, most urban people, particularly those in low income and informal settlements, are likely to resort to using water from unprotected sources, thus placing them in danger of contracting water-borne diseases (Murinda and Kraemer, 2008). Already most residential areas in Harare experience persistent water shortages and the expected changes due to climate change will increase the problem (Nhapi, 2009). Residential areas like Tafara, Mabvuku, Budiriro and Epworth are some of the worst affected. In Epworth, for example, the majority of these urban residents access water from open, unprotected and shallow wells (Murinda and Kraemer, 2008). There are a number of homeless people that are at more risk of diseases as they use untreated water from rivers such as the Mukuvisi in Harare. The cholera outbreak of 2008 and 2009 in the urban areas of the country makes evident the dangers that are likely to befall cities in the likely event of acute water shortages. The risk of contamination of water sources is also likely to increase as pollutants in the reservoirs are less diluted owing to fewer water in-flows (IIED, 2008). Increases in illness should therefore be expected, particularly where the standard of water purification may be lowered due to shortage of chemicals. In the case of Harare's reservoir, Lake Chivero, incidents of fish poisoning in the lake have frequently been reported (Chakona, 2003) and chances are that declining flows brought about by climate change will continue to increase the magnitude of the problem. The maintenance of food security in the city is therefore set to become even more precarious.

Besides water problems and the effect that this has on the food security situation of the urban population, the issue of energy is an important aspect in the climate change and urban food security discourse. Although Zimbabwe generates some of its own electricity at Lake Kariba and at Hwange Thermal Power Station, the country remains a net importer of this important resource, hence necessitating imports from such countries as the Democratic Republic of Congo, Zambia and Mozambique (Sullivan, 2011). Already most of the cities are struggling to provide their residents with adequate energy and power cuts have become more frequent in a bid to make the little that is there last longer. Load shedding has become a common practice in the country in a bid to try to make efficient use of the available power. The additional stress from climate change will likely reduce the water available for electricity generation, further limiting the urban poor's access to this crucial commodity. Lack of energy will affect food processing and storage capacity thereby affecting the quality of food available as well as its nutritional value (Mhazo et al., 2003). Already some urban residents, in a bid to find energy for their cooking needs, are resorting to collecting firewood from the peri-urban areas (Chambwera, 2004). The result is that these peri-urban areas have become heavily deforested, further fueling climate change and its detrimental effects.

Thus while Zimbabwean cities are already battling with the impact of urbanization and poverty, climate change represents an additional stress that is increasing demand on a few stretched resources. As the IPCC (2007a) points out, the stress is expected to reduce the ability of some systems to provide key goods and services needed for successful economic and social development, including adequate food, clean air and water, energy, safe shelter, low levels of disease and employment opportunities. For countries such as Zimbabwe, the ability to mitigate the impacts is limited given the few resources that are available in the country. The challenge that is left is therefore to find ways of adapting to this change, particularly for the urban poor who are faced with a multiplicity of challenges that include shortage of housing, employment, skills, finance and knowledge, as well as a lack of power to influence change in ways that would enable them to cope with food insecurity and decrease vulnerability to the vagaries of climate change. While poor urbanites generally have few assets at their disposal, they have, in this challenging environment, started using their small portfolio of assets to try and cope with the challenges brought about by climate change.

Adapting to climate change through asset adaptation

The IPCC (2007b: 869) defines adaptation as "the adjustment in natural or human systems in response to actual or expected climatic stimuli or their effects, which moderates harm or exploits beneficial opportunities". In the climate change context, adaptation connotes the actions that people take in response to, or in anticipation of, changing climate conditions in order to reduce adverse impacts or take advantage of any opportunities that may arise (Tompkins and Adger, 2003). Adaptation is considered to be successful if it reduces vulnerability of the poor to existing climatic variability, while also building in them the potential to anticipate and react to further changes in climate in the future (Davoudi *et al.,* 2009). Vulnerability is defined as insecurity in the well-being of individuals, households and communities, including sensitivity to change (Moser, 1998). According to Moser and Satterthwaite (2008: 5) "this vulnerability can be understood in terms of a lack of resilience to changes that threaten welfare; these can be environmental, economic, social and political, and they can take the form of sudden shocks, long-term trends, or seasonal cycles".

In the context of climate change and food security, asset adaptation refers to the means and ways in which people use the assets that they have to anticipate and deal with challenges resulting from the change in climate (Moser and Satterthwaite, 2008). When people have assets, they have the "capability to be and to act" (Bebbington, 1999: 2029). These assets therefore enable them to decide what to do, when to and how to do whatever is necessary for them to survive through adverse changes. Although assets are central in climate change adaptation, the ability of households and communities to adapt sufficiently is mediated by the environment in which such adaptation is taking place. This environment includes external factors such as government policies, political institutions, regulatory and legal frameworks as well as the formal and informal context within which actors operate (Moser, 2009).

While human communities have generally been able to adapt to natural climate variability for millennia (Green, 2008), the changes were such that they allowed adequate time for humans to devise new ways of coping and adapting. The speed, scale and intensity with which current human-induced changes are occurring now is, however, worsening the plight of the poor as it is not allowing them sufficient time to adjust to the changes. Societies and communities are finding themselves hard-pressed to respond to new challenges that they are ill-prepared to face. Their survival only lies in their being able to acquire "information, resources, infrastructure, influence and opportunities to diversify livelihoods" as well as building social institutions that help them to share the risk and confront the threats together (Green, 2008: 262).

For the urban poor, the degree to which they are able to adapt and enhance their resilience to climate change largely depends on the bundle of assets that they have and the extent to which these assets can be used to minimize the risks that they face in their environment (Moser and Satterthwaite, 2008). To that end, urban adaptation to climate change is therefore the sum of all physical and organizational adjustments to urban life that are required to cope with the profound changes in weather and climatic patterns (Bigio, 2003). Major determinants of this adaptive capacity include the availability of financial resources, technology, specialized institutions and human resources, access to information, and the existence of legal, social and organizational arrangements (Burton and van Aalst, 1999). Most of these assets are typically scarce in the cities of developing countries. Despite this scarcity, some communities in the developing world cities are resorting to using whatever few assets they have to adapt to changing conditions and demands to enhance their resilience and survival. The following sections discuss how some poor urban households in Zimbabwe's urban areas are adapting to climate change challenges by growing part of their own food and using alternative energy sources to prepare their food in an environment where electricity has become a scarce resource.

Exploring alternatives: the use of sawdust as an energy source

There are thousands of residents in the urban areas of Zimbabwe that are unable to access safe and clean energy in the form of electricity for their everyday use. Power cuts in the country have been so frequent that they may be experienced three or four days a week, sometimes consecutively (Dongozi, 2010). While rich households in the urban areas usually switch to using generators, most of the poor have no recourse to such energy and end up resorting to using firewood. Most of this firewood is gathered from peri-urban areas (Dongozi, 2010; Kanda et al., 2010). This is further destroying the environment and enhancing further climate change challenges by increasing greenhouse gases and reducing forests that act as carbon sinks. While power cuts have become the norm in the country, climate change is likely to exacerbate the shortages. Without guaranteed access to electricity there is very limited opportunity for economic and social advancement in the country and the poor will continue to face energy problems that will also curtail their ability to cook and store food. What is therefore needed in order to adapt to further climate change challenges is a move to promote energy efficiency, increased renewable energy technologies and cleaner conventional energy use.

In Mutare, in the eastern border town of the country, households have been using sawdust for cooking and heating purposes since the early 1990s (Chinyowa, 1997). The popularity of this kind of energy in the city is a result of the abundance of sawdust in the area. It is estimated that timber-based industries account for close to 80 per cent of industrial activities in the city (Chinyowa, 1997). The proliferation of timber industries is, however, not matched by a corresponding waste management and disposal system, which leaves many companies with mounds of sawdust, shavings, off-cuts and bark in their yards or dumping grounds. Poor residents in the city have thus resorted to using these waste products for their energy requirements. Since the sawdust is a waste product and no economic benefits are derived from it by the timber industries, the Timber Producers Council in the city has been encouraging the community to take the sawdust for their own use.

The stoves used to burn the sawdust are easy to construct, low cost, environmentally friendly and very efficient. They are made from recyclable materials – scrap metal sheets, round bars and empty tins that can be easily collected from dumpsites. The tins are perforated and designed in such a way that heat is channelled towards an opening to increase heating efficiency. A bottle is pushed into the centre of the tin and sawdust is packed in and heavily compacted. The bottle is then removed, creating an air hole through which the stove will be lighted, producing a blue flame with enormous amounts of energy. The proliferation of timber industries in the area as well as the huge amount of waste that is generated and the fact that local residents have already started using this technology makes it imperative that government and local authorities support such initiatives. In the absence of reliable electricity supply, energy from sawdust will serve as a viable alternative to which poor households resort in times of energy shortages.

The use of sawdust as a source of cooking energy is not limited to Mutare alone. In cities such as Harare, residents of low income areas such as Mabvuku, Tafara, Epworth, Budiriro and Kuwadzana affected by frequent power cuts have also resorted to using innovative low-demand stoves for their household needs. It is therefore logical for the government to invest in improving this energy source to make it more efficient and cleaner. Such investment is poised to get a higher uptake as residents are already using this technology and would welcome any improvements in making the stoves more efficient.

Urban agriculture: adjusting to climate change demands

Urban agriculture is a significant component of the livelihoods of the poor in Zimbabwe's cities. In Harare, for example, gardens covered around 8 per cent of the land in the city in 1990 and the area increased to 16 per cent by 1994 and by 2001 urban agriculture pervaded 25 per cent of the city's total area (Kisner, 2008).

There is no clearly laid down policy that spells out policy makers' views on urban agriculture in Zimbabwe (Hungwe, 2004). Both government and local authorities have traditionally been averse to the practice of farming in urban areas (Chaipa, 2001). The Urban Councils Act does not specifically provide for the practice of urban agriculture although there are several by-laws that are used to deal with the practice. However, during election years, particularly local council and parliamentary elections, legislators and councillors have generally condoned the practice of urban farming even in areas that are environmentally unsuitable for the activity (Hungwe, 2005).

In recent years, the economic crisis in the country has seen a relaxation of some of the more stringent by-laws that prohibited any form of farming in the city. In most cases, local authorities have not amended their by-laws, but rather have largely turned a blind eye to this practice, which supports an increasing proportion of poor urbanites (Mavhumashava, 2006). Despite the absence of legal frameworks to support urban agriculture, farming in the cities of Zimbabwe has become prevalent. An increasing number of poor households have taken to the activity in order to grow food to feed their members in demanding economic times.

These urban farmers have not been immune to the challenges brought about by climate change. Just like their rural counterparts, urban farmers have been exposed to prolonged drought years that have adversely affected them in their farming activities. Without access to adequate rainfall, urban farmers have resorted to a variety of strategies to make sure that their activities are viable. One of the strategies is that of growing crops that are drought resistant. In Harare's suburb of Marimba, a group of urban farmers have shifted to growing crops such as rapoko and pumpkins (Mhike, 2010). Having concentrated on maize and groundnuts for a long time, these farmers, prompted by rain shortages and declining yields have sought to maximize their benefits by concentrating on those crops that are likely to give them better yields under such conditions (Mhike, 2010).

In other parts of Harare, there are farmers' organizations that have long been lobbying the council for the increased participation of urbanites in urban farming. The Musikavanhu project, which started in the local low-income residential areas of areas of Budiriro and Glen Norah, has now spread to other low-income suburbs in Harare, namely Warren Park, Glen Norah, Mufakose, Kuwadzana, Tafara and Mabvuku (Sedze, 2006). With over a hundred members, this group has been at the forefront of leading communities in growing their own food despite the numerous challenges that they face in the urban environment (Kisner, 2008). Agricultural projects by Musikavanhu members are mostly done on land owned by the city council, and council by-laws are adhered to. The by-laws include prohibition of stream bank cultivation, cultivation areas more than 30 metres from rivers and ploughing not less than 20 metres from roads (Sedze, 2006).

While urban farmers in the urban areas of Zimbabwe have shown innovativeness in adapting to the demands of climate change and are making remarkable progress in this direction, there is still a need for help to be afforded to these farmers by both government and local authorities. The first step in helping the poor to adapt is for government and local authorities to modify their approach and adopt policies that legitimize urban farming. These policies should support rather than merely accept the practice as an integral component of the poor's livelihoods through which they gain access to food and income that greatly enhances their food security situation. Current efforts by groups of households in Harare's low-income residential areas of Budiriro and Glen Norah in Harare (for example, the Musikavanhu urban farming project), for example, have shown that urban farming can be effective in provisioning urban households even with low investments. In addition the government should also make an effort to supply agricultural extension workers who will provide urban farmers with up-to-date information on rainfall patterns, advise the farmers on proper farming methods and monitor their activities so that there are no detrimental effects to the urban environment.

Knowledge as power: increasing knowledge about climate change

While the impacts of climate change are unavoidable for the urban poor and adaptation is no longer a choice but a necessity, the majority of underprivileged people do not always have the best information on how to deal with the impending challenges. Climate change debates and policies are usually of little relevance to them as they, more often than not, fail to make a clear link between the long-term impact of climate change and their immediate needs and challenges. Nampinga (2008) argues that despite wide-scale publicity and debates at the international scale, the concept of climate change is still novel at most local levels where the majority of the people are excluded from participation in this critical issue. Any adaptation measures at local level must therefore begin to engage with the poor in terms of what they know, what they can do and how they can be helped to effectively adapt to the challenges.

Although Zimbabwe is a signatory to various climate change treaties and protocols, the dissemination of information to local levels has not been that significant. Mutekwa (2009), for example, argues that despite the fact that the majority of the poor people in the country are being affected by the change, few are aware of the broader issues surrounding the debates. Increasing the effectiveness of asset adaptation by the poor will therefore need to bring on board the poor urbanites so as to build on what they already know. Their full participation underlies the degree to which they will become active and knowing participants in the adaptation process. In this way their local knowledge, ideas and ways can be fused into the larger scope of the climate change adaptation agenda. Their better awareness of future climate impacts will make them aware of the risks and therefore prompt them to initiate their own means of confronting the situation. The value of knowledge in facilitating adaptation has been recognized at an international level. The former United States Vice-President Al Gore and the IPCC, for example, were awarded the joint 2007 Nobel Peace Prize partly for "their efforts to build up and disseminate knowledge about man-made climate change", thus underscoring the importance of knowledge in climate change adaptation (Hulme, 2009).

Conclusions

This chapter has sought to highlight the food security problems confronting poor people in the urban areas of Zimbabwe as well as showing how these are likely to be exacerbated by the additional impact of climate change. It has argued that Zimbabwe's urban areas are already overburdened by various challenges that include increasing demand for housing, water and jobs that government and urban authorities are battling to tackle. The burden of climate change is therefore likely to be felt more by the poor who are unable to adapt at a pace fast enough to offset the speed of climatic changes. While the poor are already adapting to the needs and challenges of climate change, it is the contention in this chapter that their efforts need to be complemented by input from both the national government and local authorities. Low-interest finance, for example, can be made available to assist urban farmers in adopting low-technology irrigation schemes so that they are able to continue growing other crops that are unable to thrive under the current rain-fed conditions. Integrated policies and programmes also need to incorporate food security, climate change and asset adaptation measures in order to enhance the capacity of the urban poor to respond to change.

References

Bebbington, A. (1999) 'Capitals and capabilities: a framework for analysing peasant viability, rural livelihoods and poverty', *World Development*, 27: 2021–2044.

Bigio, A. G. (2003) 'Cities and climate change', *Background Paper for the World Development Report 2003*. http://www.bvsde.paho.org/bvsacd/cd46/cap7-cities.pdf (accessed 20 April 2011).

Bryceson, D. F. (2006) 'Fragile cities: fundamentals of urban life in East and Southern Africa', in Bryceson, D. F. and Potts, D. (eds), *African Urban Economics: Viability, Vitality or Vitiation*, New York: Palgrave Macmillan.

Burton, I. and van Aalst, M. (1999) 'Come hell and high water – integrating climate change vulnerability and adaptation into Bank Work', *ESSD Climate Change Series*.

Chaipa, I. (2001) 'Institutional bottlenecks in urban poverty alleviation: the case of urban food production by the poor and the local governance system in the city of Gweru', unpublished thesis, Department of Rural and Urban Planning, University of Zimbabwe.

Chakona, A. (2003) *Impacts of Raw Sewage Spills in Manyame Park Residential Area (St Mary's) Chitungwiza*. Harare: University of Zimbabwe and the Zimbabwe Environmental Law Association.

Chambwera, M. (2004) 'Economic analysis of urban fuelwood demand: the case of Harare in Zimbabwe', unpublished thesis, Department of Environmental Sciences, Wageningen University.

Chasi, M. (2009) 'Climate change and food security in Zimbabwe', Paper presented at Trade and Development, Agro-Biodiversity and Food Security Workshop, Harare, May 2008.

Chetsanga, C. J. (2000) 'Zimbabwe: exploitation of biotechnology in agricultural research', www.cgiar.org/biotech/rep0100/chetsanga.pdf (accessed 9 August 2011).

Chikozho, C. (2010) 'Applied social research and action priorities for adaptation to climate change and rainfall variability in the rain fed agricultural sector of Zimbabwe', *Physics and Chemistry of the Earth*, 35: 780–790.

Chinyowa, M. (1997) 'Sawdust utilization: experiences in Mutare, Zimbabwe', *Boiling Point*, 39.

Climate Change Office (2004) *Technology Transfer Needs Assessment in Zimbabwe.* Harare: Zimbabwe Climate Change Office.

Crush, J., Grant, M. and Frayne, B. (2007) 'Linking migration, HIV/AIDS and urban food security in Southern and Eastern Africa', *African Migration and Development Series*, 3. Cape Town: IDASA.

Davoudi, S., Crawford, J. and Mehmood, A. (2009) *Planning for Climate Change: Strategies for Mitigation and Adaptation for Spatial Planners.* London: Earthscan.

Dongozi, V. (2010) 'Urban poor's struggle for survival limits options for curbing climate change', http://www.trust.org/alertnet/news/urban-poors-struggle-for-survival-limits-options-for-curbing-climate-damage (accessed 19 April 2011).

Drakakis-Smith, D., Bowyer-Bower, T. and Tevera, D. (1995) 'Urban poverty and urban agriculture: an overview of the linkages in Harare', *Habitat International*, 19, 2: 183–193.

FEWSNET (2009) 'Zimbabwe food security update', March. http://www.fews.net/docs/Publications/Zimbabwe_2009_03.pdf (accessed 30 March 2009).

Frayne, B., Pendleton, W., Crush. J., Acquah, B., Battersby, J., Bras, E., Chiweza, A., Dlamini, T., Fincham, R., Kroll, F., Leduka, C., Mosha, A., Mulenga, C., Mvula, P., Pomuti, A., Raimundo, I., Rudolph, M., Ruysenaar, S., Simelane, N., Tevera, D., Tsoka, M., Tawodzera, G. and Zanamwe, L. (2010) 'The state of food insecurity in Southern Africa', *Urban Food Security Series, 2.* Cape Town: IDASA.

Government of Zimbabwe (2005) *Response by Government of Zimbabwe to the Report by the UN Special Envoy On Operation Murambatsvina (Restore Order)*, Harare: Government of Zimbabwe.

Government of Zimbabwe (2006) *Poverty Assessment Study Survey, Main Report.* Harare: Ministry of Public Service, Labour and Social Welfare.

Green, D. (2008) *From Poverty to Power: How Active Citizens and Effective States Can Change the World.* Auckland Park, South Africa: Oxfam International/Jacana.

Gumbo, B. (2000) 'Urban agriculture in Harare, integrating the past, present and the future perspectives', *IFNFS-UZ/IAC Food and Nutrition Security in Urban Areas Regional Course: Strengthening Food and Nutrition Training in Southern Africa*, 4–16 December, Harare.

Gumbo, D. (2006) 'Working together to respond to climate change', Annex I, expert group seminar in conjunction with the OECD Global Forum on Sustainable Development: Zimbabwe: country case study on domestic policy frameworks for adaptation in the water sector. http://www.oecd.org/dataoecd/58/58/36318866.pdf (accessed April 2011).

Gwebu, T. D. (2002) 'Urban water scarcity management: civic versus state response in Bulawayo', *Habitat International*, 26, 3: 417–431.

Hammill, A., Mathew, R. and McCarter, E. (2008) 'Microfinance and climate change adaptation', *IDS Bulletin*, 39, 4: 113–122.

Hulme, M. (2009) *Why We Disagree about Climate Change: Understanding Controversy, Inaction and Opportunity.* Cambridge: Cambridge University Press.

Hungwe, C. (2004) 'Urban agriculture as a survival strategy: an analysis of the activities of Bulawayo and Gweru urban farmers'. http://www.cityfarmer.org/ZimbabweSecurity.html (accessed April 2011).

IFRC (International Federation of Red Cross and Red Crescent Societies) (2009) *Zimbabwe Food Insecurity, Emergency Appeal Number MDRZW003*, An International Appeal for Food Aid by the International Federation of Red Cross and Red Crescent Societies, 10 March, Harare.

IIED (International Institute for Environment and Development) (2008) *Climate Change and the Urban Poor: Risk and Resilience in 15 of the World's Most Vulnerable Cities*. London: The International Institute for Environment and Development.

International Crisis Group (2005) Zimbabwe's Operation Murambatsvina: The Tipping Point?, *Africa Report*, 97, 17 August, Harare. www.crisisgroup.org/~/media/files/africa/zimbabwe.

IPCC (2007a) *Climate Change 2007: The Physical Science Basis: Contribution of Working Group I to the Fourth Assessment Report of the Intergovernmental Panel on Climate Change* (Solomon, S., Qin, D., Manning, M., Chen, Z., Marquis, M., Averyt, K. B., Tignor, M. and Miller, H. L. (eds)). Cambridge, UK: Cambridge University Press.

IPCC (2007b) *Climate Change 2007: Impacts, Adaptation and Vulnerability. Contribution of Working Group II to the Fourth Assessment Report of the Intergovernmental Panel on Climate Change* (Parry, M. L., Canziani, O. F., Palutikof, J. P., van der Linden, P. J. and Hanson, C. E (eds)). Cambridge: Cambridge University Press.

Kanda, F., Mushandikwa, W. and Mutariswa, T. (2010) *Understanding Livelihoods of Households Displaced to Peri-urban Areas in Zimbabwe: An Insight from Rainham Farm, Dzivarasekwa Extension PRP LIME Baseline, ZCDT/IOM Zimbabwe*, Harare: GRM International.

Kessides, C. (2005) 'The urban transition in sub-Saharan Africa: implications for economic growth and poverty reduction', *Urban Development Unit, Transport and Urban Development Department, Working Paper Series, Africa Region,* 97. The World Bank, Africa Region. http://www.worldbank.org/afr/wps/wp97.pdf (accessed 18 November 2008).

Kisner, C. (2008) *Green Roofs for Urban Food Security and Environmental Sustainability, Urban Agriculture Case Study: Harare*. Washington, DC: Climate Institute.

Kutiwa, S., Boon, E. and Devuyst, D. (2010). 'Urban agriculture in low income households of Harare: an adaptive response to economic crisis', *Journal of Human Ecology*, 32, 2: 85–96.

Maslin, M. (2009) *Global Warming: A Very Short Introduction*. New York: Oxford University Press.

Mavhumashava, K. (2006) 'Stakeholders call for regulated urban farming', *Chronicle Newspaper*, Zimbabwe, 24 January.

Mazambani, D. (1982) 'Peri-urban cultivation within Greater Harare', *Zimbabwe Science News*, 16, 6: 134–138.

Mbiba, M. (1995) *Urban Agriculture in Zimbabwe: Implications for Urban Agricultural Policy*, Harare, Avebury: Ashgate Publishing Limited.

Mhazo, N., Hanyani-Mlambo, B., Proctor, S. and Nazare, R. M. (2003) 'Constraints to small scale production and marketing of processed food products in Zimbabwe – the case of fruits and vegetables', *Food Africa, Internet Forum* Internet paper for Agro-Enterprise Theme, 31 March – 11 April. http://foodafrica.nri.org (accessed April 2011).

Mhike, N. (2010) 'Supporting Urban Farmers: Challenges of Finance', address to Ruwa Urban Farmers, 26 October 2010, Mavambo, Ruwa.

Moser, C. (1998) 'The asset vulnerability framework: reassessing urban poverty reduction strategies', *World Development*, 26, 1: 1–19.

Moser, C. and Satterthwaite, D. (2008) 'Towards pro-poor adaptation to climate change in the urban centres of low and middle income countries, climate change and cities', *Human Settlements Discussion Paper Series*, 3. University of Manchester: Global Urban Research Centre (GURC).

Moser, S. C. (2009) 'Governance and the art of overcoming barriers to adaptation', *IHDP Update*, 3: 31–36.

Mugara, T. (2007) *The Impact of Operation Murambatsvina (Clean Up) on Urban Livelihoods of Informal Vendors in Harare, Zimbabwe*, paper prepared for the Living on the Margins Conference in Stellenbosch, Cape Town, South Africa, 26–28 March.

Murinda, S. and Kraemer, S. (2008) 'The potential of solar water disinfection as a household water treatment method in peri-urban Zimbabwe', *Physics and Chemistry of the Earth*, 33: 829–832.

Mutonhodzo, C. (2005) 'The socio-economic implication of urban agriculture on food and livelihoods security in Harare, Zimbabwe', unpublished thesis, University of Zimbabwe.

Nampinga, R. (2008) 'Gender perspectives on climate change', written statement to the Commission on the Status of Women Fifty-second Session, Emerging Issues Panel, 25 February – 7 March, New York.

Nhapi, I. (2009) 'The water situation in Harare, Zimbabwe: a policy and management problem', *Water Policy* 11, 2: 221–235.

Nyambara, P. S. (2003) 'Rural landlords, rural tenants and the sharecropping complex in Gokwe, North-Western Zimbabwe: 1980s–2002', Harare: Centre for Applied Social Sciences.

Nyoni, M. (2007) 'Bulawayo faces water crisis', *Mail and Guardian*, 14 September. http://www.southernafricatrust.org/docs/Water%20a%20pipe%20dream.pdf (accessed 19 April).

Potts, D. (1997) 'Urban lives: adopting new strategies and adapting rural links', in Rakodi, C. (ed) *Urban Challenge in Africa, Growth and Management of its Large Cities*, New York: United Nations University Press, pp447–494.

Potts, D. (2006) 'All my hopes are shattered: urbanization and migrancy in an imploding African economy – the case of Zimbabwe', *Geoforum*, 37, 536–551.

Potts, D. and Mutambirwa, C. C. (1991) 'Rural–urban linkages in contemporary Harare: why migrants need their land', *Journal of Southern African Studies*, 16, 4: 676–696.

Ravallion, M., Chen, S. and Sangraula, P. (2007) 'New evidence on urbanization of global poverty', *Population and Development Review*, 33, 4: 667–701.

Sedze, V. T. (2006) 'An examination of a community based urban agriculture project: the case of Musikavanhu in Budiriro, Harare', unpublished thesis, University of Zimbabwe.

Shongwe, M. E, van Oldenborgh, G. J, van Den Hurk, B. J. J. M, de Boer, B., Coelho, C. A. S and van Aalst, M. K. (2009) 'Projected changes in mean and extreme precipitation in Africa under global warming, Part I: Southern Africa', *Journal of Climate*, 22: 3819–3837.

Sullivan, F. (2011) 'Increase in electricity imports provides temporary solution to Zimbabwe's power crisis'. http://www.pressreleasepoint.com/power-crisis (accessed 19 April 2011).

Tawodzera, G. (2010) 'Vulnerability and resilience in crisis: urban household food insecurity in Harare, Zimbabwe', unpublished thesis, University of Cape Town.

The Standard (2005) 'Government stocking suspicions of neglect', *The Standard*. http://www.thestandard.co.zw/opinion/15557.pdf (accessed 19 April 2011).

Tibaijuka, A. (2005) *Report of the Fact-finding Mission to Assess the Scope and Impact of Operation Murambatsvina in Zimbabwe*, UN-HABITAT Special Envoy on Human Settlement Issues in Zimbabwe, 18 July. http://ww2.unhabitat.org/documents/ZimbabweReport.pdf (accessed 19 April 2011).

Tompkins, E. L. and Adger, W. N. (2003) 'Building resilience to climate change through adaptive management of natural resources', *Tyndall Working Paper*, 27. Norwich: Tyndall Centre.

Tshuma, D. T and Mashoko, D. (2010) 'Urban farming: its relevance, sustainability and policy implications: a case study of Gweru and Masvingo Urban Areas', *Journal of Sustainable Development*, 12, 3: 361–372.

UNFCCC (United Nations Framework Convention on Climate Change) (2011) Full text of the Convention. http://unfccc.int/essential_background/convention/background/items/2536.php (accessed March 2011).

UNFPA (2007) *State of the World Population 2007: Unleashing the Potential of Urban Growth.* New York: UNFPA.

Unganai, L. S. (1996) 'Historic and future climatic change in Zimbabwe', *Climate Research*, 6: 137–145.

United Nations (2007) *World Population Prospects: The 2006 Revision.* New York: United Nations.

USAID (2009) 'Fighting disaster-induced urban poverty in Zimbabwe'. http://urbanhealthupdates.wordpress.com/2009/09/28/usaidofda-success-story (accessed 28 September 2009).

Watson, V. (2007) 'Urban planning and twenty-first century cities: can it meet the challenge?', in Garland, A. M., Massoumi, M. and Ruble, B..A. (eds) *Global Urban Poverty: Setting the Agenda*, Washington: Woodrow Wilson International Center for Scholars, Comparative Urban Studies Project, pp205–237.

WFP *et al.* (2009) 'Climate change, food insecurity and hunger, key message for UNFCCC negotiators: technical paper for the IASC task force on climate change'.

Zimbabwe Red Cross Society (2007) *Climate Change Workshop Report*, 24 July, Harare.

ZimVac (Zimbabwe National Vulnerability Committee) (2003) *Zimbabwe Emergency Food Security and Vulnerability Assessment Report No 3*, Zimbabwe National Vulnerability Committee in Collaboration with the SADC/FANR Vulnerability Committee, Harare.

ZimVac (Zimbabwe National Vulnerability Committee) (2004) *Zimbabwe Urban Areas Food Security and Vulnerability Assessment, Urban Report Number 1*, Harare: Zimbabwe National Vulnerability Committee.

ZimVac (Zimbabwe National Vulnerability Committee) (2009) *Zimbabwe Vulnerability Assessment Committee Urban Food Security Assessment January 2009 National Report*, Harare: Zimbabwe National Vulnerability Committee.

4

MOBILITY AND MIGRATION
The missing link in climate change and asset adaptation

Belinda Dodson

Introduction

If thinking on climate change, asset adaptation and food security in African cities is to reflect the lived reality of those cities and their inhabitants, then it is essential to think beyond urban boundaries. This is important for a number of reasons. First, urban biophysical environments are not discrete bounded entities, but rather are "nested" within larger-scale and interlinked processes: geomorphological, hydrological, biological and of course atmospheric. Larger-scale environmental change affects local urban environments; city-scale environmental change contributes to regional and larger-scale processes. Second, cities must be considered in their wider political, economic and social context. This includes provincial, national and regional spheres of governance; flows of capital and commodities; and systems of transport and communication. Third, and perhaps most important for the purposes of this volume, are the flows of people – and with them goods and assets – that characterize urban life on the continent.

In Southern Africa, as in Africa as a whole, mobility and migration have long been part of individual and household livelihood strategies in what are commonly unpredictable and precarious social, economic, political and indeed natural environments (Francis 2000; Crush and Frayne 2010; Potts 2010). Some of those livelihood strategies involve different members of the same household living in different places in order to hedge their bets, minimizing risk by deploying their collective asset bundle in multiple geographical locations – for example in both urban and rural settings or in more than one country. Others involve mobility itself as a livelihood or asset accumulation strategy, as individuals seek out employment or market opportunities in different locations at different times, such as in seasonal labour migration or itinerant trading, or in various forms of circular migration. Permanent relocation from one place to another is also both common and widespread, for example from rural to urban locations, and thus new lifestyles and livelihood opportunities, or in the growing international African diaspora (Okpewho and Nzegwu 2009).

Already a region of high human mobility, Africa is likely to see additional migration in response to climate change. Geographically, climate change is expected to have an especially severe impact on the African continent, as outlined elsewhere in this volume and in the growing literature on climate change impacts and adaptation (Stern 2006; Parry *et al*. 2007). Changes in temperature and rainfall patterns are disrupting agricultural systems and threatening food security. Modifications to the distribution of disease vectors pose threats to human and animal health. Both droughts and floods are predicted to become more widespread and intense, while sea level rise threatens the permanent inundation of low-lying coastal areas, including large coastal cities such as Lagos and Accra. These environmental changes are making vulnerable livelihoods even more precarious. As in other parts of the world, African people too will employ various forms of mobility as means of adaptation to the depletion or destruction of assets such as land, livestock or housing as a result of climate change (Black *et al*. 2008; Boano *et al*. 2008; Brown 2008; Kniveton *et al*. 2008; Tacoli 2009; Warner 2010). Such migration will include rural–rural, rural–urban, urban–rural and urban–urban flows, some of these permanent and some short term or circular, some internal and some international. Thus in assessing the likely impact of climate change on African cities, migration has to be taken into account.

The focus of this chapter is on the linkage between climate change and migration. The chapter begins by reviewing current thinking on climate change and migration, tracing the dominant strands of discourse and identifying gaps, omissions and misrepresentations. The chapter goes on to present examples of recent work that adopts an alternative conceptual framework for integrating mobility and migration into climate change adaptation. Instead of starting with climate change, forecasting its wider biophysical impacts and predicting possible migration outcomes, such work suggests starting with an examination of existing patterns and processes of migration and thinking about how these might themselves be affected by climate change. This alternative conceptualization of climate change and migration lends itself to location within an asset adaptation framework, as migration is perceived in terms of household strategies to secure sustainable livelihoods rather than simple push and pull factors. An asset adaptation framework provides a basis both for critiquing simplistic understandings of the climate change–migration nexus and for developing more robust and sophisticated approaches. The chapter proposes that mobility is a key strategy in individuals' and households' asset adaptation and urges the mainstreaming of migration in climate change policy and planning, including at the urban scale.

Current thinking on climate change and migration: climate refugees and climate wars?

Migration occupies a curiously bipolar position in academic and policy discourses on climate change impacts and adaptation, tending to be either centralized or marginalized. Examples of the latter can be found in many cities' climate change policy documents, including the City of Cape Town's *Framework for Adaptation to Climate Change* (Mukheibir and Ziervogel 2006). Sectoral impacts are identified in that document under the following headings: urban water supplies, storm water, biodiversity, fires, coastal zones, livelihoods and health. Having defined climate change impacts at the urban scale and effectively ring-fenced the city's boundaries, the human dimensions too are similarly, and artificially, downscaled and limited to effects on "the population". There is brief acknowledgement of population growth and the fact that there are "many people who originally come from other countries or provinces" (ibid.: 44); but no mention of regional climate change impacts themselves being possible drivers of migration to the city, nor of the complex oscillating and circular patterns of migration between the city and "other countries or provinces". Instead, migration is viewed only as something that reduces the social networks and capital of people recently arrived in the city, thereby (it is implied) exacerbating their vulnerability to the effects of climate change on their lives and livelihoods.

At the opposite pole are narratives that seek to locate human displacement and refugee flows at the very centre of climate change discourse (El-Hinnawi 1995; Myers 2005; Smith 2007; Boano *et al.* 2008; Brown 2008; Warner 2010). The notion of climate refugees is even beginning to enter the popular imagination. Publicity for a recent documentary film called *Climate Refugees* includes the following:

> There is a new phenomenon in the global arena called "Climate Refugees". A climate refugee is a person displaced by climatically induced environmental disasters. Such disasters result from incremental and rapid ecological change, resulting in increased droughts, desertification, sea level rise, and the more frequent occurrence of extreme weather events such as hurricanes, cyclones, fires, mass flooding and tornadoes. All this is causing mass global migration and border conflicts. For the first time, the Pentagon now considers climate change a national security risk and the term climate wars is being talked about in war-room like environments in Washington D.C.
>
> Nash, 2010

Note the crude conflation of climate change, "mass global migration and border conflicts". This cannot simply be dismissed as the hyperbole of film advertising, as beneath such popular dramatizations lie numerous academic publications and policy reports at the highest levels. An estimate that has become entrenched in both academic and policy writing is the figure of "200 million climate refugees by 2050" put forward by renowned British ecologist Norman Myers (2005, cited in Brown 2008). As Oli Brown observes in that 2008 report, published by the International Organization for Migration (IOM), this represents a tenfold increase of the 2008 global refugee population, as well as more than the current total number of all international migrants of any sort worldwide. Norman Myers is still widely recognized as an authority on the subject, despite criticism of his methods and findings (e.g. Tol 2006; Tacoli 2009). Dissenting expert views notwithstanding, his prediction forms the basis of assessments in both the 2007 Intergovernmental Panel on Climate Change (IPCC) report and the influential 2006 Stern Review, *The Economics of Climate Change*. The IPCC report of Working Group II, *Impacts, Adaptation and Vulnerability* (Parry *et al.* 2007) draws on Myers and others (including McLeman and Smit 2006) to suggest that:

> Negative impacts of climate change could create a new set of refugees, who may migrate into new settlements, seek new livelihoods and place additional demands on infrastructure... A variety of migration patterns could thus emerge, e.g., repetitive migrants (as part of ongoing adaptation to climate change) and short-term shock migrants (responding to a particular climate event).
>
> Parry *et al.* 2007: section 9.4.8

In the next line, the IPCC report goes on to admit that "few detailed assessments of such impacts using climate as a driving factor have been undertaken for Africa". Indeed much of the climate refugee discourse is based on prediction of the submersion of low-lying coastal areas in countries such as Bangladesh and island states like Tuvalu and the Maldives, resulting in an emphasis on the Asia-Pacific region to the neglect of Africa. The Stern Review, also citing Myers, is alarmist and neo-Malthusian in its predictions: "Severe deterioration in local climate could lead, in some parts of the developing world, to mass migration and conflict, especially as another 2–3 billion people are added to the developing world's population in the next few decades" (2006: 104).

The IPCC Report and the Stern Review exemplify the two main strands that have become established in the academic and policy literature on climate change and migration. One is a humanitarian and legalistic strand, focused on the plight of environmental refugees and the lack of international instruments to ensure their protection. The origins of the concept "environmental refugees" lie with Lester Brown and the Worldwatch Institute in the 1970s (Kniveton *et al.* 2008), but gained more widespread attention through the United Nations Environment Programme (UNEP) and in particular UNEP researcher Essam El-Hinnawi (1985, cited in Bates 2002). In the quarter century since El-Hinnawi wrote, the growing concern and consensus about global warming has added impetus to the argument to broaden the definition of refugees to include those displaced by climate change. Neither the United Nations 1951 Convention Relating to the Status of Refugees nor the 1967 Protocol includes environmental grounds as a basis for refugee status, defined instead in terms of political and other forms of persecution. Scholarly and legal debate continues around whether people displaced by climate change or other forms of environmental degradation or disruption should be considered to be refugees per se, with all the related rights of protection and asylum, or merely as ordinary migrants, albeit along a spectrum from voluntary to forced or distress migration (Bates 2002; Brown 2008; Kniveton *et al.* 2008;

Andersen *et al.* 2010; Barnett and Webber 2010). Often neglected in this environmental refugee discourse is the fact that "the number of people who cannot migrate in response to climate change (for reasons of poverty, remoteness, ill-health, or age, for example) may far exceed the number that do, and so may pose a far larger humanitarian problem" (Barnett and Webber 2010: 13).

Alongside the intellectual and legislative dimensions of this debate are some fundamental issues that make extension of the refugee definition problematic (Brown 2008; Kniveton *et al.* 2008). For a start, most of the people displaced by the direct and indirect impacts of climate change are likely to be internally displaced rather than moving across international borders, and existing refugee law is restricted to movement from one country to another. A second fundamental basis for the recognition and treatment of refugees is the idea of the right of return once fear of persecution has passed, something that is obviously not possible for irreversible environmental damage or destruction and the resulting loss of land or livelihood. A third concern raised by those arguing against the "environmental refugee" concept is that it risks undermining the mechanisms and instruments for the protection of "genuine" refugees fleeing persecution or conflict, as recognized by the UN Convention (Brown 2008; Hartman 2010). Climate change migrants, and environmental migrants more generally, thus inevitably fall between the cracks in existing refugee and asylum law.

A second main strand of thinking on the climate change–migration nexus draws on predictions of mass migration and "climate refugees" to construct a politicized, securitized and even militarized narrative emphasizing migration as a source of conflict and "climate wars". Brown and McLeman (2009) note that both the African Union and European Union have begun to frame climate change in security terms, and that "climate change has become a core foreign policy priority of many governments, including the [Obama] administration's programme in the US, a move that is rationalized, at least in part, by the security threat it presents" (p. 290). Focusing on the UK case, Trombetta (2008) provides an insightful critical analysis of this increasing securitization of climate change discourse, noting its crude incorporation of migration and potentially problematic mechanisms of prevention and control within conventional security institutions: "[I]t is possible that the securitization of climate change would result in confrontational politics, with states adopting policies to protect their territory against sea-level rise and immigration" (p. 599).

Within this powerful emerging consensus on climate change as a security threat, migration features prominently. The UK Ministry of Defence's *Climate Change Strategy* (2008), for example, clearly identifies climate change-induced migration as a potential security threat, as does a burgeoning academic and policy literature. Brown and McLeman (2009) list "destabilizing and unregulated population movements (so-called 'climate refugees')" amongst "at least five ways in which climate change could undermine peace and stability" (p. 293). The other four are scarcities of food, water and energy; increase in natural disasters and disease burdens; international disputes over access to "unfrozen" Arctic resources; and the effects of salinization, sea level rise and "mega-droughts" on the very habitability of parts of the earth's surface. The precise mechanisms by which these environmental changes threaten security, and exactly whose security is threatened, are left opaque. There is, furthermore, considerable slippage between the terms "stability" and "security" as well as ambiguous use of the term security itself to denote either its social (human security) or political (military security) senses.

Typical of the treatment of migration in this securitized climate change discourse is a paper by Rafael Reuveny titled "Climate change-induced migration and violent conflict", published in a special issue of *Political Geography* on the theme of climate change and conflict that came out in 2007. Reuveny links climate change-induced migration not only to local or regional conflicts over resources but to global terrorism:

> The political fallout may extend beyond LDCs. The inevitable feeling of hostility may foster a fertile atmosphere for global terrorism recruitment, which may already be underway. For example, British and Italian authorities have recently identified Eritrea, Ethiopia and Somalia as fertile recruiting grounds for terrorists. This area has already experienced bouts of environmental migration in recent decades.
>
> Reuveny, 2007: 669

As in the above example, much of this discussion takes place at a disconcertingly superficial level, riddled with problematic assumptions, spurious correlations, over-reaching extrapolation and much sheer speculation. In the more sophisticated versions of such scholarship, the difficulty of attributing causation in the climate change–migration–security triangle is more fully acknowledged, but usually in the form of caveats and cautions rather than any fundamental rethinking of the underlying assumptions about migration or conflict, either independently or in causal conjunction. Brown and McLeman, for instance, note that "the picture is nuanced and the relationships not necessarily linear" (2009: 300). Elsewhere, in a 2009 study for a Nordic–African Foreign Ministers Meeting, Brown and Crawford set out the "more nuanced" picture as follows:

> Migration itself is not inherently problematic, and indeed it can be an important way of adapting to the impacts of climate change. However, experience shows that migration can increase the likelihood of conflict in transit and target regions (WBGU, 2007). Barnett and Adger (2005) argue that the influx of migrants into new areas has been a significant factor in many "environmental conflicts".
>
> Brown and Crawford, 2009: 19

Beyond the broad-brush continental picture and the global estimates of between 200 million and 1 billion people being displaced by climate change by 2050, attempts are being made to produce more refined, disaggregated and regional estimates of "climate migrants". Oli Brown (2008) sets out three scenarios of migration related to climate change: "the good" (p. 27), "the bad" (p. 28) and "the ugly" (p. 29). He derives these based largely on emissions scenarios set out by the IPCC's Working Group II in 2007 in a series of "storylines" of economic, technological and demographic developments under different "energy mix" futures. The "good" scenario is based on a best case of a stable total global population, significant reductions in greenhouse gas emissions and effective climate change adaptation worldwide. Still, this scenario suggests global migration increasing by between 5 and 10 per cent, predominantly along "existing routes" and "largely manageable, if not indistinguishable, within existing patterns of migration" (p. 28). The "bad" scenario is also based on a stable total global population, but with lower reductions in greenhouse gas emissions and more variable success in climate change adaptation in different parts of the world. This scenario does not state a specific percentage increase in migration figures, but anticipates "dramatic increases in internal rural to urban migration and also emigration to richer countries, particularly of young, skilled people" (p. 29), as well as temporary displacement by extreme weather events. The "ugly" scenario is based on "business as usual", without any "emission reductions or serious attempts at adaptation" (p. 29). The predicted numbers of migrants exceed even the 200 million figure put forward by Myers:

> Under this scenario, predictions of 200 million people displaced by climate change might easily be exceeded. Large areas of southern China, South Asia, and the Sahelian region of sub-Saharan Africa could become uninhabitable on a permanent basis. Climate forced migration would be unmistakeable with tens of millions of people at a time displaced by extreme weather events … and many millions more displaced by climate processes such as desertification, salinization of agricultural land and sea level rise.
>
> Brown, 2008: 29

Plausible predictions of migration related to climate change lie between Brown's two extremes. Many people will indeed be driven to leave their homes, either suddenly in the face of physical damage or destruction from extreme events such as floods or cyclones, or, eventually, following a gradual decline in livelihood security as a consequence of a slower erosion of economic and natural assets and capital, for example through drought, land degradation or shifts in seasonal temperature and rainfall patterns (Black *et al.* 2008; Boano *et al.* 2008; Brown 2008; Kniveton *et al.* 2008; Tacoli 2009; Andersen *et al.* 2010; Barnett and Webber 2010). Before such "distress" migration takes place, some people in areas affected by climate change are likely to move as labour migrants, employing migration as a means of asset redeployment and asset accumulation in the face of livelihood decline (Andersen *et al.* 2010). Given what we already know about the embeddedness of migration within social networks and its operation within political–economic, institutional and legislative frameworks, people are more likely to move locally or nationally than internationally, and are also more likely to move within established migration channels (Castles and Miller 2009; Andersen *et al.* 2010). Furthermore, the multi-causal and intersecting explanations for migration make it virtually impossible to distinguish environmental or climate change migrants from other, long-established categories of migration, such as labour migrants, economic migrants and asylum seekers. Such understandings of migration are far from the prevalent image of hundreds of millions of "climate refugees", and require very different forms of analysis and policy response.

Integrating mobility and migration into climate change and asset adaptation

Population geographers such as Graeme Hugo (2008) are amongst those urging recognition of a more complex, two-way relationship between environmental change and migration, even before considering how that relationship might lead to or exacerbate conflict. Hugo notes that numerical estimates of people at risk of displacement "have little empirical basis but gain a totally unwarranted credibility with repetition" (ibid.: 31). Further, "how migration and environmental concerns interact and impinge upon economic development, social change and conflict is little understood" (ibid.: 7), despite a growing literature. More sophisticated understanding of the climate change–migration nexus needs to be grounded in understandings of migration, development, poverty and governance.

The broad contours of such an approach are beginning to be mapped out, for example in work by Cecilia Tacoli and others at the London-based International Institute for Environment and Development (IIED) (e.g. Tacoli 2009); by Richard Black, Dominic Kniveton, Ronald Skeldon and others at the University of Sussex's Development Research Centre on Migration, Globalisation and Poverty (e.g. Black *et al.* 2008); by Koko Warner at the United Nations University Institute of Environmental and Human Change (e.g. Warner 2010), and by Camillo Boano, Roger Zetter, Tim Morris and others at Oxford University's Refugee Studies Centre (e.g. Boano *et al.* 2008). The IOM has produced a number of studies and reports (e.g. Brown 2008; Hugo 2008), and a special issue of *Forced Migration Review* that came out in October 2008 summarized much of the key literature on climate change and displacement (Couldrey and Herson 2008). Recent policy-oriented work published by the World Bank also presents more balanced accounts than the simplistic dual refugee/security narratives outlined above (Andersen *et al.* 2010; Barnett and Webber 2010). While this emerging work is not always explicitly framed in terms of asset adaptation, its explanations of migration are themselves grounded in considerations of assets, capacity, resilience and livelihoods, incorporating individual, household and community scales. Such analyses thus provide a useful basis for integrating migration into the climate change, asset adaptation and food security nexus that informs this volume (Moser and Satterthwaite 2010).

Cecilia Tacoli is one of the growing group of critics who caution against catastrophist thinking, in her case by examining current migration patterns and flows, including in response to environmental drivers (Tacoli 2009). Arguing that "alarmist predictions of massive flows of refugees are not supported by past experiences of responses to droughts and extreme weather events" (ibid.: 513), she observes that temporary migration is far more common than permanent migration, and also that rural–rural migration within national borders is the predominant pattern. Tacoli emphasizes the role of migration and mobility as means of adaptation to climate change:

> There is growing evidence suggesting that mobility, in conjunction with income diversification, is an important strategy to reduce vulnerability to environmental and non-environmental risks – including economic shocks and social marginalization. In many cases, mobility not only increases resilience but also enables individuals and households to accumulate assets.
>
> Tacoli 2009: 514

Similarly, Kniveton *et al.* (2008) review literature on drought-induced migration in Africa and conclude:

> First, drought seems to cause an increase in the number of people who engage in short-term rural to rural types of migration. On the other hand, it does not affect, or even decreases international, long-distance moves. Second, the conceptualization of drought-affected people as helpless victims who are left with no choice but to flee seems to be false. Depending on their socio-economic position, they might have the choice between a variety of coping strategies, including migration. On the other hand, they may be too poor to migrate at all.
>
> Kniveton *et al.* 2008: 34

Kniveton *et al.* (2008) see promise in two complementary methodologies for conceptualizing and researching the relationship between climate change and migration: sustainable livelihoods approaches (SLA) and the new economics of labour migration (NELM). The former emerged in the field of development studies (for a review see Scoones 2009), while the latter has become influential in migration scholars' analysis of contemporary migration flows (Castles and Miller 2009). Each of these approaches is based firmly within considerations of assets and asset adaptation. In SLA,

> [t]he underlying idea is that families possess a variety of natural, physical, financial, human and social assets, which are all used to maintain a family's livelihood. If one of the assets suffers a loss, it can be compensated for by falling back on the other available assets in the so-called asset-pentagon.
>
> Kniveton *et al.* 2008: 38

83

In NELM, the key insight is that migration decisions are made not by atomistic individuals but jointly by the migrant and family members,

> who expect remittances in return for investment in the initial migration of a household member. Migration is thus not a strategy to maximize individual income, but a means to diversify sources of household income and reduce risk.
>
> Kniveton *et al.* 2008: 39

From a sustainable livelihoods approach, migration can be seen as one amongst a bundle of climate change adaptation strategies, and indeed as a means by which some of those strategies (e.g. livelihood diversification) are themselves achieved. NELM approaches, by contrast, make migration the "output" and consider climate variability one of the "inputs", along with social, economic and institutional drivers and constraints to migration decisions (Figure 4.1).

One of the most thorough and systematic attempts to explain the climate change–migration nexus, drawing on the models outlined above, is by Black *et al.* (2008), in work funded by the UK's Department for International Development (DFID). First, they disaggregate the biophysical effects of climate change, initially into the main categories of slow-onset and abrupt changes. The main subcategories of slow-onset change identified are: increased atmospheric CO_2, temperature increases, sea level rise, changes in precipitation, increased frequency and length of heat waves, decline in frost days, changes in the number and intensity of tropical cyclones, and fewer mid-latitude storms. For catastrophic or abrupt changes,

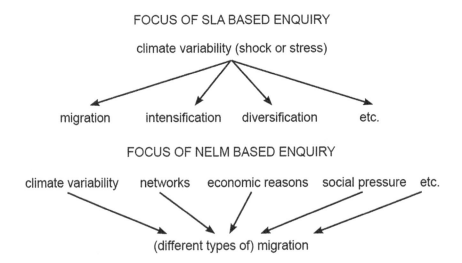

Figure 4.1 Different approaches to understanding the climate change–migration nexus

they list the following: collapse of the thermohaline circulation, rapid melting of high-latitude ice sheets, emissions of methane and carbon from soil and vegetation, and a switch to a permanent El Niño situation. Then, for each category, they delineate a range of more specific biophysical and related societal impacts, for example on crop production, biodiversity, disease distributions and infrastructure. For these, in turn, they provide an estimate of the regional distribution of impacts, before putting this all together to determine the main types of migration that are likely to be affected.

Depending on the particular biophysical impact and geographical location, the predicted changes to migration include multiple permutations: rural to urban, rural to rural, urban to rural, and urban to urban; coastal to urban and rural; seasonal and longer term; intra- and international; and forced, internally displaced and distress migration. In the analysis by Black *et al.* (2008), the main forms of climate change-induced migration affecting cities include both in-migration and out-migration possibilities. Coastal cities, for example, may see out-migration to inland urban or rural areas, either as a gradual trend or as emergency evacuation following cyclones or storm surges. Changes such as temperature increases or increased risk of drought or flooding that negatively affect crop and livestock production are likely to increase both rural to rural and rural to urban migration, while increased growing season length in some areas may actually produce an increase in migration from urban to rural areas. The key point is that linkages between climate change and migration are not only complex but also geographically specific, and thus need to be considered as such. As Black *et al.* note (2008: 24), "this is ... an area in which more specific local research in regions most likely to be heavily impacted by climate change would be welcome".

A second main component of the Black *et al.* analysis is to examine the climate change–migration nexus from the opposite direction, identifying the primary drivers of current migration flows before examining their sensitivity to climate change. As their starting position, they make three key points:

> First, short-distance, circulatory migration often has different drivers to long-distance, more permanent migration. Thus, whilst the former is often a response to shocks – food shortage, or flooding, or a temporary or cyclical shortage of employment or income – the latter is more usually planned, often as part of a household decision to "invest" in the migration of certain household members in order to bring longer-term benefits to other household members through remittances, investment in schooling or development of a small business.
>
> Black *et al.* 2008: 24

This is clearly in line with NELM approaches, with migration portrayed as a means of asset redeployment and risk reduction. Their second starting point is that urban and rural areas differ in the extent to which the effects of climate change are mediated by economic, social and political factors, with urban dwellers being less directly or immediately dependent on "natural factors of production" (ibid.: 25). Third, drawing on historical analogues of environmentally induced migration such as the 1930s US Dust Bowl, as well as an established body of literature on natural hazards, they observe that "the extent of vulnerability of individuals and families to migration is highly dependent on their asset base, understood in a wide sense to include not only physical capital ... but also human and social capital" (ibid.: 25) – in other words, their capacity for asset adaptation.

The main migration drivers listed by Black *et al.* (2008) are political instability and conflict, lack of economic opportunities, lack of access to natural resources, labour demand, wage differentials, transportation networks, family and social ties, government emigration and immigration policies, and trade and economic ties. For each of these, they argue, climate change could exacerbate or compound existing problems, thereby further undermining livelihoods and adding to the "push factors" driving migration. As a positive corollary, interventions that reduce political instability, enhance economic opportunities, strengthen environmental protection and protect the rights of migrants will augment the adaptive capacity of individuals, households and communities in the face of climate change. From a policy perspective, this demands climate sensitive development policies in both urban and rural areas:

> These should include new policies to build specific adaptive capacity amongst some of the most affected populations in areas such as the African Sahel, as well as the integration of climate change concerns into existing policies, to ensure that programmes do not further undermine the resilience of the poor when faced with climate change.
>
> Black *et al.* 2008: 61

Together, SLA and NELM approaches "provide a way of understanding how households respond to climate shocks, and the extent to which migration is part of their response" (Kniveton *et al.* 2008: 39). They also serve to highlight the centrality of migration in any understanding of climate change adaptation, and thus in effective policy responses.

The climate change, asset adaptation and food security nexus that informs the present volume is similarly based in sustainable livelihoods approaches. Yet without adding migration into such frameworks, we risk not only failing to grasp a crucial element of people's own adaptation to climate change, but also overlooking the policy implications of addressing the needs of a variety of migrant populations, including those moving to, from and between urban areas.

Climate change, migration and asset adaptation in African cities

Long-established in African households' livelihood strategies, migration on the continent will be – and likely already is being – affected by the impacts of climate change. The IPCC presents a range of potential impacts of climate change on Africa (Figure 4.2).

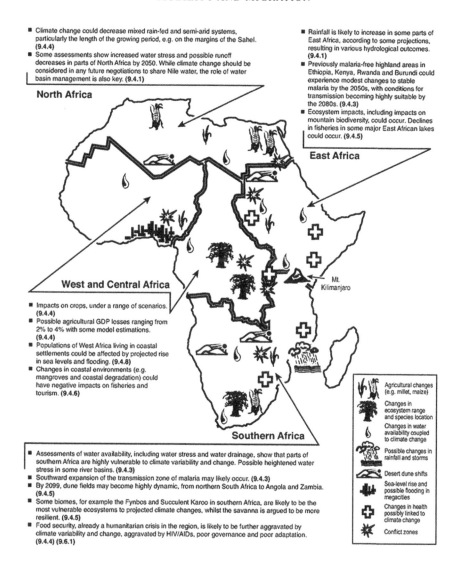

Figure 4.2 Examples of current and possible future impacts and vulnerabilities associated with climate variability and climate change for Africa

Generally, climate change literature in the African context emphasizes the effects of alterations in temperature, rainfall and seasonality along with sea level rise. These are effectively summarized in the 2007 IPCC Report (Parry *et al.* 2007). Increased water stress and shorter growing seasons are strongly predicted in many parts of the continent, with generally negative consequences for water supply, agricultural production and food security. Changed temperature and rainfall regimes will also change the distribution of biological vectors of diseases affecting people or livestock, such as malaria, schistosomiasis (bilharzia) and trypanosomiasis (sleeping sickness). Also predicted is an increase in severe weather events such as floods and storms, along with sea level rise causing inundation of low-lying coastal settlements.

Perhaps most directly significant for urban areas, sea level rise and flooding threaten low-lying areas, especially coastal cities. McGranahan *et al.* (2007) present a global overview of population and settlement patterns in low-lying coastal zones, and observe that Africa comes off relatively lightly, with only 1 per cent of its land area and 7 per cent of its total population in the low elevation coastal zone (LECZ). Yet, as they go on to observe, this represents 12 per cent of Africa's urban population, and it includes some of the largest and most rapidly growing cities in Africa, such as Lagos and Accra. Thus:

> Africa, although it contributes much less to the statistics on largest cities, has higher shares of its population in cities of 100,000 to 5 million people living in the LECZ than does Asia, Europe or the Americas. This is noteworthy because Africa's medium-to-large cities are growing at much higher rates than cities in these other continents. Given that the African cities tend to be much poorer than cities elsewhere, this raises the question of their potential vulnerability.
>
> McGranahan *et al.* 2007: 30

The multiple environmental changes arising from climate change will affect urban and rural areas in different ways, and some areas more than others, with likely consequences for migration patterns and volumes. Methods are currently being developed and strengthened that allow for downscaling of global climate models to the local scale. Although downscaling of climate models to the urban scale has not yet become widespread, a small but expanding literature does consider the likely impact of climate change on cities, along with the interaction between urbanization and global environmental change (for example, Parnell *et al.* 2007; Adamo 2010; Seto and Satterthwaite 2010; Hallegatte and Corfee-Morlot 2011). Much of this work begins by predicting possible physical changes at the urban scale, such as increased flooding, storm surges and sea level rise, and then considering the potential impacts of those changes on other components of urban physical and human environments, including housing and infrastructure. These impacts, in turn, can lead to migration and displacement both within cities and away from cities to other cities or non-urban areas. Overlooked in some of this work is the chain reaction between climate change in non-urban areas, consequent threats to rural livelihoods and food security and, in response, the migration of people, temporarily or permanently, to urban areas:

> GEC events can increase migration flows to urban areas temporarily or permanently. Large and sudden increases in the inflow of migrants can lead

to an accelerated urbanization – particularly the expansion of slums or neighborhoods in vulnerable areas – which may overwhelm the city's capacity to deliver services (education, health, public safety, etc.) and increase the population at risk.

Adamo 2010: 163

Already a challenge to housing, services and infrastructure provision in many African cities, further new in-migrants from rural areas are likely to have environmental, social and economic impacts at least as significant as urban-scale climate change impacts per se. Indirect consequences of climate change will thus affect even cities and regions that are not themselves significantly impacted by the predicted biophysical changes. At the same time, rural–urban migration is an important adaptation strategy for rural populations experiencing increased livelihood insecurity as a result of climate change, and therefore cannot be treated as something to be prevented or contained.

Few studies of climate change and cities focus on Africa, but there are African examples in the literature on climate change and migration that include cities in their analysis. In their 2008 study, Black et al. present summary scenarios for Ghana, Ethiopia and Sudan. In Ghana, they note that there may be a "double impact" (ibid.: 42), with climate change-induced migration increasing the slum populations of Accra while increased storms and flooding make those areas more vulnerable to damage. Black et al. also note the positive effects of migration, encouraging the mobilization of the Ghanaian diaspora to invest in areas most affected, such as the drought-prone north of the country. For Ethiopia and Sudan, although taking pains to counteract the direct linkage of conflict to climate change, Black et al. acknowledge the mutually confounding nature of climate change and conflict in driving human displacement in these two countries, and predict that rural–urban migration will accelerate as "distress" migration takes on more permanent form:

Projections of urban growth, and the likely acceleration of rural-urban migration as a result of climate change impacts … suggest the need for special attention to be paid to urban slums. This is not to say that there should not be investment in basic services – health and education, for example – in rural areas, as these areas are likely to maintain at least a relatively constant population. Additionally, the rural chronically poor are in most need of access to basic services and social investment, as they are least able to migrate. However, it seems that no matter how strong investment is in rural areas, urban slums will continue to grow, making it urgent that these areas also see investment

Black et al. 2008: 60

Tacoli (2009) and Adamo (2010) present further African examples. Throughout Africa, migration and mobility are long established as key means of asset adaptation and asset accumulation, especially where there is limited financial capital at the individual and household scale (Francis 2000; Frayne 2004; Tacoli 2009; Potts 2010). Crucially, migration is one of the main processes that link urban to rural areas, allowing for flows of money, goods (including food) and knowledge between them.

In urban centres in Africa, research shows that both wealthy and poorer groups tend to invest in property in rural areas, often their home villages, as a safety net against economic and political crises. Recognizing these investments and ensuring that both short- and long-term migrants retain rights in their home areas is important, especially for the groups most vulnerable to loss of property and income (Tacoli 2009: 521).

This is certainly the case in Southern Africa, where various forms of circular migration and spatially stretched household are common, including across international borders, and the combination of rural and urban livelihood strategies provides an insurance policy against the failure of one or the other. Urban employment, for example, can provide income to purchase food for rural household members during years of poor harvests, while family members in rural areas can provide food to urban-based members should they experience unemployment or other income shocks. Frayne (2004) identified complex patterns of such mutual food provisioning between urban and rural areas in Namibia, while research conducted by the Southern African Migration Project (SAMP) in numerous Southern African countries clearly demonstrates the importance of urban migrants' remittances to food provisioning in rural households (Pendleton *et al.* 2006). In explaining the linkages amongst climate change, asset adaptation and urban food security in an African context, migration is thus not merely an additional component to be considered but essential to understanding the processes by which asset adaptation is achieved and food security in urban and rural areas is sustained.

African examples can provide pointers for the integration of migration into theoretical, methodological and policy approaches to climate change adaptation. This is the case in three primary ways. First, the long history, deep socio-cultural embeddedness, and profound economic significance of migration in this region are widely documented and fairly well understood, as a voluminous literature attests (for example in work by the SAMP). Second, the African continent provides examples of marginal physical environments and variable climates in which people have managed to sustain themselves over generations without abandoning their land, thus perhaps diminishing fears of widespread "climate refugees". Third, African cities have already seen high levels of in-migration from multiple causes – economic, environmental and political – often in mutually reinforcing intersection. This makes them effective laboratories in which to study the effects of rural–urban migration, including its effects on both rural and urban areas. Following the example of Black, Kniveton, Tacoli and others, starting with existing patterns, trends and processes of migration and then assessing their sensitivity to climate change, drawing on sustainable livelihoods and new economics of labour migration approaches and incorporating an asset adaptation frame-work, may prove more useful than attempts that begin with downscaling climate change to the local scale and then trying to predict the societal impacts, including migration.

Conclusions

As discussed above, migration has been factored into climate change scenarios in a limited way, as a source of "climate refugees" and potential cause of conflict; but it remains a missing link in much of the literature on climate change impacts and adaptation, especially at the city scale. It is my contention in this chapter that the climate change, asset adaptation and urban food security nexus cannot be properly conceptualized or effectively applied without adding migration and mobility into the equation. For, as noted by the IOM:

> Migration ... is and always has been an integral part of the interaction of humans with their environment. It should therefore also be recognized as one possible adaptation strategy, especially at early stages of environmental degradation. Migration reduces reliance on the environment for livelihoods by allowing, for example, for income diversification through remittances. The contributions of migrants through the transfer of knowledge and skills upon return can also significantly strengthen the livelihoods of families and communities facing environmental challenges.
>
> IOM 2009: 2

Migration is thus not merely an adaptive strategy in and of itself, but should be seen as a key means of asset adaptation more broadly, allowing the deploy-ment of individual, household and community assets in multiple, or new, loca-tions. Obviously such mobility is impossible for most natural assets, and many physical assets, too, tend to be "lumpy" and spatially fixed – although these can be liquidated through sale. Financial, human and (to a lesser extent) social capital, by contrast, are mobile, if to varying degrees in different contexts. Migration "mobilizes" capital by allowing the translation of assets from one form, and location, to another – for example by selling physical assets to provide money to enable a household member to move to a location where their human capital can be deployed in remunerative labour, thus generating income that can be remitted to replenish and augment physical and other assets at the place of origin.

While much of the climate change and migration discourse, as for climate change more generally, is cast in terms of forecasting and future scenarios, human displacement from climate change is almost certainly already occurring, if hard to identify or distinguish given the multiple and intersecting personal, social, economic, political and environmental forces that drive migration – even forced migration – in any context. Migration is also starting to make its way into international institutional responses to climate change, for example in discussions surrounding the UN Framework Convention on Climate Change (UNFCCC) and any successor to the Kyoto Protocol (Gilbert 2009). Warner (2010) identifies several governance challenges that emerge from the relationship between climate change and migration, while also seeing the potential of migration as an adaptive strategy and pointing to a number of opportunities to "enhance resilience of both migrants and those who remain behind". These include fostering adaptive capacity through migrant networks:

> Migrants often remain linked to communities that remain behind, whether as individual migrants or as larger groups such as environmentally displaced people. These links may be material (remittances), cultural/social, or political, and shape the resilience and adaptation capacity of those who leave and those who stay
>
> Warner 2010: 411

Yet in addition to being a missing link in most of the academic writing on climate change adaptation, migration occurs within "a policy context that does not generally recognize nor support the positive potential of migration" (Tacoli 2009: 515). Tacoli calls for "a radical change in perceptions of migration" (ibid.: 523), from seeing migration in negative terms, something to be restricted and controlled, to seeing it as "an essential element of adaptation to climate change" (ibid.: 523), and thus to be accommodated and even, where necessary, supported. It is those who cannot migrate in the face of having their assets and livelihoods eroded by climate change who are the most disadvantaged, not those who are able to adopt migration as part of their adaptation strategy. Restricting mobility limits poor people's livelihood options and adaptive capacity. Nor are neo-Malthusian disaster and conflict scenarios of hundreds of millions of climate refugees especially helpful. What is required is both further, better-informed research and more coordinated and coherent policy responses. In academic terms, this "needs to involve contributions from a number of disciplines including sociology, development studies, economics, geography, informatics and climate science, while encompassing processes acting on scales from local to global" (Kniveton et al. 2008: 57). In policy terms, this means taking steps to "strengthen the adaptive capacity of communities at risk from climate change impacts" (ibid.: 57) – including, as appropriate, their capacity to move. Linking climate change to asset adaptation in urban and rural areas, highlighting the interconnectedness of urban and rural livelihoods through migration, and doing so across scales from the local community to international flows of people and their assets are important, in both academic and policy discourses, as steps towards "putting resilience, sustainability and adaptation first" (Boano et al. 2008: 18) and thinking beyond "climate refugees".

References

Adamo, S. (2010) 'Environmental migration and cities in the context of global environmental change'. *Current Opinion in Environmental Sustainability*, 2, 3: 161–165.

Andersen, L., Lund, L. and Verner, D. (2010) 'Migration and climate change', in Verner, D. (ed.) *Reducing Poverty, Protecting Livelihoods, and Building Assets in a Changing Climate*. Washington DC: World Bank.

Barnett, J. and Adger, N. (2005) 'Security and climate change: Towards an improved understanding', paper presented at International Workshop on Human Security and Climate Change, Oslo, June.

Barnett, J. and Webber, M. (2010) 'Accommodating Migration to Promote Adaptation to Climate Change', *World Bank Policy Research Working Paper*, 5270.

Bates, D. (2002) 'Environmental refugees? Classifying human migrations caused by climate change'. *Population and Environment*, 23, 5: 465–476.

Black, R., Kniveton, D., Skeldon, R., Coppard, D., Murata, A. and Schmidt-Verkerk, K. (2008) *Demographics and Climate Change: Future Trends and Their Policy Implications for Migration*. University of Sussex, Brighton: Development Research Centre on Migration, Globalisation and Poverty.

Boano, C., Zetter, R. and Morris, T. (2008) 'Environmentally Displaced People: Understanding the Linkages between Environmental Change, Livelihoods and Forced Migration'. *Forced Migration Policy Briefing*, 1. University of Oxford: Refugee Studies Centre.

Brown, O. (2008) 'Migration and Climate Change', *IOM Migration Research Series*, 31. Geneva: International Organization for Migration.

Brown, O. and Crawford, A. (2009) *Climate Change and Security in Africa. A Study for the Nordic–African Foreign Ministers Meeting*. Winnipeg, Manitoba: International Institute for Sustainable Development.

Brown, O. and McLeman, R. (2009) 'A recurring anarchy? The emergence of climate change as a threat to international peace and security'. *Conflict, Security and Development, 9*, 3: 289–305.

Castles, S. and Miller, M. J. (2009) *The Age of Migration*. London: Palgrave Macmillan.

Couldrey, M. and Herson, M. (eds) (2008) Special issue of *Forced Migration Review*, 31.

Crush, J. and Frayne, B. (eds) (2010) *Surviving on the Move: Migration, Poverty and Development in Southern Africa*. Cape Town: Idasa.

El-Hinnawi, E. (1985) *Environmental Refugees*. Nairobi, Kenya: United Nations Environmental Programme.

Francis, E. (2000) *Making a Living: Changing Livelihoods in Rural Africa*. London: Routledge.

Frayne, B. (2004) 'Migration and urban survival strategies in Windhoek, Namibia'. *Geoforum*, 35, 4: 489–505.

Gilbert, N. (2009) 'Climate refugee fears questioned'. *Nature News*. http://www.nature.com/news/2009/090625/full/news.2009.601.html (accessed 25 June 2009).

Hallegatte, S. and Corfee-Morlot, J. (2011) 'Understanding climate change impacts, vulnerability and adaptation at city scale: an introduction'. *Climatic Change*, 104, 1: 1–12.

Hartman, B. (2010) 'Rethinking climate refugees and climate conflict: rhetoric, reality and the politics of policy discourse'. *Journal of International Development*, 22, 2: 233–246.

Hugo, G. (2008) 'Migration, Environment and Development', *International Organization for Migration (IOM) Migration Research Series*, 35.

Intergovernmental Panel on Climate Change (IPCC) (2007) *Climate Change 2007: Synthesis Report. Contribution of Working Groups I, II and III to the Fourth Assessment Report of the Intergovernmental Panel on Climate Change* (Core Writing Team, Pachauri, R.K and Reisinger, A. (eds)). Geneva, Switzerland: IPCC.

International Organization for Migration (IOM) (2009) 'Migration, Climate Change and the Environment', *IOM Policy Brief*, May.

Kniveton, D., Schmidt-Verkerk, K., Smith, C. and Black, R. (2008) 'Climate Change and Migration: Improving Methodologies to Estimate Flows'. *International Organization for Migration (IOM) Migration Research Series, 33.*

McGranahan, G., Balk, D. and Anderson, B. (2007) 'The rising tide: assessing the risks of climate change and human settlements in low elevation coastal zones'. *Environment and Urbanization*, 19, 1: 17–37.

McLeman, R. and Smit, B. (2006) 'Migration as an adaptation to climate change'. *Climatic Change*, 76: 31–53.

Moser, C. and Satterthwaite, D. (2010) 'Toward pro-poor adaptation to climate change in the urban centers of low- and middle-income countries', in Mearns, Robin and Norton, A. (eds) *Social Dimensions of Climate Change: Equity and Vulnerability in a Warming World*. Washington DC: World Bank.

Mukheibir, P. and Ziervogel, G. (2006) *Framework for Adaptation to Climate Change in the City of Cape Town*. Cape Town: City of Cape Town.

Myers, N. (2005) 'Environmental refugees: An emergent security issue', paper presented at the 13th Economic Forum, Prague, May.

Nash, M. P. (director) (2010) *Climate Refugees*, http://www.climaterefugees.com (accessed 10 June 2010)

Okpewho, I. and Nzegwu, N. (2009) *The New African Diaspora*. Bloomington, IN: Indiana University Press.

Parnell, S., Simon, D. and Vogel, C. (2007) 'Global environmental change: conceptualising the growing challenge for cities in poor countries'. *Area*, 39, 3: 357–369.

Parry, M. L., Canziani, O. F., Palutikof, J. P., van der Linden, P. J. and Hanson, C. E. (eds) (2007) *Contribution of Working Group II to the Fourth Assessment Report of the 2007 Intergovernmental Panel on Climate Change, 2007. Impacts, Adaptation and Vulnerability*. Cambridge, UK and New York, USA: Cambridge University Press. http://www.ipcc.ch/publications_and_data/ar4/wg2/en/contents.html (accessed May 2011).

Pendleton, W., Crush, J. and Campbell, E. (eds) (2006) *Migration, Remittances and Development in Southern Africa*. Cape Town: IDASA and Kingston, Ontario: Southern African Migration Project.

Potts, D. (2010) *Circular Migration in Zimbabwe and Contemporary Sub-Saharan Africa*. Woodbridge, Suffolk: Boydell and Brewer (James Currey).

Reuveny, R. (2007) 'Climate change-induced migration and violent conflict'. *Political Geography*, 26, 6: 656–673.

Scoones, I. (2009) 'Livelihoods perspectives and rural development'. *Journal of Peasant Studies*, 36, 1: 171–196.

Seto, K. and Satterthwaite, D. (2010) 'Interactions between urbanization and global environmental change'. *Current Opinion in Environmental Sustainability*, 2, 3: 127–128.

Smith, P. J. (2007) 'Climate change, mass migration and the military response'. *Orbis*, 51, 4: 617–633.

Stern, N. (2006) *The Economics of Climate Change: The Stern Review*. London, UK: HM Treasury.

Tacoli, C. (2009) 'Crisis or adaptation? Migration and climate change in a context of high mobility'. *Environment and Urbanization*, 21: 513–525.

Tol, R. S. J. (2006) *The Stern Review of the Economics of Climate Change: A Comment.* Hamburg: Economic and Social Research Institute, Vrije and Carnegie Mellon Universities.

Trombetta, M. J. (2008) 'Environmental security and climate change: analysing the discourse'. *Cambridge Review of International Affairs*, 21, 4: 585–602.

UK Ministry of Defence (2008) *Climate Change Strategy*. London, UK: Ministry of Defence.

Warner, K. (2010) 'Global environmental change and migration: governance challenges'. *Global Environmental Change*, 20, 3: 402–413.

5

IMPACTS OF CLIMATE CHANGE ON MIGRATION AND FOOD SECURITY IN MAPUTO, MOZAMBIQUE

Inês Raimundo and Bruce Frayne

Introduction

Mozambique emerged from a 15-year civil war in 1992 and the country's first multi-party elections were held in 1994 (Christie and Hanlon, 2001). Since then, the country has enjoyed positive economic growth and is developing at a fast pace. However, coupled with this ongoing period of relative prosperity is sustained population growth and rapid urbanization. The country has had a population growth rate of approximately 2.2 per cent over the past two decades, with an increase in the urban population from 21 to 35 per cent of the total population between 1990 and 2007 (World Bank, 2011). Over the same 17-year period, the percentage of households living in slums has risen from 75 per cent to 80 per cent. While per capita income has more than doubled since the end of the war, inequality remains entrenched with an income Gini coefficient of 47.1 for the last decade (World Bank, 2011). In fact Mozambique has fallen two places on the 2010 Human Development Index (HDI) (ibid.), and is now ranked 155 out of 159 countries (Zimbabwe being 159).

Poverty is increasingly associated with urbanization in the context of Mozambique as rural populations continue to migrate into the towns. The capital city of Maputo has experienced significant growth over the past two decades, with the large majority of the population living in informal conditions. The city's rate of urbanization is the highest in Mozambique, increasing from 1.2 per cent in 1970 (DNE, 1980) to 2.7 per cent in 1997 and peaking at 3.5 per cent (INE, 2009, 1998). This trend is expected to continue, with an estimated rate of urbanization of 4 per cent over the coming decade (CIA, 2011). The latest estimates of poverty in Maputo indicate that more than half (53.5 per cent) of the urban population live below the poverty line (Matusse, 2009; INE,

2003). Moreover, food poverty is severe in the city; a recent survey amongst poor residents in Maputo found that 85 per cent of households are chronically food insecure (Frayne et al., 2010).

In addition to rapid urban growth and widespread poverty in Maputo, the city faces a number of significant environmental challenges. Much of the city's population is housed informally, and services are limited. This makes much of the urban population highly vulnerable to extreme weather events, and directly impacts their assets and livelihoods. Cyclones and floods are commonplace, and affect the city, which is both coastal and largely flat. Flooding is mainly attributed to the city's location in the coastal zone and at the confluence of five rivers – the Incomati, Umbeluzi, Maputo, Matola and Tembe – all of which empty into Maputo Bay (Indian Ocean). There is also the Infulene River, a small stream only 24 km in length, and this too ends in Maputo Bay. The poorest residents of the city are concentrated in these rivers' floodplains, and are largely made up of rural to urban migrants who began to migrate during the civil war and have continued to do so since (Raimundo, I. M., 2009). These floodplains are also where much of the city's urban agriculture takes place, which is periodically destroyed by severe storms and cyclones, further exacerbating the negative impacts of environmental factors on local resident's livelihoods. Research indicates that the occurrence and intensity of storms are increasing as a result of climate change, as are mean temperatures and net rainfall (Tadross, 2009). In addition to rapid urban growth and widespread poverty in Maputo, the city faces a number of significant environmental challenges (Araújo, 2003, 2005; Muanamoha, 2002).

It is within this vexing confluence of rapid urbanization, widespread and rising urban poverty, and increasingly severe weather patterns that this chapter examines the links between migration, food security and climate change in Maputo.

Methodology

In addition to a range of secondary data sources, this chapter is based on two recent studies in Maputo. The first is the African Food Security Urban Network (AFSUN) Urban Food Security Baseline Survey undertaken in Maputo in late 2008.[1] AFSUN also undertook the same survey in 10 other cities in Southern Africa, collecting data on 5453 households and 28,771 people (data were collected on all people living in the household). The sample in Maputo was drawn from poor neighbourhoods, with a total size of 397 households. In this chapter, the survey households are classified by food security status (food secure, food insecure).[2]

The second study conducted a series of focus group discussions and 148 in-depth life history interviews in both migrant sending and receiving areas in Mozambique, including Maputo. The focus of this study was on household dynamics and urbanization, with a focus on gender, choice and migration issues (Raimundo, I. M., 2009).

Food insecurity and poverty in Maputo

The AFSUN survey (Frayne *et al.*, 2010) shows that 85 per cent of poor urban households in the city are chronically food insecure. The Lived Poverty Index (LPI) (Frayne *et al.*, 2010) is a reliable, self-reported, multidimensional measure of deprivation ('going without'). When the food security status of the sample is cross-tabulated with the LPI, it is clear that food insecurity is a reasonable proxy measure for poverty (Figure 5.1). Although the sample is split about equally between households who 'go without' and those who do not, more than 91 per cent of food secure households have an LPI score of 0–1 (never – seldom go without). In contrast, 50 per cent of those households that are food insecure are also those that 'go without' (LPI score of 1.01–4.0).

Education and food security

Within the context of rising poverty, it is not surprising that the AFSUN survey (2008) found that only 13 per cent of the sample population had completed high school and/or obtained higher education qualifications. About half of the people surveyed had no formal schooling (10 per cent) or had not completed primary school (38 per cent). Functional literacy levels amongst the city's poor are therefore low, and compare similarly to the estimated adult literacy rates in Mozambique as a whole (44 per cent; WHO, 2007). The data show that education levels and food security are related; those with no formal schooling and only primary schooling are the most insecure, whereas those with high school and tertiary education enjoy greater levels of food security (Figure 5.2).

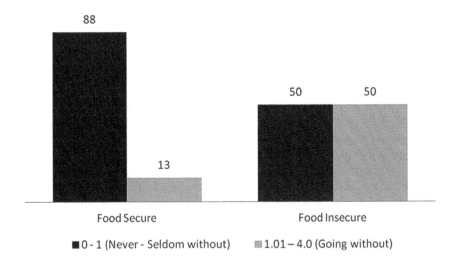

Figure 5.1 Lived Poverty Index by household food security status (per cent)

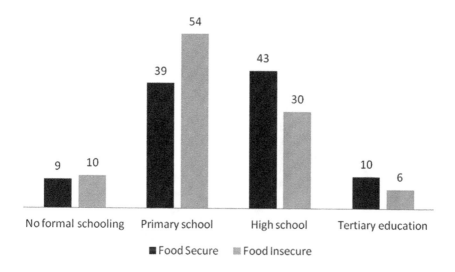

Figure 5.2 Education by household food security status (per cent)

Occupation and food insecurity

Mozambique has a population pyramid with a very large base, indicating that the majority of the population are young. In the case of Maputo, the data show that 72 per cent of the survey population are below 30 years of age, and that about half are younger than 20 years (Figure 5.3). It is therefore not surprising that 39 per cent of the sample population are scholars. However, and indicative of high levels of poverty, the survey found that one third of the sample (including scholars) was under or unemployed. Figure 5.3 shows that unskilled workers, those in the informal sector, those looking for work and unpaid domestic workers totalled 33 per cent, compared to 19 per cent who are employed in professional roles, the military and skilled occupations.

Moreover, the survey shows that having a household member(s) in full-time work (income) is positively correlated with greater levels of food security for that household. As illustrated in Figure 5.4, the greatest proportion (59 per cent) of food secure households have income from full-time work, whereas households that derive an income from part-time and casual work have a greater proportion of food insecure households. As expected, the trend is similar for households with unemployed members who are looking for work, with higher levels of insecurity. However, it is noteworthy that almost as many households with income from full-time work are food insecure as not; this speaks to the generalized nature of urban poverty in Maputo.

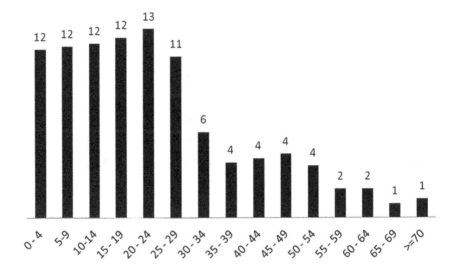

Figure 5.3 Age groups of sample population (per cent)

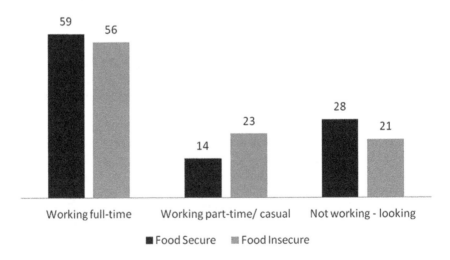

Figure 5.4 Work status by food security status (per cent, excluding those 'not looking for work')

Income and food insecurity

Just as work status and source of work have been shown to be important in determining household security status, income and food security are also positively correlated. Income terciles have been computed against food security status, and the data show that those households with the lowest incomes experience the greatest levels of food insecurity (Figure 5.5). More than half (54 per cent) all food secure households are in the highest income category, with the greatest proportion of food insecure households (30 per cent) in the poorest income tercile. This pattern is consistent with the regional picture (Frayne *et al.*, 2010).

Food price shocks and food security

Sharp food price increases in 2007–2008 were experienced in Maputo, and it therefore comes as no surprise that when asked about the impact on food availability as a consequence of recent food price increases, 50 per cent of households in the region reported going without food in the past six months as a *direct outcome* of food price increases. As shown in Figure 5.6, the vast majority (80 per cent) of food insecure households have had to go without food as a result of food price increases. The fact that more than almost two thirds (60 per cent) of households categorized as food secure also go without food is a reflection of the reality that, although relatively better off, the food secure in this sample are still largely poor and therefore very sensitive to price shocks. Indeed, more recent price hikes in bread and fuel in 2010 have led to food riots in Maputo.

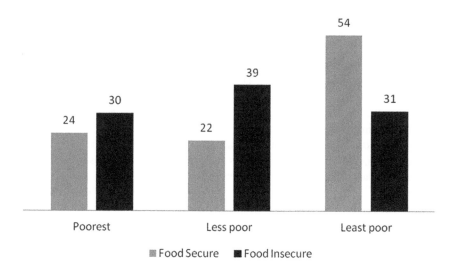

Figure 5.5 Household income terciles by food security status (per cent)

101

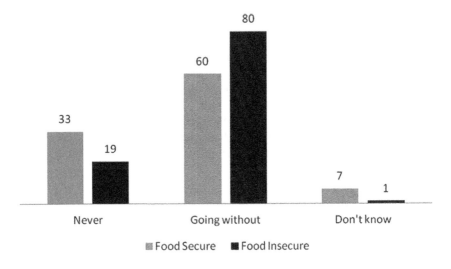

Figure 5.6 Impact of food price changes: frequency of households going without food (unaffordable) in past six months by household food security status (per cent)

Migration and food security

Mozambique has a long history of migration, both internal and cross-border. In addition, the rate of urbanization in Maputo is estimated to be 4 per cent for the period 2010–15, which is higher than the natural population growth rate of 2.4 per cent (CIA, 2011). With this high rate of urbanization in Maputo, it would be expected that many households in the city would be migrant households. While the AFSUN survey (migrant households) found that only 11 per cent of households in the sample are first generation migrant households (in other words, no one in that household was born in that city, but has migrated there during their lifetime), the majority of households had migrants living in them (78 per cent). Therefore the largest proportion of households comprised a mix of migrants and non-migrants, which illustrates the significance of migration in the socio-economic make-up of the city, a pattern that is mirrored in other urban centres in Southern Africa (Frayne *et al.*, 2010) indicating the temporal and geographic fluidity of household structure across all cities in the region (Table 5.1).

Given this large-scale migration process evident in Maputo, it is surprising that migration appears to have little influence on households' food security status. Figure 5.7 shows that having migrants in the household does not make much difference to the levels of food security in the household. However, where household migration status does make an important difference is with regard to inter-household food transfers. Only 13 per cent of food secure households in the survey reported receiving food transfers from elsewhere, whereas 87 per cent of food insecure households receive food transfers. This is significant and demonstrates the important social capital that operates between poor households as part of their survival strategies.

Table 5.1 Lifetime migration

Migrant status of household	Total per cent
Migrant HH	11
Non-migrant HH	11
Mixed HH*	78
Total	100

Notes
N=397
HH – households
* Has both migrants and non-migrants.

Source: Frayne *et al.*, 2010

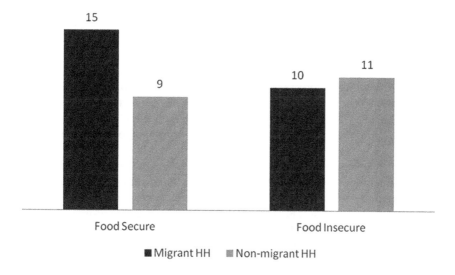

Figure 5.7 Household migration status by food security status (per cent)

Climate change and assets in Maputo

Climate change scenarios are a new concern for politicians and researchers. According to the UN-HABITAT report (2008), climate change is likely to become an important driver for both internal and external migration, putting huge pressures on urban settlements. Additionally, climate change can lead to greater impoverishment since the soil is becoming more unproductive and crops are also failing because of extreme drought and flooding. This situation is more critical in those countries where the urban population will double between 2000 and 2030. Since many African cities are located within disaster prone zones, the UN-HABITAT report urges decisions to be made immediately, in preparation for expected increased migratory flows into cities as a result of weather variability and severity.

In the case of Mozambique, climate change models indicate a clear warming trend with increased rainfall and intensity. These climate change expectations are based on analysing observed data collected from 32 weather stations across Mozambique since 1950; the outputs from seven global circulation models (GCM); and the results of downscaling these GCM outputs to a number of station locations (using the observed data record to do this) for two periods in the future: 2045–2055 and 2080–2100 (Tadross, 2009). In both cases temperatures will rise and rainfall will increase (although not uniformly). In addition, rising sea levels may also impact the country negatively as large coastal areas have little elevation, including Maputo.

Planning for these climate change impacts on Maputo, which has already experienced giant waves that have flooded neighborhoods such as Pescadores, Costa do Sol and Inhaca Island, is a daunting challenge. What makes matters worse is the fact that those who should be dealing with the issue are distracted by other pressing matters and are not prioritizing climatic change. City planners must cope with a mix of factors including poverty reduction, resettlement of people who live in areas of economic interest (near roads and industry plants), as well as dealing with people who have been displaced by floods or heavy rains.

What the AFSUN survey (Frayne *et al.*, 2010) data show is that poverty and food security in Maputo are directly related, and that migration is a major demographic force in the city's growth and social economy. However, the data do not provide any evidence of environmentally induced migration. When asked for their reasons for migrating to Maputo, less than 1 per cent of the respondents ranked environmental reasons first. In contrast economic and family reasons dominated the responses. This is typical of migration findings elsewhere in the region.[3] Nonetheless, I. M. Raimundo's (2008) and J. C. J. Raimundo's (2009) in-depth qualitative research with migrants suggests that environmental factors are becoming an important reason for migration. What is important in this discussion is the impact of weather related events on the assets of the urban poor, who are largely first generation migrants. Of particular importance is the impact of extreme weather events on the ability of households to maintain food related assets that directly support their food security – as the data presented have shown, the majority of the urban poor are already highly vulnerable to external shocks as they are already food insecure. The question is to what extent longer-term climate change expectations are likely to impact on food production (and security) in the city of Maputo.

A UN-HABITAT report (2008) points out that due to global warming, coastal cities such as Maputo and Beira in Mozambique are at substantial risk of sea levels rising, and, to date, that appears not to have been fully captured in city plans. Indeed, within Southern Africa, Mozambique is the most at risk from flooding, cyclones and sea levels rising. Almost half of the country is a flood plain with major rivers such as the Zambezi, Limpopo, Save and Pungoe flowing into the Indian Ocean from various parts of the country. As discussed in the introduction, multiple major rivers terminate in Maputo. Furthermore, the city of Maputo, due to its location in a coastal area, is exposed to surge flooding.

It is the urban poor in Maputo who live on the flattest land (and therefore most prone to flooding) and who are already the most impacted by these disasters. Experience has shown the need to develop plans to mitigate disaster vulnerability. However, a programme to relocate and resettle households away from the flood plains has failed as people have returned to the old sites, indicating the huge gap between policy makers' and poor residents' perception of risk.

Food security is a concern in Mozambique since floods, drought and cyclones mean people have regularly lost their crops. According to INGC *et al.* (2003), food production within Maputo has been impacted by these events, reducing output for household use and for sale at the market. In both cases, these losses represent an erosion of poor urban households' assets. This erosion of assets is fundamental to the ongoing and rising poverty and food insecurity evident in Maputo, and places households in a state of permanent vulnerability since agriculture is an activity that increases income by producing produce for sale or providing food to eat.

I. M. Raimundo (2009) points out that those who are involved in rural agriculture are wives/spouses who travel and live away from their home in Maputo. These women travel far distances to places such as Vilanculos in order to engage in agriculture to feed the members of their households. Others also make daily journeys of distances of up to 30 km to places such as Boane or Marracuene. Some of these women often travel to fishing villages in order to buy seafood that they then sell in the city. The produce they bring back home serves to supplement the family diet, or is sold to obtain cash for domestic needs.

Areas such as Vilanculos (a coastal district), Funhalouro and Chicualacuala (interior districts that are extremely dry) are prone to recurring cyclones, floods and drought and there is no longer any certainty that agricultural crops or seafood harvesting will adequately meet consumer demand. In this way, migration and food security are linked, not only within Maputo but also between households in Maputo and households living elsewhere in the country. Assets impacted in locations far from Maputo may therefore still have direct and negative impacts on poverty and food insecurity in the city, so also linking climate change with multi-spatial livelihoods.

Scarcity of rain has adversely impacted urban agriculture because of the lack of rainwater to nurture crops. The rainy season has become irregular and even water from nearby streams and swamps is not plentiful enough to sustain cultivation. The soil is also becoming more and more unproductive due to increasing salt contamination. Resulting fallow land is particularly prevalent on Inhaca Island and in Catembe; both are administrative posts of the city of Maputo. Since 2007, giant waves[4] washing in from the ocean have flooded crops and houses including the backyard of a four star hotel. According to the islanders and fishermen, this is a new phenomenon in Maputo with no collective memory of similar historical events.

Aside from agriculture, these tidal waves have also impacted the local fishing industry. After the occurrence of such waves, ocean habitat is disrupted and the fish normally harvested in the area have migrated elsewhere. Without enough fish to catch, fishermen were not able to harvest enough to feed their families, or even sell it. In Maputo, apart from natural inherent problems related to management of people and crumbling infrastructures, the municipal administration must now also cope with climatic impacts such as floods, drought and giant waves – all of which impact urban agriculture, fishing and livelihoods, eroding the natural capital stocks available to the local population.

Crush and Frayne (2010) state that urban agriculture is generally seen as an important source of income and food for poor urban households in Africa. While the practice of urban agriculture is uneven in the region, it is important in Maputo, with approximately 50 per cent of city dwellers involved in urban agriculture as a supplement to their income or for their own consumption (Ministry of Planning and Development, 2009; National Institute for Statistics, 2003). Urban agriculture serves to furnish the city with vegetables and fruit while generating household income for the seller. Most city dwellers involved in agriculture do their cultivation alongside the Infulene River, in the low lands, on "free-land",[5] "waste ground" or in their backyards. This is particularly true of those who have large portions of land not occupied by houses.

The J. C. J. Raimundo (2009) study shows that those who cultivate near the Infulene River, do so in association with other farmers, sharing an irrigation system. As a collective, they pay "right of use fees" to the city Municipality of Maputo. Twenty per cent of this group is made up of people who do agriculture while the majority are urban farmers (about 80 per cent) who use so called "free-land" in schoolyards and even within the grounds of the University of Eduardo Mondlane.

The first group was formed by long-established settlers in the city. Those presently involved were born in Maputo and enjoy better living conditions. The second group is made up of those who came to the city as immigrants/migrants or were internally displaced persons.[6] In both situations, the agricultural work is done by women. However, in the case of agriculture done alongside the Infulene River, the land is registered in the name of the head of household, which in most cases is a man although the actual farming is done by women (Raimundo, J. C. J., 2009).

The poor, who are cultivating on school or other public land, in reality, have no legal rights to that land. However, there are some "squatter farmers", who, for whatever reason, have had to move away from Maputo. They are now charging new users rent for land inside school and University property. The spirit of entrepreneurship – legal or not – is alive and well in Maputo city (ibid.). Security of tenure remains a key multigenerational asset building block, and needs to be addressed within the prevailing context of poverty and food insecurity in Maputo.

Conclusions

Ongoing urbanization and population growth are major challenges for Maputo. Moreover, with the majority of households living below the poverty line, deepening poverty in the city is eroding the capacity of the poor to maintain existing livelihood strategies, let alone develop new ones. The primary source of livelihoods for the urban poor is small-scale agriculture and fishing, yet levels of household food insecurity amongst the city's poor are close to 90 per cent.

Within this context, and given the low-lying topography of Maputo, climate change may already be exerting significant stresses on the livelihoods of the poor. Storms, cyclones, unpredictable rainfall patterns and increasing weather intensity are all eroding productive household assets through wind damage, flooding, crop losses and changes in fish availability in and near the city. In addition to this, the high levels of informality in the urban fabric and housing in poor neighbourhoods translate into regular flooding and housing and other infrastructure damage, all of which are key productive assets (Moser, 2009). The ability of the poor to recover from these impacts is limited; for example, many houses that have been damaged in major cyclones remain unrepaired in the city. Climate modelling confirms that the frequency and intensity of these weather events is likely to increase in the coming decades, together with a net increase in mean temperatures, all of which will again impact both agriculture and fisheries in ways that are not yet fully understood.

Whereas migration is considered to be a development pressure within Maputo, it may very well also be an important adaptive response to climate change and its impacts on livelihoods. This chapter argues that geographic fluidity as a result of the migration process makes it possible for households to diversify their productive activities between different places. In so doing, households can buffer the shocks to their assets that are brought on by extreme weather events in one location. In one sense this is simply a complex coping strategy employed by poor and vulnerable households; on the other hand, it may yet offer a viable way to protect and build assets in an increasingly unpredictable and poor context. This does not, however, negate the responsibilities of government to engage meaningfully in pro-poor urban development in Maputo, although, as this chapter recognizes, authorities face many competing challenges, which place pressure on the poor to continue to strive for asset building strategies as they negotiate their lives in complex ways.

Notes

1   The African Food Security Urban Network (AFSUN) is supported by funding from the Canadian International Development Agency (CIDA) under its University Partners in Cooperation and Development (UPCD) Tier One Program.
2   A full explanation of this methodology can be found at Frayne *et al.*, 2010.
3   For migration research in Southern Africa, see the Southern African Migration Project (SAMP) at Queen's University, Canada (www.queensu.ca/samp).

4 Information gathered in August of 2008, during fieldwork with students who were attending a training programme on Climatic Changes and Adaptation to Climatic Changes in Africa. This programme was sponsored by the Organization of Social Sciences Research in Eastern and Southern Africa (OSSREA) to Lusophone countries.
5 This land is "free" until the Municipality takes it for implementation of urban planning. In fact there is no longer any free land or free space because Maputo City owns every bit of space including the swamps and slopes.
6 This is mainly due to civil war and the floods of the late 1980s as well as in recent years.

References

Araújo, M. G. M. (2003) 'Os Espaços Urbanos em Moçambique', *GEOUSP – Espaço e Tempo*, 14: 155–182.
Araújo, M. G. M. (2005) A População das Cidades da Matola e Maputo: espaços urbanos multifacetados. Centro de Estudos da População. Faculdade de Letras e Ciências Sociais. Maputo: Imprensa Universitária.
Christie, F. and Hanlon, J. (2001) *Mozambique and the Great Flood of 2000*. London: Zed Books.
CIA (Central Intelligence Agency) (2011) *The World Factbook, Mozambique*, https://www. cia.gov/library/publications/the-world-factbook/geos/mz.html (accessed March 2011).
Crush, J. and Frayne, B. (2010) 'Pathways to Insecurity: Urban Food Supply and Access in Southern African Cities', *Urban Food Security Series, 3*. African Urban Food Security Network (AFSUN) IDASA Publishing, Cape Town.
DNE (1980) *Moçambique: Recenseamento Geral da População*, Maputo.
Frayne, B., Pendleton, W., Crush, J., Acquah, B., Battersby-Lennard, J., Bras, E., Chiweza, A., Dlamini, T., Fincham, R., Kroll, F., Leduka, C., Mosha, A., Mulenga, C., Mvula, P., Pomuti, A., Raimundo, I., Rudolph, M., Ruysenaar, S., Simelane, N., Tevera, D., Tsoka, M., Tawodzera, G. and Zanamwe, L. (2010) 'The State of Urban Food Insecurity in Southern Africa', *Urban Food Security Series, 2*. African Urban Food Security Network (AFSUN) IDASA Publishing, Cape Town.
INE (Instituto Nacional de Estatísticas) (1998) *II Recenseamento Geral da População e Habitação 1997: Indicadores Sócio-Demográficos – Maputo cidade, Maputo*. Maputo: Instituto Nacional de Estatísticas.
INE (Instituto Nacional de Estatísticas) (2003) *Inquérito nacional aos Agregados Familiares sobre orçamento 2002/3*. Maputo: Instituto Nacional de Estatísticas.
INE (Instituto Nacional de Estatísticas) (2009) *Cidade de Maputo: Resultados definitivos do III Recenseamento geral da População e Habitação 2007*. Maputo: Instituto Nacional de Estatísticas.
INGC, FEWSNET and Eduardo Mondlane University (2003) *Atlas for Disaster Preparedness and Response in the Limpopo Basin*.
Matusse, C. (2009) 'Políticas públicas de redução da pobreza em Moçambique', unpublished paper presented at the Conference on Urban Poverty in Southern Africa, Maputo 16 April 2009.
Ministério da Planificação e Desenvolvimento (2009) *Políticas de Redução da Pobreza em Moçambique*. Maputo: Direcção Nacional de Planificação.
Moser, C. O. N. (2009) *Ordinary Families, Extraordinary Lives: Assets and Poverty Reduction in Guayaquil, 1978–2004*. Washington, DC: Brookings Press.

Muanamoha, R.C. (2002) 'Dinâmica do crescimento populacional no período pós-Inde-pendência em Maputo', in Oppenheimer, J. and Raposo, I. (eds), *Urbanização acelerada em Luanda e Maputo – Impacto da guerra e das transformações sócio-económicas (década de '80 e '90)*, CesA: Estudos de Desenvolvimento nº 7, 11–19.

National Institute for Statistics (2003) *Statistical Yearbook 2003*. Maputo.

Raimundo, I. M. (2008) 'Famílias, Secas e Implicações nas Migrações Internas em Moçambique: O que é que Existe e o que é que não Existe?', paper presented at SEMILUSO Conference, Brazil, University of Paraiba, João pessoa, June.

Raimundo, I. M. (2009) 'Gender, choice and migration – household dynamics and urbanisa-tion in Mozambique', unpublished thesis, University of Witwatersrand, Johannesburg, Graduate School of Humanities, Forced Migration Programme.

Raimundo, J. C. J. (2009) 'Environmental degradation and food insecurity in the city of Maputo', paper presented at AISA (Africa Institute of South Africa) Conference on Revitalizing African Value Systems for Sustainable Continental Integration: Perspectives from Emerging Scholars, Johannesburg, June.

Tadross, M. (2009) 'Climate change modelling and analyses for Mozambique', final report. Mozambique: Instituto Nacional de Gestãde Calamidades.

UN-HABITAT (2008) The State of African Cities 2008 – A Framework for Addressing Urban Challenges in Africa. Nairobi: United Human Settlements Programme, ECA-CEA.

WHO (World Health Organization) UNData (2007) *World Health Statistics*, http://data.un.org/ (accessed March 2011).

World Bank (2011) World Development Indicators, Washington, DC: World Bank, http://data.worldbank.org/data-catalog/world-development-indicators/wdi-2011 (accessed September 2011).

6

ASSET ADAPTATION AND URBAN FOOD SECURITY IN A CHANGING CLIMATE

A case study of Kalingalinga and Linda Compounds in Lusaka, Zambia

Danny Simatele

Introduction

Zambia has been experiencing repeated adverse weather conditions ranging from severe droughts to extreme precipitation in recent years. The frequency in these events have negatively affected food production, availability and distribution including consumption for both rural and urban households (Kasali, 2007; IUCN, 2007). This is because agriculture, especially the production of cereal crops, which provides over half of all calories consumed in Zambia, is dependent on rainfall. Given these erratic weather conditions, and the high dependence of urban population on rural production, chronic malnutrition (stunting) has become prevalent and has affected an estimated 53 per cent of the urban households. Malnutrition, on the other hand (wasting), has affected about 5 per cent of all urban households (CSO, 2005).

In Lusaka the capital of Zambia, for example, an estimated 48 per cent of the 1.3 million people live in poverty, with 29 per cent and 19 per cent of these being classified as living in extreme and moderate poverty respectively (CSO, 2006). In view of these poverty levels, an estimated 30 per cent to 40 per cent of all the households in Lusaka are affected by malnutrition (ibid.). At the household or individual level, the poverty and food insecurity situation is the result of the urban poor households lacking the means of production (i.e. stock of assets), and their inability to secure decent wage employment and incomes to purchase food. An estimated 74 per cent of the population in Lusaka, for example, are employed in the informal sector, while 21 per cent are unemployed (CSO, 2006; LCC, 2008). These varying circumstances have subjected a significantly large proportion of the urban poor to different vulnerabilities, among which include: substandard housing, poor roads, poor sanitation, and poor waste management and service provision.

The recent changes and variability in weather conditions in Lusaka, for example, have resulted in reductions in crop yields and agricultural productivity both in the intra- and peri-urban areas. For the majority of the urban poor, the gradual impacts of the changing weather patterns have manifested themselves through increased food and energy prices, and the slow erosion of their livelihood assets. An elderly male participant in Linda Compound for example, commented that: "People can always withstand bad harvests and bad rain, but when it happens so often, like now, it is hard. Every year it happens, we become a bit weaker. Every year we become poorer. This is the big problem."

This chapter draws upon recent field-based research in two informal settlements in Lusaka, and discusses the way in which changes in weather patterns are negatively impacting the livelihoods of the urban poor, and how different asset adaptation strategies of poor households and communities contribute to their food security or, alternatively, reduce their food security.

A conceptual note: asset adaptation and food security

Asset adaptation, according to Moser and Satterthwaite (2008), refers to actions that people take in response to, or in anticipation of, projected or actual changes in weather conditions. These actions are usually taken in order to reduce adverse impacts, or to take advantage of the opportunities posed by these changes. The argument is based on two premises: firstly, the assumption that a large portion of people's assets, particularly the urban poor, are vulnerable to different stresses, which may either be a result of internal or external processes. Secondly, the assumption that the poor are not passive residents or actors, but that they are actively involved in protecting and modifying their assets against the impacts of extreme weather events at all times.

It is, however, important to note that the types of asset adaptation strategy and action that are normally available to the urban poor are often influenced by a number of factors, which can either facilitate or impede their efforts to adapt to different weather conditions. Moser (2009), for example, is of the view that asset adaptation strategies of the urban poor do not occur in a vacuum because the lives of the urban poor are predisposed by a number of factors and processes. She observes that asset adaptation, in the context of climate change, is based on three basic principles:

1   Firstly, that external factors such as government policies, political institutions and government legislation can either block or facilitate asset access[1] and asset accumulation,[2] and this has implications on the type of asset adaptation[3] strategies embarked on by the urban poor.
2   Secondly, the formal and informal contexts in which actors operate can either facilitate or erode asset adaptation efforts in the sense that the assets that the urban poor own are interrelated. The erosion of one asset, for example, will inherently affect the other assets.

3   Thirdly, she observes that household asset portfolios change over time, and these changes can occur either suddenly or gradually, as in the case of death of the household's breadwinner.

In view of the asset and food vulnerability context of the poor, Maxwell (1998) argues that for many of the vulnerable urban households, the strategy to sustain their livelihood options and food security in a changing environment is often fox-like. It does many things: sniff around and look for opportunities, diversify by adding enterprises and multiply activities and relationships. It uses not one but many means to gain food and cash, reduce vulnerability and improve the quality of life. Prowse and Scott (2008) are of the view that asset adaptation, in the context of climate change, determines the extent to which a household will be food secure or insecure. They further point out that assets and asset accumulation, which includes asset protection, tell us "who will adapt and recover quickly from the impacts of climate change" and who will not (ibid.).

In summary, therefore, it is important to note that the bundle of assets owned by the urban poor can facilitate greater adaptation and resilience to the impacts of extreme weather conditions because various assets, and the ways in which they are adapted against adverse weather events, can be used to analyse the multiple risks that urban residents are exposed to, and identify entry points for policy formulation.

The case studies: Kalingalinga and Linda Compounds

Kalingalinga[4] Compound is a settlement, east of the city of Lusaka, while Linda is located on the southern part and straddles Lusaka and Kafue districts (see study sites in Figure 6.1). Both settlements originally developed as farming sites for a group of Asian and European farmers before Zambia attained political independence from Britain in 1964. From the 1940s until the early 1960s, both settlements increasingly became recognised as residential areas as more new native migrants took up urban residence in Lusaka. With increased demand for housing, coupled with institutional failures in colonial structures in providing housing for the local people, European and Asian farmers with vast pieces of farm land started engaging in what become known as kafir[5] farming (Williams, 1986). With the attainment of independence, a number of travel restrictions imposed by the colonial government were removed and this paved the way for new levels of migration into the urban centre of Zambia. By the 1970s, both settlements were gazetted as illegal settlements.

Although Kalingalinga and Linda are both informal settlements and share a number of characteristics, some significant differences exist. Kalingalinga, with an estimated population of between 35,000 and 45,000, and which was previously omitted from the Lusaka Urban District (LUD)/World Bank (WB) upgrading programme, benefited from the LUD and Deutsche Gesellschaft für Technische Zusammenarbeit (GTZ) project. The upgrading scheme included: the provision

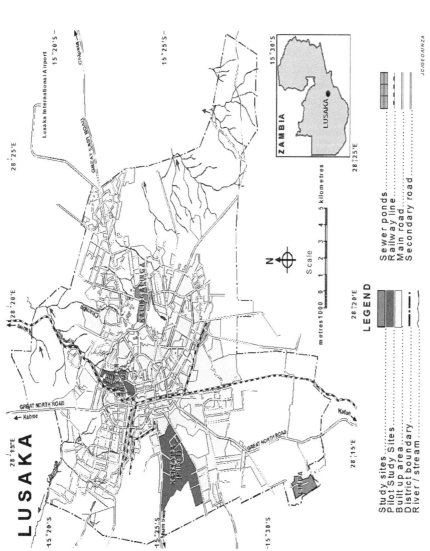

Figure 6.1
Location of Kalingalinga
and Linda Compounds in
Lusaka

of a school, clinic, market and community centre; installation of water standpipes to groups of families, roads, street lighting, house improvement loans and a core house material loan programme through a community revolving fund; secure title to land; and promotion of informal economic activities and income generation through micro-loans for use in the informal sector, in which about 80 per cent of the population are presently employed. The scheme also included the realignment of dwellings and efforts to lower densities and allow for widening of streets.

Linda Compound is a settlement that has not benefited from any government development efforts or strategies since being established as a residential area. The area is normally described as having a split personality because it straddles two planning authorities, which raises questions as to which local authority is responsible for the provision of both social and economic facilities. With an estimated population of 25,000 people, only 2000 of these have any form of formal employment. The limited socio-economic services available in this community, such as the installation of public water standpipes, roads and health amenities, are normally a result of community-based initiatives in collaboration with external organisations and concerned citizens. Thus, Linda Compound, compared to Kalingalinga Compound and other informal settlements in Lusaka, has continued to lag behind in terms of development and is a community that exhibits significant rural characteristics. One such feature is the heavy dependency of the residents of this community on peri-urban agriculture and the natural environment for their livelihoods. The dependency on natural resources has placed many of the residents in this settlement at high risk to any changes in weather conditions, especially drought or heavy rainfall.

Methodology

As stated earlier, this chapter is based on information collected from Kalingalinga and Linda Compounds (see Figure 6.1) in Lusaka. It is based on discussions with 51 focus groups. Each focus group consisted of an average number of six participants. Of the 51 focus groups, 13 comprised adult female-only participants aged between 19 and 85 years, 17 were male-only participants, 19 consisted of both male and female participants, and 2 comprised schoolchildren aged between 13 and 16 years old.

The Participatory Climate Change Asset Adaptation Appraisal (PCCAA) framework, developed by the Global Urban Research Centre (GURC) and the University of Manchester, and which builds on the accumulation of assets, was the main methodological and analytical framework that was used for data collection and analysis. The PCCAA uses the principles and practices of participatory research (PR), and is an extension of the asset-based vulnerability and adaptation framework, initially developed by Moser and Satterthwaite (2008). The asset-based vulnerability framework highlights the role that assets play in building the adaptive capacity of the most vulnerable groups of people to severe weather conditions (Prowse and Scott, 2008; Moser and Satterthwaite, 2008). It consists of two components: firstly, the asset analytical framework, which identifies the links between different vulnerabilities and assets of the urban poor, including the various practices employed to cope with, recover and build resilience against internal and external stressors. Secondly, the asset adaptation operational framework, which identifies concrete measures taken by individuals or households to increase their resilience and reduce vulnerability in the face of long-term changes as well as immediate shocks that result from changes in climatic conditions (Moser and Stein, 2010).

In light of the above, two basic data collection instruments were employed: focus group discussions and semi-structured interviews. The two data collection techniques facilitated the use of various PCCAA tools, among which included: transect walks, participatory community risk mapping, Venn (or institutional) diagrams, different matrices, brainstorming, causal flow diagrams and community workshops. In additional to focus group discussions, open-ended questions were frequently used to solicit additional information from the participants using the 'six helpers' – What? When? Where? How? How much? Why? It is important to note that the purpose of using the PCCAA tools was manifold. Firstly, to engage in cumulative learning of all stakeholders involved in the study (i.e. both the participants and the researchers). Secondly, to have multiple perspectives on the social dimension of severe weather conditions affecting the urban poor in the two study sites and how they adapt to these conditions using different assets. Thirdly, the process of understanding the complexity of the world of lived experiences is often context specific, and group analysis and interaction is one possible avenue through which to unveil this complexity.

Local perceptions of extreme weather conditions and climate variability at the sites

Lusaka has been experiencing some adverse impacts of climate including climate variability, extreme events and other systematic changes in climate variables over the last several decades. Extreme weather events such as floods and droughts, as well as El Niño induced events have become more frequent and intense, with serious consequences for the socio-economic and livelihood activities of the urban population. Between 1972 and 1996, for example, Lusaka and several other parts in Zambia suffered severe droughts, with at least eight droughts being observed in less than three decades (Kasali, 2007). And since the dawn of the new millennium, the city has been experiencing severe floods, which have had devastating impacts on the general well-being of the urban poor.

The changes in weather patterns have not gone unnoticed by the local people. Participants in both study locations mentioned having experienced changes in rainfall patterns and temperature during the last 10 years. Many participants, using various participatory methods, argued that the rains start late, but they tend to bring severe flooding that lasts several months, and displaces them when they finally commence. They also pointed out that the temperatures have become warmer during both the rainy season and the dry season, and that there are more droughts than before.

In terms of factors attributed to these weather changes, a clear distinction in perception between older[6] and younger participants could be observed. Many of the older participants argued that contemporary extreme weather events being experienced were a result of a curse from the "gods" because society had committed some unpardonable sins. This perception was clearly articulated during a focus group discussion, when an elderly female participant, who has lived in Linda Compound for more than 50 years, commented:

> These frequent heavy rainfalls that come year after year, and the heat, including the sudden shifts between them, are clear signs of a curse from the gods. Women must stop wearing trousers, playing football, boxing and going to taverns. They should respect their husbands. And the wealthy must help the poor.

On the contrary, many younger participants claimed that they had heard of climate change through the radio, and understood it as referring to changes in weather patterns. They, however, argued that they had not heard about the causes of this problem, and did not know if this was a local or a global phenomenon. However, in-depth discussions, with a group of four young men, aged between 25 and 35 years, and trading in building sand in Kalingalinga Compound, revealed that they had heard of climate change as being a man-made phenomenon. This assertion made one of the four participants question the combined wisdom of the world's scientists when he commented:

> How can man change the climate or weather and make it stop raining or rain heavily like it does these days? It is God's will that has brought all these changes and not man. Who is man? God made the world and He is in charge of all the seasons.

The heavy inclination on divine intervention as the main driver for changes in weather patterns by participants in the two study sites is not surprising in a city and country that is deeply religious and traditional, and where one's faith and beliefs are used as the basis for understanding different events or processes that take place in the community. During a discussion with another focus group consisting of two men and three middle-aged women in Kalingalinga Compound, a male participant who learned the trade of tinsmithing from his father, and is a practising Muslim, stated that "the rampant destruction of the environment is prohibited in Islam because everything is connected to the environment. Environmental destruction is to blame for all these changes in the weather patterns."

Despite the varied perceptions on the causes of extreme weather events and, in some instances, the lack of clearly stated reasons for the causes of such events, it was apparent that many participants, using the listing and ranking exercise, identified increased precipitation, often leading to severe flooding, as the single most extreme weather related event that greatly impacted their livelihood and physical well-being. Many participants argued that heavy rainfall and flooding have become more frequent in recent years and, because of this, adapting to its impacts has become problematic. Some participants, especially those in Linda Compound, and whose main form of livelihood is dependent on urban cultivation, pointed out that extreme heat (i.e. drought) and the habitual, but sudden, shifts to flooding make it virtually impossible for them to grow enough food and have any surplus for income generation.

In view of the above observations expressed by participants in the two study sites, a review of the existing scientific data on weather revealed that Kalingalinga and Linda Compound, and Lusaka in general, lie in agro-climatic Zone IIa (see Figure 6.2), which is normally characterised by an annual precipitation level ranging between 800 and 1000mm (Kasali, 2007). However, Chipeta and Mumba (2000), using rainfall variability analysis of Zambia for the baseline period of 1970–2000, observe that Zone IIa has experienced 15 seasons of heavy precipitation above the 30-year average (830mm), while 13 seasons have had rainfall below the average. This observation is supported by the International Union for Conservation of Nature (IUCN, 2007), who state that, although Zone IIa is increasingly beginning to experience lower precipitation, it is also prone to sporadic heavy rainfall and floods. The immediate and long-term outcomes of these changes in weather have to a large extent been responsible for determining the vulnerability trajectory of people in Kalingalinga and Linda Compounds to climate variability and change.

Figure 6.2 and Table 6.1 show the agro-climatic zones of Zambia and the drought and floods years for Lusaka, respectively (see the inset map of Zambia on Figure 6.1 for the geographical position of Lusaka). The general picture depicted in Table 6.1 is that since the 1970s, Lusaka has suffered repeated severe droughts and floods. However, the most striking feature from the information in this table is the frequency in the occurrences of floods, especially during the post-millennium period. During this period, scientific data show that six of these years were characterised as years of severe floods, therefore occurring almost on a yearly basis.

Although scientific data for Lusaka, and Zambia in general, are somewhat scanty, the limited information as seen in Table 6.1 is consistent with the reported weather changes that participants in the two study sites have observed.

Other scientific information, such as shown in Figure 6.3, shows the rainfall variations over Zambia from 1950 to 2005. Between 1950 and 1979, for example, Lusaka experienced a precipitation of between 6000mm to slightly above 7000mm. And between 1976 and 2005, the city experienced an estimated 7000mm to almost 9000mm of precipitation. And changes in the concentration of rainfall in all the zones can be noticed, with areas in the north and north-west of the country receiving more rainfall since the 1950s. Even in zones of heavy precipitation, and those experiencing less precipitation, significant shifts can be observed. The variations in rainfall patterns, as depicted in Figure 6.3 are indicative of the fact that climate variability is a reality for many of the urban population in Lusaka and Zambia in general.

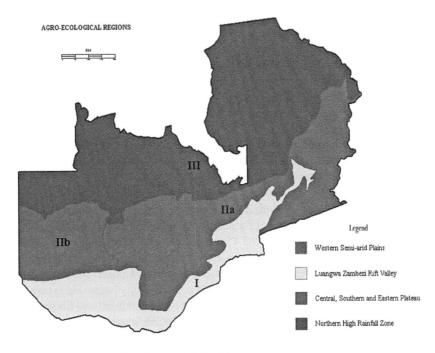

AGRO-ECOLOGICAL REGIONS

Legend

■ Western Semi-arid Plains

□ Luangwa Zambezi Rift Valley

■ Central, Southern and Eastern Plateau

■ Northern High Rainfall Zone

Figure 6.2 The agro-climatic zones of Zambia

Table 6.1 Years of severe droughts and floods in Lusaka

Drought years	Years of heavy precipitation
1972/73	1973/74
1981/82	1977/78
1986/87	1980/81
1991/92	1989/90
1994/95	–
1995/96	1997/98
1998/99	–
2000/01	2003/04
2001/02	2005/06
2002/03	2006/07
2004/05	2007/08
–	2008/09
–	2009/10

Source: MTENR, 2008

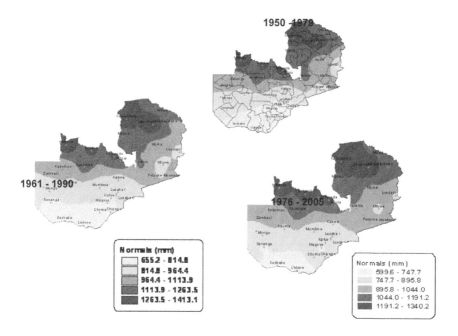

Figure 6.3 Rainfall variations over Zambia from 1950 to 2005

Climate change variability, asset portfolios and food security in Kalingalinga and Linda Compounds

Changes in weather patterns have had some significant implications on the assets and livelihoods options of the urban poor in Lusaka. Many participants in the two sites argued that events such as floods normally lead to low crop yields and poverty. They argued that crops like maize, millet and vegetables usually rot when they are subjected to too much water or the lack of it. A male participant, for example, in his early forties and engaged in urban agriculture (UA), commented during a focus group discussion in Kalingalinga that: "Cassava has not started making tubers yet, because there is too much water in the soil. And as a result, we cannot harvest anything at the moment." A similar view was presented in Linda Compound, where a group of five female participants aged between 25 and 40 years, and deriving a livelihood from UA, demonstrated, using the listing and brainstorming exercise, how the different extreme weather conditions impact them. The information in Table 6.2 shows that different extreme weather events impact negatively on the livelihood options of the urban poor, particularly on UA.

What is evident from the information in Table 6.2, however, is that the participants in Linda Compound are increasingly taking advantage of weather events such as floods by growing crops like rice, which can withstand being waterlogged

119

and have traditionally been confined to rural areas. Rice is customarily culti-vated in the western part of the country, which experiences annual flooding (see Kajoba, 1993).

Despite the consequences of extreme weather on the livelihood options of the urban poor in Lusaka, participants at both sites argued that the impacts and impli-cations of these weather related events on household food security are not homo-geneous. Households with limited access to resources are considered to be more likely to suffer food insecurities than those with access to different assets and resources. This argument is reflected in Table 6.3, which shows the main character-istics of households or individuals considered more or less vulnerable to extreme weather conditions, from the perspective of the five participants all engaged in UA and other informal systems of livelihoods in Kalingalinga Compound.

Table 6.2 Vulnerability context of food security to extreme weather events in Linda Compound

Extreme weather hazard	Impacts on food production	Coping strategy
Increased precipitation often leading to floods (*Mvula yamatalala)	Destruction of crops, leading to decreased crop yields and hunger	Selling less crops and growing crops like rice that can withstand being waterlogged Collecting wild fruits/vegetables
	Decreased income due to poor harvests from UA	Income diversification (e.g. charcoal production, housekeeping in town etc.)
	Loss of life (animals and humans, due to diseases)	Buy medicines or use traditional herbal medicines
	Seeds/crops do not mature	Buying seeds for next season
Drought (*Chilala)	Crop loss and hunger	Earlier planting
	Decreased soil fertility	Avoid late burning of grass, shrubs and other organic materials
	Soil erosion	Avoid burning and incorporate crop residues in cultivating
High temperature (*Kupyasha)	Increased health problems and diseases making it difficult to be productive	Buy medicines/traditional herbal medicine
	Increased loss of crops and yields	Earlier crop planting and planting drought resistant crops
	Decreased livestock feed (mostly goats)	Taking animals out early in the morning

Note
* Expressions of the weather event in Nsenga, one of the local languages spoken in Lusaka, Zambia.

Source: Based on discussions with six women in Linda Compound.

The table is based on a listing and wealth or well-being ranking exercise. From the information in Table 6.3, we can speculate that the presence of a critical mix of assets and production activities can have a big positive impact on ensuring secure livelihoods for households that are vulnerable to extreme weather events.

Conversely, the absence of a critical mix of assets and production activities or their replacement with the "wrong" mix of assets and production activities can exacerbate the food insecurity situation of a community. The critical mix of assets that distinguishes households or individuals that are less vulnerable from their more vulnerable counterparts is made up both of resources in the community itself and external interventions such as remittances from relatives or friends. In view of this observation, therefore, what would make a significant difference in the food security situation for the urban poor would be an emphasis on the different assets that are available to them, identifying how these assets can be supported, strengthened or enhanced in order to provide secure and sustainable livelihoods.

Table 6.3 Characteristics of households and individuals vulnerable to extreme weather events

Type of assets	Features of most vulnerable	Features of less vulnerable
Natural assets	Cultivate and own small pieces of land, no title to land, no or very little inputs. Mostly depend on the environment like UA for food	Access to and cultivation of relatively large tracts of land, have title to land, access to a wide agro-inputs, access to other food sources
Physical assets	Own houses made from mud or grass, no piped water and depend on pit latrines	Concrete houses with in-built facilities and sanitation services
Social and human assets	Inexperience of crop production, high incidence of alcoholism and laziness, and theft	Active participants in private sector organisations promoting urban agriculture production
Financial assets	Very limited liquid capital and little or no remittances	Access to financial capital and may have health remittances from relatives
Activities	Producing low value crops that require heavy doses of fertiliser. Low incidences of high value crops	Growing high value crops including livestock
Marketing	Low levels of production, so little is left for marketing after consumption	Majority of high value crops are marketed
Consumption	Nearly all that is produced is food crops grown for consumption	Food crops grown alongside high value crops for sale and for consumption

Source: Based on views expressed by three men and two women engaged in UA and petty trading in Kalingalinga Compound.

Table 6.4, for example, shows different livelihood sources and the resources and assets that participants in the sites considered as playing important roles in their procurement. It is evident that 36 per cent of all the responses identified natural, physical and human assets as being the most important in facilitating the practice of UA, an activity identified as the single most important source of primary livelihood. The perception of UA as an important source of livelihood for the urban poor is consistent with views expressed in official documents such as the Lusaka City State of the Environment report, in which it is explicitly stated that:

> urban agriculture has become an important part of city life in Lusaka ... [and there] has been an increase in informal agricultural activities within residential areas and road reserves in [the] form of maize cultivation, vegetable gardens and even poultry rearing.
>
> LCC, 2008

See also Simatele and Binns, 2008.

Table 6.4 Food sources, resources and assets important in the procurement of food in the study sites

Primary source of livelihood	Important resources for obtaining the livelihood	Important assets for the procurement of food	No. responses	% responses
Selling charcoal	Trees, health, road and transport	Natural, human and physical	5	3
Urban agriculture (selling vegetables and maize)	Small piece of land, health, water and house	Natural, physical and human	68	36
Beer brewing	Maize, water, house, pots and health	Natural, physical and human	9	5
Carpentry	Wood, machinery and health	Productive and human	4	2
Shoe repair	Rubber, wire, string and health	Productive and human	3	2
Wage labour	Health	Human	7	4
Government employment	Skills and health	Financial, social and human	6	3
Bricklaying	Skill, equipment and materials	Financial, social and human	3	2
Self-employment	Money and health	Financial and health	35	19
Relatives, neighbours and friends	Kinship and friends	Social	47	25
Total			187	

Source: Based on 51 focus group discussions in Linda and Kalingalinga Compounds.

Social, financial and health assets were identified as the second (25 per cent) and third (19 per cent) most important assets respectively. Emphasising the importance of social networks or interactions in a community, a male participant in his early thirties, resident in Linda Compound and self-employed, and whose house had collapsed in the night due to heavy rainfall, commented

> had it not been for my neighbours and friends, my family and I would have been in a lot of problems. The old lady gave us one of her houses, and the neighbours and friends contributed food, beddings and everything that we needed to pull through the crisis.

It is important to note here that social capital both at community and the household level was significantly associated with household food security during discussions with different focus groups at the sites. Many participants expressed the view that having a household member participating in a social or civic activity in the community increases the level of social capital available to a household. Also, social assets, particularly in terms of reciprocity among neighbours, relatives and friends, contribute significantly to household food security. Moser (2008), for example, writing on assets and livelihoods, echoes this argument when she observes that households may have limited financial or food resources, but households with higher levels of social capital are less likely to experience hunger. And the Central Statistics Office (CSO), through the Living Conditions Monitoring Survey, reported that an estimated 65 per cent of the urban population in Zambia depend on asking for food and other basic needs from friends and relatives as a coping strategy during times of need (CSO, 2005).

Despite the role of assets in facilitating different livelihood options, a close scrutiny of Table 6.4 reveals that the resources and assets required are highly susceptible or vulnerable to changes in weather conditions. A discussion with a group of schoolchildren, aged between 15 and 17 years in Kalingalinga, for example, revealed that events such as heavy rainfall, which in the context of Kalingalinga often results in severe flooding, has serious consequences on the general welfare and household food security. Using the cause–impact technique of participatory research, the pupils demonstrated that flooding has multiple consequences for the livelihoods of poor urban households.

They argued, for example, that flooding leads to the lack of food, which in turn results in loss of income and promiscuity. Promiscuity can lead to contracting diseases, which eventually may result in death. They further illustrated that flooding damages can lead to houses collapsing and this in turn can result in injury and death. Death, according to Moser (2009), will affect a household's asset portfolio, thereby subjecting its members to suddenly insecurities and vulnerabilities, and in the context of this chapter, to poverty and food insecurity.

The general picture presented in the flow diagram (Figure 6.4), is that extreme weather events, particularly floods, can trigger combined impacts resulting in a number of consequences, among which poverty and the lack of household food are the most significant.

In summary therefore, it can be argued that the changes in weather patterns in Lusaka are having a slow and almost invisible impact on the food security of residents at the sites and in Lusaka city in general. This is because the impacts of weather related events erode the assets of the poor in a gradual way. Thus, with their assets getting slowly eroded year after year, their adaptive capabilities against extreme weather are also slowly becoming compromised. In view of this observation therefore, it would not be an exaggeration to argue that changes in weather patterns are making it difficult for the urban poor to access different resources and/or assets that would enable them to gain a sustainable livelihood.

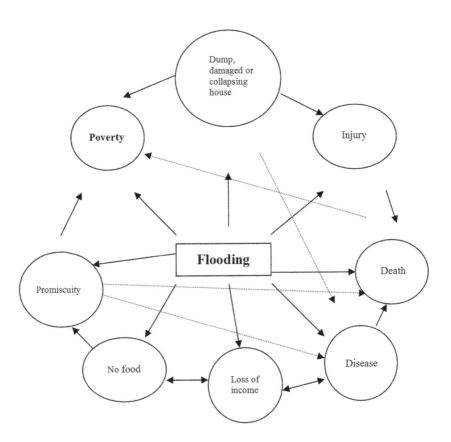

Figure 6.4 Cause and impact flow diagram showing the relationship between floods and poverty

What would make a difference, therefore, is to identify measures that would complement the efforts of the poor in facilitating asset protection and recovery. Such measures would also facilitate the identification of different assets or resources that are critical to a secure livelihood system and the barriers that may exist in obtaining them.

Asset adaptation and food security in a changing context

Despite the impacts of extreme weather events on food security, the urban poor in Linda and Kalingalinga Compound are not passive. They are actively involved in protecting and adapting their assets against the impacts of extreme weather conditions. At both sites, discussions with the 51 focus groups revealed that 61 per cent of the participants had some form of household asset protection and adaptation measures in place before the occurrence of a weather event; 53 per cent claimed to be engaged in household asset protection and adaptation during the occurrence of a weather event; and 57 per cent said they adapted their household assets after the event occurred. A further 27 per cent of the participants said they engaged in collective asset protection and adaptation, with 24 per cent claiming to be engaged in collective asset protection and adaptation before and after the occurrence of an event. Only 20 per cent said they engaged in collective asset adaptation during the occurrence of a weather related event. And of the 51 focus groups, 41 per cent said they had business asset protection and adaptation measures, with 39 per cent claiming to do this before the occurrence of an extreme weather event, while 37 per cent said they adapted their business assets during and after the event.

Table 6.5 is a summary of some of the asset adaptation measures, commonly practised by participants in Kalingalinga and Linda Compounds, which are aimed at reducing the impacts of floods on their assets. It is evident, from the perspective of the participants, and as illustrated in Table 6.5, that asset adaptation is important in ensuring household food security. In the context of the challenges posed by severe flooding for example, the urban poor tend to protect and adapt different assets available to them at different stages during the crisis. These efforts, as alluded to earlier, are aimed at safeguarding not only those assets that are at high risk to adverse weather conditions but also those that can suffer indirectly and may have either direct or indirect implications on the critical assets that play a significant role in households or individuals obtaining a livelihood.

In view of this argument, it would not be an exaggeration to argue that protecting and adapting one set of assets can actually lead to the protection and adaptation of other assets that are important to the general welfare of a household or community. A female participant, with six children in Linda Compound for example, pointed out that:

> The most important thing in life and worthy of protecting is a house. If a house gets damaged or collapses due to heavy rainfall or other calamities,

Table 6.5 Asset adaptation measures against flooding in Kalingalinga and Linda Compounds

Type of asset	Type of asset adaptation measures			Impacts on household food security (if asset adaptation not done)
	Long before	During	Immediately after	
House	Build house using cement and concrete blocks Put building plastic on the slab to avoid water coming into contact the foundation Raise the foundation of the house to 50m Put crushed stones and soil around the house to improve drainage Dig drainage channels around the house	Dig drainage channels Add more crushed stones and soil to raise the base of the house and improve drainage Put out sandbags to act as barriers against the rising water	Clean up and repair the damage Build house using cement and concrete blocks Move out of the house and rent out the house Sell the house	Loss of stored foodstuff Loss of income to buy food Cut down on number of meals to save money to rebuild house or make repairs More money to look for another house to rent, meaning less to spend on food
Pit latrine	Build upwards with cement block Raise the base of the pit latrine to at least 50m Dig drainage channels Build on raised ground	Dig drainage channels and cover the hole for the pit latrine to avoid spillage of human pathogens	Clean up and repair the damage and build upward with cement blocks	Move money from food to building or repairing the toilet Poor health making it difficult to work
Children	Teach them not to play with dirty water Immunisation	Keep them indoors Keep a close eye on them Take them to the clinic	Take them to the clinic Buy medicine from chemist	Reduced labour working in the field resulting in low productivity Money spent on health when they get sick

Type of asset	Type of asset adaptation measures			Impacts on household food security (if asset adaptation not done)
	Long before	During	Immediately after	
Household goods (e.g. TV, sofa, radio, beddings and clothes)	Cover them with plastic Put them on raised tables or move them to another safe location	Cover them with plastic Put them on raised tables, or move them to another safe location	Clean up and repair house and bring the goods back in the house	Reduced food expenditure to save money for repairing or replacing household goods
Food	Store in safe place	Store in safe place	Store in safe place	More expenditure on food
Money	Deposit it at a bank or post office	Keep it in the bank or post office	Keep it in the bank or post office	No money for food
Health	Clean up the surroundings Improve the drainage	Boil drinking water Keep the house clean	Clean up the surrounding area	Poor health making it difficult to work
Crops	Plant crops on raised ground Dig drainage channels	Nothing	Save surviving crops Engage in other livelihood activities Seek waged employment	Limited access to food No food at all

Source: Based on 51 focus group discussions in Kalingalinga and Linda Compounds.

then one is in a lot of trouble. A house is the basis for all aspects of life; it is a source of food, security, income generation and even protection against diseases.

Because of the high vulnerability context of poor people's livelihood systems, protecting and adapting priority assets, such as housing, are key to attaining some form of food security. However, other assets, such as natural and human capital, also play a significant role in facilitating the multiple livelihood activities that the urban poor depend on for sustenance. Thus, the poor, as earlier pointed out, are usually preoccupied, whether consciously or otherwise, in making sure that the few assets that they own are protected against the impacts of both internal and external stressors.

The combination of different assets, according to participants on the sites, enables the urban poor to engage in various livelihood activities as seasons and urban processes change over time and space. With UA coming under increasing pressure from changes in weather conditions and planning policies, for example, the urban poor are now combining this informal sector activity with other activities such as petty trading, moonlighting, collecting and selling used bottles, cleaning sewers in better-off housing areas, street-hawking, undertaking piece-work (e.g. laundry, housework, slashing grass, pruning trees, carrying water), and even small-scale quarrying, involving crushing stones for the burgeoning construction industry.

These menial activities do not only provide supplementary income for poor households, but also keep people active and conscious that they can actually do something to improve household livelihoods and ensure their food security in the face of a changing climate. It must be emphasised that the combination of extreme weather events and other processes that erode the assets of the urban poor, such as lack of government support, has left the urban poor in Kalingalinga and Linda Compounds rather overwhelmed by the frequency in extreme weather events.

Conclusions

It is clear that extreme weather-induced impacts pose a considerable challenge to the food security of the urban poor in Linda and Kalingalinga Compounds, and indeed Lusaka in general. This is because the impacts of weather related events have undoubtedly become more acute in recent years, and we must only assume that they are likely to intensify further. Identifying appropriate responses to these challenges, focusing on the role of assets in building the adaptivity and resilience of the most vulnerable groups of people should therefore be a key element of the sustainable urban development strategies adopted by affected cities and countries.

Despite this observation, at present we seem to have little experience of how to manage this adaptation process. There is a paucity of systematic risk assessments predicting who will be affected and when this is likely to happen (IUCN, 2007; Mukheibir and Ziervogel, 2008). What is certain, however, from the information collected in the study sites, is that the negative impacts of extreme weather will be felt disproportionately more severely by poor people in cities of the South, particularly those with the least adaptive capacity due to their lack of financial and technical resources. The poor people are particularly vulnerable because they are often directly dependent on a number of assets that are very vulnerable to changes in weather conditions. The erosion of these assets often makes it impossible for the urban poor to switch to alternative sources of livelihood. And as the impacts of extreme weather progressively worsen, it seems likely that the livelihoods of poor people will also deteriorate.

In Lusaka and Zambia, as in many other urban centres of Africa, the challenges of extreme weather conditions are by no means a new phenomenon, and there is a wealth of literature on how local people have developed a wide range of strategies to manage the environment in a sustainable way (see, for example, Leach and Mearns, 1996; Mortimore, 1998; Reij and Waters-Bayer, 2001). However, in light of both their speed and intensity, the changes predicted for the coming decades could possibly exceed the adaptive capacities of poor households and communities. Traditional adaptation methods and mechanisms may no longer be adequate, and vulnerable members of communities that are most affected by weather related impacts are likely to become progressively more vulnerable.

Field-based research on pro-poor climate change adaptation and UA in Lusaka suggests that local government should adopt pro-poor policies that will help reduce the vulnerability of poor households and enhance the resilience of the urban poor. From the work that has already been undertaken on the impacts of extreme weather conditions on the assets of society, there are clear synergies between successful climate change adaptation and poverty reduction strategies (Huq, 2007; Moser, 2008; Prowse and Scott, 2008). But what is urgently needed in Lusaka is for the city's developers and planners to undertake a detailed inventory of households in order to ascertain levels of resources and vulnerability, and to evaluate the role of assets in contributing to food security both now and in the future. Planners need to be much more aware of what is happening at the grass roots level, and should strive to introduce a more democratic form of planning that engages with local communities and utilises the considerable amount of knowledge and resources that they have. In Lusaka, as in many other African cities, it is a fact that planning strategies have barely changed since the colonial period (Simatele and Binns, 2008). The negative attitude to activities such as UA, which originated during colonial times, seems to be inappropriate in situations where it now plays such an important role in sustaining the livelihoods of poor households. Local authorities must evaluate the significance of informal sector activities in light of possible extreme weather adaptation measures, and it is vital that government institutions should work much more closely with local people, non-governmental organisations and community-based organisations.

Notes

1   Access to assets is used here to refer to the ability of the poor not only to have access to different resource endowments but also to own the means of production (Prowse and Scott 2008).
2   Asset accumulation refers to the ability of an asset(s) to generate future flows, to be transformed and used in different contexts, and transferred across generations (Moser, 2008).
3   Asset adaptation consists of actions to reduce the vulnerability of an asset(s) to either short-term or long-term weather shocks and to climate variability (Satterthwaite et al. 2007).
4   The name refers to someone with no fixed abode. It literary means someone who moves from place to place.
5   A derogatory term used by the white settler community to refer to the native people during the colonial era.
6   Especially respondents aged above 70 years.

References

Chipeta, G. and Mumba, S. L. (2000) 'Rainfall indices of Zambia', in *State of the Environment in Zambia 2000*. Lusaka: Environmental Council of Zambia.

CSO (Central Statistical Office) (2005) *Living Conditions Monitoring Survey Report 2002–2003*. Lusaka: Central Statistical Office.

CSO (Central Statistical Office) (2006) *Living Conditions Monitoring Survey Report, 2004*. Lusaka: Central Statistical Office.

Huq, S. (2007) 'Community based adaptation: a vital approach to the threat climate change poses to the poor'. *IIED Briefing*. London.

IUCN (International Union for the Conservation of Nature) (2007) *Climate Change and Development: Examples from Zambia*. Geneva: International Union for the Conservation of Nature.

Kajoba, G. (1993) *Food Crisis in Zambia*. Lusaka: ZPC.

Kasali, G. (2007) *Historical Overview of Climate Change Activities in Zambia*. Harare: IUCN.

LCC (Lusaka City Council) (2008) Lusaka City State of Environment Outlook Report. Lusaka: Lusaka City Council.

Leach, M. and Mearns, R. (eds) (1996) *The Lie of the Land: Challenging Received Wisdom on the African Environment*. Oxford: James Currey.

Maxwell, D. (1998) 'The Political Economy or Urban Food Security in Sub-Saharan Africa', *FCND Discussion Paper*, 41. Washington, DC.

Mortimore, M. (1998) *Roots in the African Dust: Sustaining the Drylands*. Cambridge: Cambridge University Press.

Moser, C (2008) 'Assets and livelihoods: a framework for asset-based social policy', in Moser, C. and Dani, A. (eds) *Assets, Livelihoods and Social Policy*. Washington DC: World Bank.

Moser. C. (2009) 'A conceptual and operational framework for pro-poor asset adaptation to urban climate change', unpublished paper, Manchester: Global Urban Research Centre.

Moser, C. and Satterthwaite, D. (2008) 'Towards pro-poor adaptation to climate change in the urban centres of low- and middle-income countries', *GURC & IIED Discussion*

Paper Series, Climate change and cities 3. Manchester and London.

Moser, C. and Stein, A. (2010) 'Implementing the urban participatory climate change adaptation appraisals: a methodological guideline', *Global Urban Research Centre Working Paper* 5, Manchester: University of Manchester.

MTENR (Government of Zambia, Ministry of Tourism, Environment and Natural Resources) (2007) *The Zambia National Policy on Environment*. Lusaka: Ministry of Tourism, Environment and Natural Resources.

MTENR (2008) *Formulation of the National Adaptation Programme of Action on Climate Change*. Lusaka: Ministry of Tourism, Environment and Natural Resources.

Mukheibir, P. and Ziervogel, G. (2008) 'Urban adaptation planning', *Tiempo*, 67, 3–14.

Prowse, M. and Scott, L. (2008) 'Assets and adaptation: an emerging debate', *IDS Bulletin*, 39, 4: 42–52.

Reij, C. and Waters-Bayer, A. (eds) (2001) *Farmer Innovation in Africa: A Source of Inspiration for Agricultural Development*. London: Earthscan Publications.

Satterthwaite, D., Hug, S., Reid, H., Pelling, M. and Lankao, P. (2007) 'Adapting to climate change in urban areas: the possibilities and constraints in low- and middle-income nations'. *IIED Human Settlements Group and the Climate Change Group Working Paper*. IIED, London.

Simatele, D. and Binns, T. (2008), 'Motivation and marginalisation in African urban agriculture: the case of Lusaka, Zambia', *Urban Forum*, 19, 1: 1–21.

Williams, G. (1986) 'The physical growth of Lusaka: past and projected', in Williams, G. (ed.) *Lusaka and Its Environs: A Geographical Study of a Planned Capital City in Tropical Africa*. Lusaka: Associated Printers Ltd.

7

THE ITHEMBA FARMERS'
STORY OF CLIMATE AND FOOD
SECURITY ADAPTATION IN CAPE
TOWN, SOUTH AFRICA

Housing versus food?

Gareth Haysom

Introduction

The world food situation is being rapidly redefined by new driving forces. Changes in food availability, rising commodity prices and new producer–consumer linkages have crucial implications for the livelihoods of poor and food insecure people (von Braun, 2007). The doubling of grain output globally between 1965 and 1990 was a remarkable achievement that drew on the skills and innovations of thousands of scientists, extensionists and farmers,[1] backed by the supportive decisions of policy makers (Uphoff, 2002). The current predominantly rural industrialized approach to food production was reviewed in 2008 by the United Nations International Assessment of Agricultural Knowledge, Science and Technology for Development (IAASTD)[2] process and found to have significant flaws. The IAASTD report argues for fundamental changes in the world's agricultural systems. These challenges have a profound impact on the food security and food systems of cities. The implications of these challenges to food production, distribution and processing require that urban leadership significantly review how the city relates to its food supplies. This is specifically relevant to a city such as Cape Town, South Africa.

Worldwide the impacts of a multitude of cumulative and interacting crises require that food production, access and agricultural approaches increasingly need to support sustainability (see Annexure 1 for the interlinking crises, or poly-crises, explanation). This food challenge is interpreted by many to be a rural challenge. However, the urbanization trend in developing countries, and specifically in South Africa, requires that city planning and development are approached in fundamentally different ways.

The great challenge for a city such as Cape Town is that food is viewed in a traditional sense and that the policy and management structures are ill prepared to address the contemporary food related challenges being faced by the poor communities within the City. The general assumption, understood through practice as opposed to explicit policy articulations, is that food should be procured at some distant large scale industrialized system, processed and then transported through a multiple of distribution systems to arrive at retail centres accessible to the resident of the City.

The challenge of food access and the approaches to food by the various bodies within the city and regional governments reflect a trend evidenced in many developing urban areas: that food is only politically expedient in a time of crisis and, as such, is posited low on the political urgency scale in respect of delivery and support.

This challenge was evidenced in a recent process launched by the province of the Western Cape. The project was one that links to the theme of this book, where the officials were attempting to remedy the consequences of increased flooding in poor urban areas; flooding that was becoming more extreme and frequent, driven by greater extremes in weather events. This is, however, not a case study of best practice but rather a reflection on the realities of governance processes that do not consider food a priority within the urban environment, or, it is argued here, as being something that is not politically expedient. This is a case study of an adaptation response, not on the part of communities but rather by officials responding in ways that are not sensitive to local practice. The case study reflects on responses that are short term and do not suitably build resilience and long term sustainability. The adaptation responses selected and detailed in this case study, it is argued, would have a detrimental impact on the overall viability of the communities within the case study site. It must, however, be made clear that the reason for these choices is not to deliberately prejudice one community over another, but that the reasons are far more complex, embedded in political expediency, ignorance, governance pressures and, most importantly, practice that is embedded in an outdated business as usual approach to urban issues and challenges.

Adaptation response

Managing flooding has always been a challenge in the lower lying areas within the area known as the Cape Flats in the Cape Town Metropolitan area. The area, where one of the main settlements is Philippi, is settled by predominantly poor urban dwellers with high levels of informality. These informal dwellers face the brunt of the adverse weather conditions, specifically in the Cape winter. Over this period, flooding is commonplace and while certain local interventions have been used to mitigate the impacts of this flooding, the scale and frequency of flooding are increasing.

The cause of the increase in flooding can be ascribed to a number of possible reasons. However, one of the main causes of the increase in frequency and severity of the flooding is attributed to climate change. The adaptation strategy of the regional housing department has been to develop a plan to relocate the residents of the flood prone areas to a site on the outskirts of the City of Cape Town. This area is currently occupied by a group of farmers who refer to themselves as the Ithemba farmers.

The provincial housing department's relocation plans involve the development of a transitional relocation area (TRA) at or near the current Ithemba farmers' site. This plan has been met by planned and active resistance by the farmers who have real concerns associated with the relocation to this area. The area is also questionable as it is in itself an area that experiences flooding. It is also far further from employment opportunities, specifically in relation to the areas from which the relocated residents will be moved. In addition, it is also significantly removed from other social infrastructure such as clinics and places of worship.

Food production is a key challenge in South Africa and, as such, the following section of this chapter will argue that in the light of the agriculture, urbanization and food security challenges, different paradigms are required for the development of sustainable cities.

The South African agricultural and food security challenge

Food prices are expected to rise rapidly in the next year[s] as input costs escalate (Schalkwyk, 2008). There are a number of agricultural systems present in South Africa and they should be recognized for the role that they play in generating food and livelihoods. The fact that a group of small farmers, the Ithemba farmers, have been able to establish a viable and vibrant community and are able to generate sufficient produce to address livelihood needs on land that has been "reclaimed", needs recognition. The fact that the farmers have productively enhanced the land is evidence of the diversity and skill of farmers that are generally seen by many to be hobbyists or insignificant in the generalized perspectives of agriculture and food supply. This is very wrong.

Food security and all facets of South African agriculture are interlinked. In South Africa 35 per cent of the land surface receives sufficient rain for dryland crop production, but only 13 per cent (or 14 million hectares) is suitable arable land. Most of this land is marginal with only 3 per cent of the land considered high potential land (Swilling, 2006).

Cape Town's food security and sustainability challenge

Estimating Cape Town's food needs, based on the above, means that Cape Town's 2006 population of 3,240,000 (Provincial Government of the Western Cape, 2006a) required 1.3 million hectares to sustain its population, or 9.2 per cent of arable South African land.[3] In considering the anticipated growth of Cape Town's population, this figure highlights the potential scale of the challenges. Taken together, these facts speak to the claim for an alternative approach to agriculture and food security. Food supply within the City needs to be robust in the face of increasing diversity, deepening complexity, drastic shocks and rapid change. A sustainable approach needs to be locally and community adaptive, and resource building in terms of all the capitals: human, social, economic and biological, and should promote social and ecological justice.[4]

Table 7.1 demonstrates, from pro-poor research by Frayne et al. (2009), the distribution of food insecurity within the Cape Town region and serves to highlight the gender dynamic at play in respect of food security.

The challenge is compounded by the findings of the 2005 National Food Consumption Survey-Fortification Baseline (NFCS-FB) showing that 64 per cent of one- to nine-year-old South African children were vitamin A deficient, 28 per cent were anaemic, 13 per cent had a poor iron status and 45 per cent had a low zinc status (Labadarios, 2007). Findings from the 1999 National Food Consumption Survey (NFCS) (Labadarios et al. 1999) and the 2005 NFCS-FB (Labadarios, 2007) reported that the rural and urban poor bear the burden of poor health, reflected in a greater proportion of these groups having high levels of stunting and underweight children. It is estimated that poor people in South Africa may spend up to 60–80 per cent of their incomes on staple food and consistently increasing food prices are forcing these families into conditions of poorer nutrition (Naylor, 2008). While these figures reflect the national challenge, they are reflected in all poor communities in South Africa and the Western Cape and Cape Town are no exception.

In the context of this, it is argued that communities producing food within the City need support and a policy environment that ensures their recognition, allowing for processes that work to integrate these practices into the urban fabric. This, it is argued, is not the case currently in Cape Town.

Ithemba farmers' story

The Ithemba farmers' story is one of self-sufficiency, self-reliance and perseverance. These are farmers who have been actively farming the land for a number of years, with the first members settling and farming on the land from the mid-1980s.

Table 7.1 Food insecurity in Cape Town

Cape Town	Food secure (%)	Food insecure (%)
Female centered	18	83
Male centered	24	76
Nuclear	18	82
Extended	30	70
Total	20	80

Source: Frayne et al., 2009

Over the years the number of farmers has grown and today there are 157 who farm on the land and approximately 315 people are members of the Ithemba Farmers' Association (Ithemba Farmers' Association, 2010).

The Ithemba farmers farm livestock and crops with each farmer managing an area of approximately 65 × 35 metres. Almost all of the 157 farmers are actively farming although some do have other occupations and farm as a second job, or other family members farm on their behalf.

The Ithemba farmers are subsistence farmers, producing food for their own consumption with some additional livelihood support being generated from the farm. Many of the farmers have some form of shelter on the land and this is often occupied by the farmer or by a family member or possibly a farm worker and serves more to ensure security than as a specific residence.

The farmers produce a variety of agricultural products that range from dairy cattle to chickens producing eggs, as well as broiler chickens. Some of the more common items farmed include pigs and goats. Some of the farmers also keep sheep, rabbits and other smaller livestock. The Ithemba farmers generally farm a variety of livestock and crop items through mixed farming. However, most of the farmers appear to farm a specific animal.

Vegetable crops that have been farmed include a number of leafy vegetables such as spinach, cabbage and lettuce. A variety of herbs and spices are also grown, some for consumption but others for medicinal purposes, both for humans and animals. Root crops are also grown including potatoes and carrots.

A variety of materials have been used to create the structures on the various farms. Most of the structures are made from recycled items. That being said, for the vast majority, great care has been taken in the building of the various structures on the sites and, in a number of instances, projects aimed at the upgrade and general beautification of the structures were observed. The animal stalls are cleaned out regularly and the manure is either used on site to build soil health or is provided to other farmers elsewhere.

One of the most important aspects of the Ithemba farmers' group is the level of organization and the sense of community. This social capital has been built up over the years. This commitment to community and mutual success is something that is sorely lacking in other communities today.

The group is of mixed race and religion, making this community's cooperation and support all the more important in the increasingly racially segregated South African cities. The racial and faith based diversity of the group and the willingness to accept and work with one another is an example for others to follow and emulate.

One of the other great strengths of the Ithemba farmers is the fact that the land on which they have farmed for over 20 years was previously infested with alien vegetation and had very poor soil quality. These farmers have rehabilitated the land, clearing the alien vegetation and rebuilding the soil organically. These improvements have been undertaken through good agricultural practices and animal husbandry. This observation speaks to both the commitment and the skill of the farmers and while these farmers may not be successful economi-cally, they have been able to use the scarce resources available to generate livelihoods of great value. These farms are productive, well managed and well maintained areas.

The Ithemba farmers also have distinct and valuable indigenous knowledge that they use in their treatment of livestock ailments and crop related disease. The natural remedies have served the community well and the information has been shared among the farmers.

The Ithemba farmers play a role beyond the boundaries of the areas on which they farm. The Ithemba farmers represent a resource to the surrounding area providing surplus food to a number of the neighbouring communities. In addi-tion, the group plays an active role supporting the neighbouring community where excess food is dispensed free to the needy within the adjacent communities. This civic involvement further supports the argument that this is a community contrib-uting greatly to the broader fabric of society.

Although most of the farmers are considered livelihood farmers, the surplus stock from the farms is also sold to the communities neighbouring the Ithemba farming operations. This channel of fresh and affordable food is believed to be of vital importance to the communities of Electric City, Mfuleni and the nearby informal settlement. The ability of the neighbouring communities to access good quality and affordable food is critical from an economic and nutritional perspective. This is of specific importance considering the high levels of HIV/AIDS infection in the area. From a generalized food production point of view, the relationship between food production and possible areas where food could be grown within the broader region, the alternative areas require far more trans-portation to get the food to the markets. Additionally, a number of potential food production areas within the broader Cape region all present significant produc-tion challenges. Therefore, the strategic importance of the Ithemba farmers is significant. Other areas that have often been cited as food producing areas that could serve the city are listed below. It should be noted that these areas all have severe constraints:

- Malmesbury: water scarcity.
- Atlantis: water scarcity during summer.
- Joostenberg Flats: on average 5 degrees Celsius warmer than Ithemba; too warm for some vegetable types such as lettuce, cauliflower, broccoli.
- Sandveld: too warm for potatoes in January, whereas Ithemba farmers have had success in growing them in their area.

A generalized view of urban farming carried out by poor communities is that this is a remnant of the rural lifestyle and something that would pass once the "farmer" becomes more familiar with, or fully enters, the urban system. This view results in a perspective that the production areas are piecemeal and arbitrary, lacking planning and good agricultural practice. Observation of the Ithemba farming area, taking into account the level and effort of investment (even if just in person power), reflects the commitment to this area. This is a farming area where the farms are well maintained and husbandry is good, and even better than that of the animals observed in formal or industrial farming systems.

The Ithemba farmers are providing a further service to the community. The characteristics of urban agriculture are evident in the approaches adopted by these farmers who have facilitated arrangements with local fresh produce retailers, collecting all the organic waste and utilizing this as feed, either for the livestock or for the soil once decomposed. This closing of the open and linear system associated with the urban metabolism further highlights the value of this group of farms.

There are three primary resources required if farmers are to be successful: the first is soil, the second water and the third knowledge. These farmers have been at a disadvantage in that the soil is poor, water has only recently been provided and, as such, they have had to rely on knowledge in order to make a success of their operations. This knowledge is, however, site specific. Farmers may have good general knowledge but the real knowledge is specific to a farm — much of what farmers do is as a result of knowledge built up over time. In certain agricultural circles, this is referred to as dependable instinct. Dependable instinct is knowledge that is generated over time but is also knowledge that relates and interacts directly with the locality in which the farmers operate. This place-specific knowledge is often overlooked and removal of these farmers to other areas would be to their disadvantage.

The Ithemba farmers are a group of committed and highly skilled farmers, farming in a manner that makes use of natural resources, uses indigenous and traditional knowledge to support their endeavours and farm productively with minimal negative impacts on the land. The Ithemba farmers support broader city-wide goals of reducing flows of wastes to landfill and assist in the rehabilitation of the area on which they farm.

These farmers have made significant investment in the productivity of the land and the systems that they operate. It is difficult to correctly assign a value, but it is something of significant value in any event.

Why urban agriculture?

Smit and Nasr (1999) argue that cities require processes to close the open loop system and that throughput of resources in cities needs to be reduced. Typically consumables are imported into the urban areas and what remains, including the packaging, is dumped as waste into the bioregion and biosphere. It is the City of Cape Town's goal to seek the continued and aggressive reduction of throughput over time. Food is listed as being one of the main contributors to the ecological footprint of the City of Cape Town. Swilling (2006), draws on Gasson's (2002) work on the ecological footprint of Cape Town[5] and estimates that the total ecological footprint for Cape Town is 128,264 square kilometres[6] and that 41 per cent of this footprint (52,780 square kilometres[7]) can be attributed to food.

This is significant if compared to the contribution of energy to the footprint of 44 per cent. The most significant consequence of this input–output model is that it demonstrates the resource intensity of the Cape Town urban system.

Urban agriculture is core to the development of a sustainable city: an inclusive, food secure, productive and environmentally healthy city (van Veenhuizen, 2006). Because urban agriculture links cities and their environments, it is an increasingly acceptable, affordable and effective tool for sustainable urbanization (Deelstra and Girardet 2001). Urban agriculture is thus seen as a key component within the urban planning processes. If correctly implemented, it has the potential to address a variety of the urban planning and developmental challenges because of its integrative nature. This perspective is supported directly within the *Western Cape Sustainable Human Settlement Strategy* (Provincial Government of the Western Cape, 2008).

Mougeot (2005) defines urban agriculture as an industry located either within intra-urban or on the peri-urban fringes of a city. It grows and raises, processes and distributes a diversity of food and non-food products and (re)uses both human and material resources, products and services found in and around that urban area. Urban agriculture initiatives also supply human and material resources, products and services largely to that urban area (Mougeot, 2005).

What is described in the City of Cape Town *Urban Agriculture Policy* is the formal recognition of urban agriculture (City of Cape Town, 2007). However, the practice of implementing the policy is severely constrained as a result of a number of operational and institutional challenges. Urban agriculture is both an industry and a social development process that supports the sustainability objectives of the City. Urban planners commonly consider urban agriculture and livestock keeping as merely "hangovers" of rural habits, a marginal activity of little economic importance, or as a health risk and a source of pollution. Such biases, sustained by the limited exposure to information and practice in terms of urban agriculture, have meant that few authorities recognize urban farming as an urban form of land use, despite its prevalence.

The City of Cape Town's urban agriculture policy

The *Urban Agriculture Policy* for the City of Cape Town was approved by Council in December 2006. The purpose of the policy is to develop "an integrated and holistic approach for the effective and meaningful development of urban agriculture in the City of Cape Town ... to create an enabling environment wherein public, private and civil society agents can work collectively to create more real and sustainable opportunities for local area economic development" (City of Cape Town, 2007). The Policy describes its vision as being framed by the following strategic goals:

- To enable the poorest of the poor to utilize urban agriculture as an element of their survival strategy (household food security).

- To enable people to create commercially sustainable economic opportunities through urban agriculture (jobs and income).
- To enable previously disadvantaged people to participate in the Land Redistribution for Agricultural Development (LRAD) programme (redress imbalances).
- To facilitate human resources development (technical, business and social skills training).

All of the above goals are evident within the Ithemba farmers' situation.

The policy context

The attitudes displayed towards the Ithemba farmers clearly contradict a number of policies and framework documents designed to recognize and facilitate the formal and legitimate integration of the endeavours of the Ithemba farmers into the systems of governance within the City and region. At the policy and strategy levels, the Ithemba farmers' challenge appears to be one of significant contradiction. The following city policies and frameworks should be supporting such initiatives but, in reality, are not.

Human settlements and housing[8]

The national housing framework has shifted from being one of what is often referred to as the RDP[9] (Reconstruction and Development Programme) type roll-out of housing where the overarching strategy, in terms of housing or settlement, is to create sustainable communities. This approach is enshrined within the national housing framework of Breaking New Ground, or BNG, which calls for: "well-managed entities in which economic growth and social development are in balance with the carrying capacity of the natural systems on which they depend for their existence and result in sustainable development, wealth creation, poverty alleviation and equity" (Republic of South Africa, 2004). The question that then needs to be asked is: What is a sustainable community? It is the author's contention that the Ithemba farmers represent a sustainable community. While food and the relationship between food production areas and housing are not expressly stated in BNG, it is read as being implicit.

The *Western Cape Sustainable Human Settlement Strategy* (WCSHSS) is an interpretation and application of the national housing policy framework through Breaking New Ground within and for the unique conditions that pertain to the Western Cape (Provincial Government of the Western Cape, 2008).

The core focus of the WCSHSS is influenced by three major strategic shifts in emphasis that are apparent in all three spheres of governance. These shifts, which have emerged as a consequence of the gradual overall strategic shift towards a "development state" approach, are: the shift from housing construction to "sustainable human settlements"; the shift to sustainable resource use; and the shift to real empowerment. In the case of the Ithemba farmers, it is argued that all of the above strategic shifts are evidenced in the work that they currently do and thus support the need for greater recognition of the fact that they are emulating these shifts.

The shift from pre-1994 housing policy to BNG policy is necessary and should be welcomed by those who share the view that the apartheid city needs to be transformed in the interests of all South Africans, and the urban poor in particular.

BNG's goal is "sustainable human settlements". The WCSHSS interprets this in light of Section 24 (b) of the South African Constitution (Republic of South Africa, 1996), which states that there is an obligation to "secure ecologically sustainable development and use of natural resources while promoting justifiable economic and social development". This is what the Ithemba farmers are doing and it is a failure on the part of the Western Cape Department of Human Settlements that the spirit of one of the key strategic documents, drafted to provide the ethos of what settlements should represent, is ignored. Instead the opposite approach is applied and one from which the WCSHSS is trying to move away.

The WCSHSS (Provincial Government of the Western Cape, 2008) contains eight specific objectives with actions detailed to support the achievement of the stated objectives. The specific actions to achieve Objective seven are detailed in the WCSHSS as follows:

Supply 25 percent of household food requirements via neighbourhood-level "farmer-to-fork" markets, which will:

- stimulate growth of local farming businesses and employment by facilitating farmers to sell directly to consumers, thus improving their margins and lowering the prices paid by consumers;
- support, together with education and technology advice, the gradual spread of organic farming practices that will reduce the dependence on food production on oil-based chemical inputs;
- improve health levels, including boosting of immune systems specifically those with HIV/AIDS;
- contribute to the revitalisation of biological productivity of our soils and enhance biodiversity.

Provincial Government of the Western Cape, 2008

In terms of the WCSHSS, food and food supplies into the urban system are of critical importance. This link to the urban agriculture policy should result in those producing food for the City, and those acting out the very aims and objectives set out in the policies, being the communities most celebrated and valued.

It should also be noted that the notion of a sustainable community, as espoused within BNG and the WCSHSS is supported by a number of other national policy and strategy documents. As has been made clear, the WCSHSS approach is derived directly from BNG at a national level, read within the context of the Accelerated and Shared Growth Initiative – South Africa (Republic of South Africa, 2006), which is focused on public investment as the driver of growth.

Links to additional policies, plans and frameworks

The WCSHSS also supports the following national level strategies and frameworks:

- Provincial Spatial Development Framework (PSDF) 2009 (Provincial Government of the Western Cape, 2009).
- Strategic Infrastructure Plan (SIP) 2005 (Provincial Government of the Western Cape, 2005a).
- Micro-Economic Development Strategy (MEDS) 2006 (Provincial Government of the Western Cape, 2006b).
- Social Capital Formation Strategy (SCFS) 2005 (Provincial Government of the Western Cape, 2005b).
- The Human Capital Development Strategy (HCDS) 2006 (Provincial Government of the Western Cape, 2006c).
- Sustainable Development Implementation Plan (SDIP) 2005 (Provincial Government of the Western Cape, 2005c).

The WCSHSS was drafted to be consistent with the Provincial Growth and Development Strategy (PGDS). The PGDS envisages measures to ensure that the ecological footprint of the Western Cape expands at a much slower rate than the economic growth rate – something that cannot be achieved without substantial reduction in consumable throughput. By aligning itself with the PSDF, PGSD and SIP approaches, the WCSHSS is endorsing a sustainable resource use perspective.

Government Gazette Province of Western Cape: Provincial Gazette 5576: 1 September 2000

This special publication of the government gazette specifically stated that it is the vision of the Provincial Government of the Western Cape that access to land on the fringe of urban areas and rural towns, and its utilization, will contribute to sustainable agricultural and urban development. Municipalities should prohibit the establishment of residential smallholdings on land suited for agricultural purposes within the urban fringe. While the TRA is not a residential smallholding, the implicit recognition of the need to retain agricultural land on the urban fringe is clear (PGWC, 2000).

Municipal Spatial Development Framework of 2001: Principles and Goals for Planning and Development, Annexure A 2001

The Municipal Spatial Development Framework (MSDF) sets out the fundamental planning and development principles for the City of Cape Town, which include the following:

- Equal Opportunity: All in the City have the right to participate as equals in the planning and decision making process. Also the principles of Sustainable Development must inform all aspects of planning in the development of the City.
- Principle of Sustainable Development: To ensure the enhancement, sustainable utilization and appropriate conservation of the natural environment to sustain essential ecological processes as well as encourage long term environmental diversity and conservation.
- Efficient Resource Utilisation: To efficiently utilize financial, human, environmental and institutional resources to meet basic needs, whilst promoting sustainable development (adapted from City of Cape Town, 2001: 6).

All of these aspects have direct relevance to the Ithemba farmers' case in that this details the principles within which the City is intended to function or at least engage with its community, a situation that has not been enacted in the engagement with the Ithemba farmers.

Policy for Keeping of Animals and Poultry for the City of Cape Town of 2005

This policy presents an interesting case should land use change be attempted in order to accommodate the TRA in the vicinity of the Ithemba farmers. In terms of the Policy for Keeping of Animals and Poultry for the City of Cape Town of 2005 (Special Mayoral Committee 05/09/05) it states that permits to keep animals and poultry are not required for any property zoned for agricultural farming or agricultural purposes, where the primary use of the land is for farming with animals and poultry. On all other premises permits are required. Should rezoning be enacted in order to accommodate the TRA, this could potentially force the Ithemba farmers to seek permits for their existing stock, a process that would result in confrontations with officials while also precipitating the risk associated with the fact that a zoning change could potentially result in a denial of livelihood opportunity.

Conclusions

The Ithemba farmers represent a unique multicultural and multiracial group of farmers, a group whose size, length of period on the land, organizational structure and production approaches make it possibly one of the only such groups within the City. The Ithemba farmers represent arguably one of the future typologies of how food can be produced on a sustainable basis within the City. The knowledge and skill of this group is of great value to the City.

Urban agriculture is an increasing land use form within cities but is often resisted as it is both misunderstood and/or is viewed as both a health risk and something that should remain within the rural environs. This is no longer the case and more and more cities around the world are recognizing the value of urban agriculture in the functioning of the urban system.

It is believed that this is recognized, in part, within the context of Cape Town, as evidenced by the fact that Cape Town is the only city in South Africa to have a specific urban agriculture policy. However, the validity, application and importance afforded to the policy are questioned. While, in this case, the housing programme is driven by the housing department of the regional government and not the city specifically, the failure to recognize the links to the goals of the urban agriculture policy disenfranchises the farmers and undermines their existence.

The Ithemba farmers represent a unique spirit, one of perseverance and collective support. This is a case of social capital being used to build natural capital. These agro-ecological practices provide adaptation strategies that are people centred and focus on building resilience and community innovation.

Adaptation to climate change describes the adjustments people make in response to, or in anticipation of, a changing climate. This is arguably the approach being adopted by the provincial housing officials in the Ithemba case, but the motivation is driven through a need to deliver housing units. Adaptation options to those affected by the climate related challenge of urban flooding are, of course, critical but officials are clearly placing one need above another and the priorities are questioned. The core question is: Why isn't the value of the urban farmers recognized? This question is relevant as it speaks directly to how adaptation is viewed and the processes that facilitate this. Adaptation that takes place at a community level is very different from adaptation driven through official governance structures. Governance (through a top down approach) adaptation comes with other needs and embedded strategies such as political point scoring and potentially even rent seeking (though there is no evidence that this is true in the Ithemba case).

Brown and Funk (2008) argue that climate change threatens human health through, for example, its effect on under-nutrition and food insecurity. Intergovernmental Panel on Climate Change (2007) models indicate that the future climate of much of Southern Africa, and in particular its impact on food security, may have profoundly negative health outcomes. Climate change adaptation is, at best, a social learning process that equips local decision makers and communities to respond to a wide range of difficult-to-predict contingencies brought on by perturbed climates (Ziervogel et al., 2008: 4). The notion of adaptive capacity implies longer term changes in behaviour and livelihood strategies to ensure the maintenance of food and health security for the foreseeable future in the face of changes that are yet to come (Eakin 2005; Berkes and Jolly 2001). This is what is taking place within the Ithemba community and it is at risk from other top down strategies. It is argued that when the real adaptive outcome is diluted with political imperatives, the adaptation is short term and could potentially undermine more than just the affected community.

The persistent shift to an urbanized population and the failure of the region's cities to be the engines of growth associated with urbanization elsewhere implies that the urban question must establish itself firmly on the political and development agendas of national and urban governments, as well as the donor and international development communities. As an increasingly urbanized country, South

Africa's core development challenge will be in the growing towns and cities of the country, marking a major shift away from past concepts of rural development as an engine for social and economic advancement (Frayne *et al.*, 2009).

The above point linked to the dilution challenge poses interesting questions about who leads adaptation, how adaptation is facilitated and the roles played by the various actors within processes of adaptation to climate change. If cities are to have a sustainable future, are to respond to the poly-crises and are to provide the necessary opportunities for future populations, the governance roles in responding and adapting to all aspects demand a very different view of governance and leadership within the city.

Annexure 1

Six most important documents

The documents listed in Table 7.2, produced over the past 12 years, reflect the convergence of a number of crises that are already having a significant impact on the global systems. These, coupled with the global trends (Table 7.3), all point to the need for a fundamental review of how society engages with these systems and the potential consequence of ignoring the challenges.

Table 7.2 Reports reflecting the convergence of a number of crises

Report	Comment
UN-HABITAT – Challenge of Slums (2003)	Detailed the urbanization trend and how most future urbanization will be in the cities of the developing world
UNDP – Human Development Report (1998)	Detailed the fact that development has been severely unequal, where the richest 20 per cent of society account for 86 per cent of consumption expenditure
ASPO Peak Oil Analysis (ongoing) (Association for the Study of Peak Oil, 2011)	Details the fact that we are consuming more oil than we are discovering and predicts peak oil within next 10 years – linked directly to fuel price
Intergovernmental Panel on Climate Change Fourth Assessment Report (2007)	Detailed categorically that climate change was taking place and that it was driven by anthropocentric actions
Millennium Ecosystem Assessment (2005)	Global review of the state of the ecosystems and found that 16 out of 20 were being exploited unsustainably. Presented notion of ecosystem service
International Assessment of Agricultural Science and Technology for Development (2008)	Global review of food systems and argued for a shift to more localized food practice and more indigenized approaches to food security

Table 7.3 Global trends

Trends	Comment
Rapidly growing population	Largely in developing countries and within cities
Hegemonic shifts	Shifts in global economic and social power away from the US and the Organisation for Economic and Co-operation and Development to Brazil, Russia, India and China (BRICs)
Ongoing financial insecurity	Potential for ongoing financial crises and changes to economic system

The components of the poly-crisis are drawn from sources cited. The issues of rapidly growing population, hegemonic shifts and the ongoing global financial insecurities are trends observed from multiple sources by the author.

Notes

1   Farmers in this instance and through the chapter refer to males and females involved in production and beneficiation of a variety of agricultural typologies and within a wide variety of contexts. The term is used generally and refers to all farming unless specifically stated.
2   The International Assessment of Agricultural Science and Technology for Development *Synthesis Report* captures the complexity and diversity of agriculture and AKST across world regions. It is built upon the global and five sub-global reports that provide evidence for the integrated analysis of the main concerns necessary to achieve development and sustainability goals. It is organized in two parts that address the primary animating question: how can agricultural knowledge, science and technology (AKST) be used to reduce hunger and poverty, improve rural livelihoods, and facilitate equitable environmentally, socially and economically sustainable development?
3   This figure for arable land considers only food production and not food production for export, fibre and non-food items or animal feed.
4   From Bruce Frayne – note from food security colloquium Development Bank of South Africa, August 2008 (Frayne, 2008).
5   It has been estimated that Cape Town's ecological footprint is 4.28 hectares per capita (ha/cap). This compares to Canada's 4.3 ha/cap, the USA's 5.1 ha/cap, India's 0.4 ha/cap, and a world average of 1.8 ha/cap. Gasson (2002) arrived at these estimates by following the generally accepted methodology of calculating "ecological footprints", i.e. calculating the inputs and outputs and reducing these to land area equivalents.
6   This figure excludes the 2.5 billion tonnes/year of seawater used to cool the Koeberg Nuclear Power Station (input), and the return to the sea of heated seawater (output).
7   This figure has been revised from the figure used in Gasson (2002). This revision was communicated to the author by Yvonne Hansen, a senior researcher on the Gasson (2002) work. The revision, completed in 2009, was informed by a review of data used to assess the food consumption of the City in the 2002 report.
8   A large portion of the text within this section has been taken directly from the *Western Cape Sustainable Human Settlement Strategy* (Provincial Government of the Western Cape, 2008).

9   The Reconstruction and Development Programme was the housing programme of the first ANC government led by Nelson Mandela after the 1994 elections.

References

Association for the Study of Peak Oil (ASPO) (2011) Understanding Peak Oil. http://www. peakoil.net/about-peak-oil (accessed 26 May 2011).

Berkes, F. and Jolly, D. (2001) 'Adapting to climate change: social-ecological resilience in a Canadian Western Arctic Community', *Conservation Ecology*, 5, 2: 18. http://www. consecol.org/vol5/iss2/art18 (accessed 26 May 2011).

Brown M. E. and Funk C. C. (2008) 'Food security under climate change', *Science*, 319: 580–581.

City of Cape Town (2001) Municipal Spatial Development Framework. http://www.cape-town.gov.za/en/sdf/Documents/MSDF%20REDRAFT%202001%20v2.pdf (accessed 12 August 2011).

City of Cape Town (2007) *Urban Agriculture Policy for the City of Cape Town.* http:// www.capetown.gov.za/en/stats/CityReports/Documents/Population%20Profiles/City_ of_Cape_Town_Socio-Economic_Profile_-_Report_(PGWC)_181220069025_359.pdf (accessed 23 March 2011).

Deelstra, T. and Girardet, H. (2001) 'Thematic paper 2: urban agriculture and sustainable cities', in Bakker, N., Dubbeling, M., Guendel, S., Sabel Koschella, U. and de Zeeuw, H. (eds) *Growing Cities, Growing Food: Urban Agriculture on the Policy Agenda*, pp43–66. http://www.ruaf.org/book/export/html/54 (accessed 26 May 2011).

Eakin, H. (2005) 'Institutional change, climate risk, and rural vulnerability: case studies from central Mexico', *World Development,* 33, 11: 1923–1938.

Frayne, B. (2008) 'Urban food security in South Africa: case study of Cape Town, Msunduzi and Johannesburg', presentation at food security colloquium Development Bank of Southern Africa, hosted by the Development Planning Division of the DBSA, 27 August.

Frayne, B., Battersby-Lennard, J., Fincham, R. and Haysom, G. (2009) 'Urban Food Security in South Africa: Case study of Cape Town, Msunduzi and Johannesburg', *Development Bank of South Africa Development Planning Division Working Paper Series*, 15.

Gasson, B.(2002) 'The ecological footprint of Cape Town: unsustainable resource use and planning implications', paper presented at National Conference of the South African Planning Institution, Durban, September.

International Assessment of Agricultural Science and Technology for Development (IAASTD) (2008) *Synthesis Report: International Assessment of Agricultural Knowledge, Science and Technology for Development.* Washington DC: Island Press.

Intergovernmental Panel on Climate Change (IPCC) (2007) *Climate Change 2007: Synthesis Report, Summary for Policymakers.* http://www.ipcc.ch/pdf/assessment-report/ar4/syr/ar4_syr_spm.pdf (accessed 12 June 2008).

Ithemba Farmers' Association (2010) Documents prepared for legal case. Internal court documents. Cape High Court. Cape Town.

Labadarios,. D. (ed.) (2007) *National Food Consumption Survey – Fortification Baseline (NFCS-FB): South Africa, 2005.* Pretoria: Department of Health.

Labadarios, D., Steyn, N. P., Maunder, E., MacIntyre, U., Gericke, G., Swart, R., Huskisson, J., Dannhauser, A., Vorster, H. H., Nesamvuni, A.E. and Nel, J. H. (1999) 'The National Food Consumption Survey (NFCS): South Africa', *Public Health Nutrition* 2005: 8(5): 533–43.

Millennium Ecosystem Assessment (2005) *Ecosystems and Human Well-being: Synthesis. A Report of the Millennium Ecosystem Assessment.* Washington, DC: Island Press.

Mougeot, L. (ed.) (2005) *Agropolis: The Social, Political and Environmental Dimensions of Urban Agriculture*, International Development Research Centre, London: Earthscan Publications.

Naylor, R. (2008) 'The global food crisis exposes the fragility of sub-Saharan economic progress', *Science*, 323: 239–40.

Provincial Government of the Western Cape (2000) 'Policy for the establishment of agricultural holdings in the urban fringe', *Provincial Gazette Extraordinary*, 5576: 1 September. http://www.capegateway.gov.za/Text/2004/5/policy_urban_fringe_2000.pdf (accessed 23 March 2011).

Provincial Government of the Western Cape, Department of Transport and Public Works (2005a) *Western Cape Strategic Infrastructure Plan.* http://www.capegateway.gov.za/Text/2006/3/provincial_social_capital_formation_strategy.pdf (accessed 12 August 2011).

Provincial Government of the Western Cape (2005b) *The Provincial Social Capital Formation Strategy with an Emphasis on Youth.* http://www.capegateway.gov.za/Text/2006/5/sipoverview_-gate_rev3v4_1_upload2.pdf (accessed 12 August 2011).

Provincial Government of the Western Cape, Department of Environmental Affairs and Development Planning (2005c) *Towards a Sustainable Development Implementation Plan for the Western Cape.* http://www.capegateway.gov.za/Text/2005/8/sdip_august05_eadp.pdf (accessed 23 March 2011).

Provincial Government of the Western Cape (2006a) *Provincial Government of the Western Cape, Socio Economic Profile: City of Cape Town.* http://www.capegateway.gov.za/Text/2007/1/city_of_cape_town_se_profile_optimised.pdf (accessed 23 May 2009).

Provincial Government of the Western Cape, Department of Economic Development and Tourism (2006b) *Micro-Economic Development Strategy for the Western Cape (MEDS): Synthesis Report 2006.* http://www.capegateway.gov.za/eng/pubs/reports_research/M/165989/1 (23 March 2011).

Provincial Government of the Western Cape, Department of Education (2006c) *A Human Capital Development Strategy for the Western Cape.* http://www.capegateway.gov.za/Text/2006/4/hcds_english.pdf (accessed 23 March 2011).

Provincial Government of the Western Cape, Department of Local Government and Housing (2008) *The Road to Dignified Communities, Western Cape Sustainable Human Settlement Strategy (WCSHSS).* Cape Town: Provincial Government of the Western Cape.

Provincial Government of the Western Cape, Department of Economic Development (2009) *Western Cape Provincial Spatial Development Framework (PSDF).* http://www.capegateway.gov.za (accessed 23 March 2011).

Republic of South Africa (1996) *Constitution of the Republic of South Africa, Number 108 of 1996.* http://www.info.gov.za/documents/constitution/1996/a108-96.pdf (accessed 23 March 2011).

Republic of South Africa (2004) *Breaking New Ground: A Comprehensive Plan for the Development of Sustainable Human Settlements.* Pretoria: Department of Housing.

Republic of South Africa (2006) *Accelerated Shared Growth Initiative – South Africa (ASGiSA)*. http://www.info.gov.za/asgisa/asgisadoc.pdf (accessed 23 March 2011).

Schalkwyk, S.V. (2008) 'Farmers hobbled by high input costs', *Mail & Guardian*, 12 June.

Smit, J. and Nasr, J. (1999) 'Agriculture: urban agriculture for sustainable cities: using wastes and idle land and water bodies as resources', in Satterthwaite, D. (ed.) *Sustainable Cities*. London: Earthscan Publications.

Swilling, M. (2006) 'Sustainability and infrastructure planning in South Africa: a Cape Town case study', *Environment & Urbanization*, 18, 1: 23–50.

UNDP (United Nations Development Project) (1998) *Human Development Report 1998 – Overview*, New York: UNDP. http://hdr.undp.org/en/media/hdr_1998_en_overview.pdf (accessed 12 June 2008).

UN-HABITAT (United Nations Human Settlements Programme) (2003) *The Challenge of Slums: Global Report on Human Settlements 2003*, Nairobi: UN-HABITAT. http://www.unhabitat.org/pmss/getPage.asp?page=bookView&book=1156 (accessed on 12 June 2008).

Uphoff, N. (ed.) (2002) *Agro-ecological Innovations: Increasing Food Production with Participatory Development*. London: Earthscan Publications.

van Veenhuizen, R. (2006) *Cities Farming for the Future: Urban Agriculture for Green and Productive Cities*. http://www.ruaf.org/node/961 (accessed 30 June 2008).

von Braun, J. (2007) *The World Food Situation: New Driving Forces and Required Actions. Food Policy Report*. http://www.ifpri.org (accessed 11 April 2008).

Ziervogel, G., Cartwright, A., Tas, A., Adejuwon, J., Zermoglio, F., Shale, M. and Smith, B. (2008) 'Climate Change Adaptation in African Agriculture' (unpublished report), New York: Rockefeller Foundation.

8

CLIMATE CHANGE AND FOOD INSECURITY IN MOMBASA

Institutional and policy gaps

Alfred Omenya, Grace Lubaale
and Collins Miruka

Introduction[1]

The chapter discusses climate change impacts on the urban poor in Mombasa, Kenya. It discusses the relationship between climate change and food security, showing that climate change is a key factor in exacerbating food insecurity in Mombasa. Food insecurity in Mombasa has three main causes: first, the untenable land tenure arrangements; second, climate change impacts both on the island and the hinterland; and thirdly, non-responsive policy, institutional and programmatic frameworks. This leaves the small scale, inadequate efforts of households and communities as the only adaptation means for the poor on the island.

The chapter is arranged in five sections. First is the introduction. The second section discusses the conceptual framework and methodologies that were used in the original study from which this chapter is drawn. The third section discusses the interrelated issues of climate change impacts, food insecurity and land in Mombasa, showing that Mombasa's climate has indeed changed, impacting negatively on food security. The fourth section looks at the current policy and institutional responses to address the dual challenges of climate change and food security, and the intervening variable of land. The fifth, and last, section is the conclusions, and recommendations are made.

Conceptual and methodological considerations

This study was based on Moser's (2009) asset-based adaptation framework. The data were collected through a participatory climate change adaptation appraisal (PCCAA); a rapid appraisal of relevant policies (Rapid Risk Institutional Appraisal), programmes and institutions; and triangulation and validation of results.

The PCCAA was composed of two parts: the asset vulnerability analytical framework and asset adaptation operational framework. The PCCAA appraised the mechanisms through which changes in climate indirectly led to the erosion of assets. This was carried out among diverse groups of the urban poor. Data collection and analysis were undertaken using a range of participatory urban appraisal techniques. The rapid appraisal of current policies, programmes and institutions evaluated municipal, provincial and national institutions and policies, regulations and mandates.

The appraisal also investigated scientific studies, programmes and practices of the different actors in climate change adaptation in Mombasa. It used semi-structured interviews, focus group discussions, observations and workshops. Triangulation and validation involved consultations with different stakeholders and an action planning exercise.

The Rapid Risk Institutional Assessment of the City of Mombasa was divided into three broad components, namely: the biophysical analysis of Mombasa; the mapping of key institutions involved directly and indirectly in climate change adaptation; and the analysis of the policies. These various components fed into a discussion on possible action in regard to development of community adaptation strategies and programmes in low income urban areas.

Twenty-two in-depth interviews were conducted with key informants. These key informants were drawn from provincial government, the City of Mombasa, and key CSOs. The informants from provincial government included planners, and Directors of Meteorology, Environment, Roads, Geology and the Coast Development Authority. From the City of Mombasa, the respondents included the Mayor, the Town Clerk, and the Directors of Housing, Architecture and Planning. A Member of Parliament and a director of an influential philanthropic agency were interviewed. We also interviewed the Regional Director of the Red Cross – a key player in addressing climate change and food insecurity in Mombasa. The interviews focused on the relevance and effectiveness of institutional and policy frameworks and their relationships with observed and recorded changes in the biophysical situation in Mombasa.

This chapter draws on some aspects of this study that are useful in understanding climate change and food security in Mombasa. These include information showing climate change impacts on the urban poor in Mombasa, its impacts on food security, which has already been negatively influenced by land problems in Mombasa, and possible institutional and programmatic interventions.

Mombasa: climate change and food security

Mombasa is Kenya's second largest city; it is also one of the oldest. With one of the best natural deep water harbours on the Eastern African Coast, Mombasa is a key port serving over 100 million people drawn from various eastern African countries. Mombasa developed as a city in the 11th century as one of the many ports serving the dhow trade of the Indian Ocean. In the 13th century, Mombasa attracted the Shiraz from Southern Arabia and Persia as permanent settlers. A small town developed on the east side of the island facing what is now Mombasa Old Harbour (Hoyle, 2000).

The city of Mombasa is located on Mombasa Island on the Kenyan Coast. The Municipal Council of Mombasa also covers districts outside of Mombasa Island. The map in Figure 8.1 shows the areas covered by the City of Mombasa. Mombasa District has a population of 523,183; composed of 268,038 men and 255,145 women. Mombasa is located in the proposed Kilifi County, with a population of 1,109,735 (Government of Kenya, 2009).

Analysis of climatic data from the Kenya Meteorological Department (see Tables 8.1, 8.2 and 8.3) shows that Mombasa's climate has been changing. There is gradual increase in mean temperature; Mombasa has been warming up for the last 50 years. Mean temperature, mean minimum temperatures and mean maximum temperatures have all been rising.

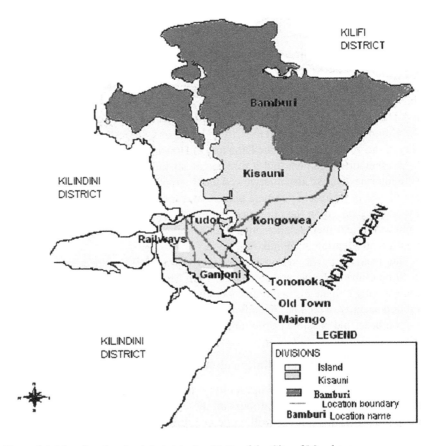

Figure 8.1 Map showing the Administrative Units of the City of Mombasa

The gradual temperature increase has been accompanied by reduction in mean humidity. This is an indication that Mombasa is getting drier on average. The pattern of rainfall is getting more erratic; making it difficult, particularly for the local communities in the hinterland, relying mainly on rain fed agriculture, to plan their agricultural activities.

The data also show significant reduction in visibility and increase in wind speeds. Reduction in visibility could be attributed to higher local pollution, reduction in ground cover, increase in wind speeds and, with that, increase in particulate matter in the atmosphere. Increase in wind speeds also has the effect of reducing the soil moisture content.

Table 8.1 Climate data for a wet month (April) in Mombasa, 1957–2009

Year	Mean temp. (°C)	Max. temp (°C)	Min. temp (°C)	Mean sea level pressure (mb)	Mean humidity (%)	Precipitation amount (mm)	Mean visibility (km)	Mean wind speed (km/h)	Max. sustained wind speed (km/h)
1957	26.3	31	23.1	1010.9	82.3	–	36.2	10.1	23.4
1966	27.1	30.2	24.3	1010.1	77.9	–	37.1	13.8	24.4
1977	26.9	30.6	24	1009.9	80.3	94.24	38.9	16.6	29.8
1987	28.4	32.2	24.7	1011.1	75.7	90.44	28.9	12.5	24.2
1997	26.8	30.8	23.1	1011	83.1	161.3	19.9	11	22.4
2007	27.9	31.8	24.2	1011.7	78	81.27	17.7	12.9	30.7
2009	28.2	32.2	24.7	1011.8	75.2	55.12	16.8	16.3	33.4

Source: adapted from Kenya Meteorology Department Climate Data

Table 8.2 Climate data for a cold month (July) in Mombasa, 1957–2009

Year	Mean temp. (°C)	Max. temp (°C)	Min. temp (°C)	Mean sea level pressure (mb)	Mean humidity (%)	Precipitation amount (mm)	Mean visibility (km)	Mean wind speed (km/h)	Max. sustained wind speed (km/h)
1959	23	27	20.3	1016.7	83.5	–	37.1	11.9	30
1966	23.8	26.7	21.3	1015.3	81.8	–	30.7	14.5	24
1979	23.6	27.9	20.4	1017.2	78.7	43.19	36	16	28.2
1989	23.6	27.5	20.3	1016.4	81.4	43.71	20.1	11.8	23
1999	23.9	27.2	19.9	1016.7	81.5	–	20	14.1	23.5
2009	24.5	28.3	21.1	1017.3	77.2	42.16	17.3	18	35.8

Source: Kenya Meteorology Department Climate Data

Table 8.3 Climate data for a hot month (December) in Mombasa, 1957–2009

Year	Mean temp. (°C)	Max. temp (°C)	Min. temp (°C)	Mean sea level pressure (mb)	Mean humidity (%)	Precipitation amount (mm)	Mean visibility (km)	Mean wind speed (km/h)	Max. sustained wind speed (km/h)
1959	26.5	31.3	23.3	1011.1	79.8	–	34.7	9.2	27.4
1966	27.2	30.9	24.1	1008.6	75.2	–	31.8	15.3	24.6
1979	27.1	31.5	22.8	1011.3	78.5	43.18	35.8	11.3	23.4
1989	26.7	30.8	24.2	1010.7	82.8	111.51	24.4	8.8	19.3
1999	26.9	31.1	22.5	1011.5	80.8	61.73	18.9	8.6	22.4
2008	27.9	32.4	24	1010.9	73.6	19.82	17.5	14.7	30.5

Source: Kenya Meteorology Department Climate Data

Mombasa is endowed with fertile loamy soils suitable for many crops. The region receives adequate rainfall, with an annual average of 1200mm. The Coast Province boasts 3,700 square kilometres of arable land. The key sources of food for Mombasa are mainly rain fed agriculture and livestock on the island and the hinterland, and fishing (Mute and Kibe, 2009).

However, Mombasa, like many parts of Kenyan urban areas, is faced with a deteriorating food security situation (Meijerink *et al.*, 2009). Mombasa is highly food insecure, comparable only to the arid and semi-arid areas of the country and parts of war torn Somalia (see Figure 8.2). Of Mombasa residents, 36.8 per cent face food insecurity. The region has a potential for grain production of 2.5 million metric tons, yet it only produces 0.5 million metric tons, accounting for 20 per cent of its annual requirements.

In their paper on the Kenyan challenges of food security and seasonal climate information, Rarieya and Fortun (2010) identify at least five ways in which climate change affects food production and, by extension, food security. First, extreme weather events such as floods may result either in waterlogged or direct destruction of crops. Similarly, water stress as a result of prolonged drought leads to crop failure. Second, increase in temperature may determine the length and the success of the growing season in terms of crop yield. Third, timing and magnitude factors of the rainy season, for example, when does the season start, how long is the season, when does it end, what is the intensity of rainfall and so forth, influence crop production. Predictability of the season may determine whether crop production succeeds or fails. Fourth, climate induced reduction in ground cover may lead to soil erosion, hence reduction in fertility and crop production. Fifth, increased incidents of weeds, pests, and diseases, because of change in the climate, may lead to use of chemicals, which may have negative impacts on the overall environment year.

There is a clear link between food insecurity and climate change in Mombasa. Mombasa experiences climate induced food insecurity every year (Rarieya and Fortun, 2010). Table 8.4 shows climate related disasters that have affected the city and their impacts on residents' food security. These impacts include: deaths of livestock and destruction of farmlands during the El Niño rains of 1947, 1961 and 1997; annual flooding leading to deaths of livestock and destruction of farmlands, especially in the hinterland on which the island relies for food supply; severe droughts accompanied by famine pushes food insecurity to disastrous levels every four to five years.

Beyond climate change per se there are other recent studies linking climate and food security in Mombasa. A case is that of the planting period for maize and the incidence of June winds. Backed with 39 years of meteorology data, the study (Mute and Kibe, 2009) argues that despite the fact that long rains fall in Mombasa, only one period, that of April and May, experiences positive soil moisture content changes. In the remaining months evaporation exceeds precipitation; thus there is net moisture loss. The paper argues that June winds create a cyclic depression in rainfall amounts, which result in decreased soil moisture content. This in turn affects cereal production, particularly maize, negatively. The paper suggests that 95 per cent of potential maize harvest losses are attributed to the June cyclic winds. The paper proceeds to suggest that maize plantation modelling should be based on the June La Niña effect, rather than on the start of the long rains, around March.

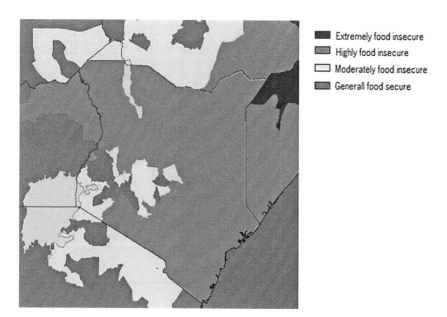

Extremely food insecure
Highly food insecure
Moderately food insecure
General food secure

Figure 8.2 Food security situation in Kenya

Table 8.4 Climate related disasters typology, trends and impacts

Disaster type	When was experienced	Frequency	General impacts	Impacts on food security
El Niño	1947 1961 1997	Approximately five years	Houses destroyed Property lost Livestock and crops lost Human lives lost Increased incidence of disease (cholera, typhoid)	Crops and livestock were destroyed both in the island and in the hinterland Food became scarce and expensive
Floods	Frequently (almost annually)	Unpredictable	Houses destroyed Property lost Livestock lost (all types) Human lives lost Increased incidence of disease (cholera, typhoid)	Affects poor neighbourhoods that have to spread their income between protecting their assets and purchase of food Farmlands off the island get destroyed, making food unavailable and expensive
Tsunami	2006	Unpredictable	Several fishing boats destroyed One human life lost	Short lived and far from the epicentre; did not have direct impacts on food security
Drought	2005/6	Every 4–5 years	All agricultural activities are affected Women spend more time looking for water	Annual droughts are the most critical cause of food insecurity, as livestock die and crops fail They are accompanied by severe famine
Hunger/ famine	Every year	Every year	Loss of human lives from starvation Gross malnutrition and underfeeding leading to poor economic productivity	Effects are felt across all age groups and gender

Source: Danda, 2006

Food insecurity and land

Food insecurity in Mombasa is not only caused by climate change, but also by land tenure problems that are synonymous with this region. Land is a major factor in agricultural production and in wealth creation, thus it is understandable that in the case of Mombasa insecure tenure, evictions, harassment and speculation on land have had the impact of reducing agricultural productivity, hence exposing the people to food insecurity.

The contentions around land were occasioned by gross abuse of the Titles Act of 1908. This resulted in the creation of the largest concentration of landless indigenous people in the Coast Province. The landless people have lived as squatters on government land, land with absentee landlords and idle land, amongst others. Although there have been several statutes governing the management of, access to and ownership of land, the entire legal framework has been perceived by most actors, including the poor and the government, as being obsolete to the extent that it cannot respond to the needs of the squatters, some of whom have occupied the land for generations (Government of Kenya, Ministry of Lands, 2007).

There are five major systems of land allocation and use in Mombasa: the traditional Mijikenda system; the Islamic Sharia law based system; adaptations of the English property law (declaration of title and private property rights in the alienated areas); the pre-independence land tenure reforms in the 'Natives Reserves'; and current systems defined in existing legal and policy frameworks. In the current legal and policy framework, three categories of land ownership exist in Mombasa. They are the government or public land, trust land and private land. Government/public land is reserved for government use, and trust land is administered by local authorities under freehold title in the name of the local authorities. Private land includes all land held on freehold or leasehold tenure by members of the public. In Mombasa, 40 per cent of the land available is government/public land. Private and trust land constitute 35 per cent and 25 per cent respectively (ILISHE Trust, 2004).

Chapter 3.6.4 of the National Land Policy (Government of Kenya, Ministry of Lands, 2007) focuses on 'Land Issues Peculiar to the Coast Province' with its 'peculiar historical and legal origins'. The Land Titles Act (Cap 282) was used to turn indigenous people at the coast into landless squatters, vulnerable to mass evictions and with no access to livelihood opportunities from the sea. Granting of freehold and leasehold tenures to beaches denied locals access to important livelihood sources. Leasing productive agricultural land to salt mining companies has rendered these lands inaccessible to the locals and agriculturally unproductive. Speculative land allocation and inappropriate land uses are threatening marine ecosystems. The new land policy promises to address all these issues and restore land, land use rights and benefits accruing from use of land to the indigenous people of the Coast Province (Government of Kenya, Ministry of State for Planning, 2009). However, this policy has not yet been implemented.

A future aspect of land that is directly related to climate change is the possibility of submergence of sections of Mombasa Island due to rising sea level. Our interviews with a municipal geologist painted a scenario as follows: due to the continued siltation of the coral polyps, the entire ecosystem will be affected, leading to the death of the coral reef. This scenario is possible given the loss of ground green cover and increased runoff and siltation into the ocean. Currently the reef protects the island from flooding. In the case of the reef being unable to renew itself due to the death of the coral polyps, which will lead to the death of the reef, the island will be exposed to flooding. The Intergovernmental Panel on Climate Change *Fourth Assessment Report* (FAR) (2007) estimates that 17 per cent of the island will be submerged with a sea level rise of just 30 centimetres. Agricultural land will not only be lost, but remaining areas will be rendered unproductive due to increased salinity from sea water contamination (Awuor *et al.*, 2008).

The food security problem in Mombasa is worsened by poverty. Table 8.5 shows that almost half the Mombasa population is composed of poor people. As discussed above, most of these people are also landless squatters, in some instances on unserviceable public land, like riparian way leaves; thus they are more vulnerable to the vagaries of climate change. Others squat on public land where adverse possession does not apply. The rest squat on private land and are always under threat of violent evictions. Their limited resources are stretched in ensuring that their basic livelihood needs, including food, are met even when they spread their resources to adapt to the impacts of climate change.

Policy and institutional responses to climate change and food insecurity in Mombasa

Policy responses

Analyses of policies suggest that various policies could help the poor in Mombasa to adapt to adverse weather conditions, and also improve their food security situation. Currently most of these are 'paper policies' and related legal instruments have limited or no impacts on the lives of the urban poor in Mombasa. A key policy

Table 8.5 Population and poverty in Mombasa

Division	Population	Poor population	Poverty (%)
Kisauni	319,104	149,979	47
Changamwe	220,736	105,953	48
Mombasa Island	188,711	64,162	34
Likoni	127,658	61,276	48
Total	856,209	381,370	

Source: Government of Kenya, 2009

gap is the fact that food security, as an urban phenomenon, has been neglected in Kenya generally, the responsibility being left to government departments that deal mainly with rural production, namely Agriculture and Livestock, and also to the emergency related ministries for example, the Ministry of Special Programmes in the Office of the President. The role of the Ministries of Agriculture and Livestock in urban areas has been marginal, while that of the Office of the President has been mainly provision of security. This leaves urban food security in Kenya in a 'no man's land' as far as policy is concerned.

The most important issue for food security, particularly production, is the need to use climate data wisely and link these with agricultural production models. Critical agricultural decisions need to be made with climate and climate change in mind. Climate modelling and prediction therefore need to feed directly into agricultural production (Rarieya and Fortun, 2010).

Kenya has only recently enacted the National Land Policy (Government of Kenya, Ministry of Lands, 2007), hitherto a complex set of land laws, some of which are incompatible, and which created a complex and inefficient land management and administration system (Olima and Kreibich, 2002). This exacerbated the problems of tenure insecurity of the urban poor in Mombasa. With particular reference to the Coast Province, it is hoped that the land policy will address historical injustices and land grievances that stretch back to colonial land policies and laws that resulted in mass disinheritance of communities of their land. Addressing the land issues will enable the poor access to land for food production. It would also enable them to access planning, infrastructure and services, which cannot happen on informally occupied land as per the Physical Planning Act (as revised; Government of Kenya, Attorney General, 2009).

The Integrated Coastal Zone Management Policy (Government of Kenya, National Environment Management Authority, 2007) is another important policy that may impact on the lives of the urban poor in Mombasa. It aims at ensuring that current and future generations of coastal communities – many of whom are poor – realize their basic needs and improve their quality of life whilst maintaining diverse, healthy and productive coastal ecosystems. It recognizes that coastal resources provide food and livelihoods to millions of poor people and if well managed can offer increased potential for nutritional and social needs while maintaining biological diversity. This policy needs to be revised with a focus on climate change adaptation and food security, amongst other things.

Institutional responses

There are gaps in institutional arrangements that need to be addressed for effective adaptation to climate change and food security. There are a number of local institutions that assist communities in Mombasa during disasters but there are no coherent institutional arrangements for these interventions. There are no financial frameworks for climate change adaptation and food security. These should be developed given the high incidence of climate related disasters. Such financial frameworks should adequately highlight climate change adaptation funds for better targeting and impacts.

In Kenya, climate change is still broadly considered as an environmental issue. Climate change related issues in Kenya are dealt with through the Ministry of Environment, especially the National Environmental Management Authority (NEMA). NEMA is a small organization making it weak in dealing with climate change impacts. Currently there are a few initiatives beyond those of the Ministry of Environment, namely efforts by members of parliament to develop climate change legislation and the setting up of a small advisory unit at the office of the Prime Minister. Nothing is being done on climate change adaptation, especially for the poor, by the Government of Kenya. In the disaster management and response sector, there is no clear delineation of general disasters as opposed to climate change induced disasters. Mombasa Municipality has neither the direct mandate nor particular programmes to deal with climate change impacts and food security for urban poor.

Community based organizations (CBOs) and faith based organizations (FBOs) are involved in aspects of food provision, particular during disasters. They approach it mainly from the perspective of relief. Our interviews showed that a number of community based organizations, kinship organizations and informal savings groups are active in helping the poor deal with food security issues particularly during droughts. They also help the poor build some resilience to climate change impacts, particular floods. They do this by providing better wells, improving sanitation, improving housing, and so forth. The support is mainly in the form of provision of food rations and emergency evacuations during floods. Support also comes in cash, mainly from saving groups. Overall, these efforts are short term, uncoordinated, unsupported by the state and therefore limited in scale, scope and impact. In Kenya, it is unclear in which government docket food security is located. The Ministry of Agriculture seems to be in charge as far as food production is concerned. However, in the case of droughts and floods, the responsibility shifts to the Special Programmes Ministry, coordinated at provincial level, through the Office of the President, Provincial Administration Office, with the Provincial Commissioner chairing all disaster response meetings at that level. Various heads of departments at the provincial level, including the Meteorology Department, attend these meetings. However, they focus on disaster response and not prevention. They offer only short term solutions (not long term adaptation) to climate change induced recurrent disasters.

Conclusions

The analysis of information in this chapter leads us to three broad conclusions and recommendations. First, that approaches to agricultural production and food security in Mombasa do not take cognizance of climate change and climate variability. This makes the entire food production system vulnerable to the impacts of climate change and climate variability. It also exposes local residents to perpetual and recurrent food insecurity. Therefore there is need to change the approaches to agricultural production and food security in Mombasa, so that they take into account climate change and climate variability.

Secondly, currently climate change impacts, especially on the vulnerable urban poor, are dealt with both by the state and non-state actors from the relief perspective. This does not address the longer term impacts of climate change, which would require that communities build resilience and adapt to the impacts of climate change. Institutional arrangements involving the Office of the President – Ministry of Special Programmes and Provincial Administration – have focused mainly on disaster response. CSOs led by the Red Cross have also focused mainly on post-disaster relief. This short term focus has left a gap in long term adaptation that needs to be dealt with. Therefore, the state and the non-state actors should develop and shift institutional and policy responses from relief to long term resilience to climate change impacts, including the development of a comprehensive climate change adaptation framework.

Thirdly, in addition to climate change, and institutional and policy challenges, food insecurity is exacerbated by poor access to, use of and planning of land, especially amongst the low income groups in Mombasa. Therefore there is need for further reforms on land use and planning policies, to incorporate climate change adaptation, especially for the poor populations in Mombasa squatting on land with no tenure security. There is a need to deal with the historical challenges that have left most of the poor residents in Mombasa squatters, as indicated in the current Kenya National Land Policy (Government of Kenya, Ministry of Lands, 2007). Planning and provision of infrastructure and services will greatly reduce the vulnerabilities of the urban poor in Mombasa to the vagaries of climate change and its climate induced food insecurity. This can only be done by finding creative ways of providing services in areas where residents still do not have security of tenure, for example, squatters.

Note

1   This chapter is based on the study of 'Pro-poor adaptation to climate change in Mombasa: rapid risk institutional assessment and participatory climate change asset adaptation appraisal in Mombasa, Kenya', by Eco-Build Africa for the World Bank, Washington. We would like to acknowledge the contributions of Professor Caroline Moser (University of Manchester), Andy Norton, the World Bank, Washington, and Titus Wamae (Eco-Build Africa).

References

Awuor, B., Orindi, V. and Adwera, A. (2008) 'Climate Change and Coastal Cities – the Case of Mombasa, Kenya'. *Environment and Urbanisation*, 20: 231.

Danda, M (2006) 'Vulnerability and Capacity Assessment in Mombasa District' (unpublished report), *Survey Report for the Kenya Red Cross Society*, Kenya, Mombasa: Kenya Red Cross Society.

FEWSNET (2009) *FEWSNET Kenya, Food Security Update, July 2008.* http://www.fews. net/ (accessed 2009).

Government of Kenya, Attorney General (2009) *The Physical Planning Act*, chapter 286, Revised edition 2009 (1996). Nairobi: National Council of Law Reporting.

Government of Kenya, Ministry of Lands (2007) *The National Land Policy.* Nairobi: Ministry of Lands.

Government of Kenya, Ministry of Planning and National Development (2008) *Mombasa District Development Plan 2008–2012.* Nairobi: Ministry of Planning and National Development.

Government of Kenya, Ministry of State for Planning (2009) *2009 Census National Development and Vision 2030.* Nairobi: Government of Kenya.

Government of Kenya, National Bureau of Statistics (2007) *Kenya National Bureau of Statistics.* Nairobi: Government of Kenya.

Government of Kenya, National Bureau of Statistics (2009). Population and housing census highlights. *Kenya National Bureau of Statistics.* Nairobi: Government of Kenya.

Government of Kenya, National Environment Management Authority (2007) *Integrated Coastal Zone Management Policy.* Nairobi: National Environment Management Authority.

Hoyle, B. (2000) 'Port Development', in J. Hoorweg, D. Foeken and R. Obudho (eds), *Kenya Coast Handbook: Culture, Resources and Development in the East African Littoral.* Hamburg: LIT Verlag.

ILISHE Trust (2004) *Mapambano: A Documented Account of Land Struggles in Majaoni and Mwembelegeza.* Nairobi: Claripress.

Intergovernmental Panel on Climate Change (IPCC) (2007) *Climate Change 2007: Synthesis Report. Contribution of Working Groups I, II and III to the Fourth Assessment Report of the Intergovernmental Panel on Climate Change* (Core Writing Team, Pachauri, R. K. and Reisinger, A. (eds)). Geneva, Switzerland: IPCC.

Lubaale, G. (2009) 'The impacts of and response to the food, fuel and financial crisis', (unpublished report), Sussex: IDS.

Meijerink, G., Roza, P. and Berkum, S. (2009) *East African Governments' Responses to High Cereal Prices.* The Hague: LEI Wageningen.

Moser, C. (2009) 'A conceptual and operational framework for pro-poor asset adaptation to urban climate change', paper presented at Fifth Urban Research Symposium 2009: Cities and Climate Change: Responding to an Urgent Agenda, June.

Mute, S. M. and Kibe, A. M. (2009) 'The Effects of East African Low Level Jet on Food Security in Horn of Africa: A Case Study of Coastal Region of Kenya'. *African Journal of Food, Nutrition and Agricultural Development*, 9, 8: November.

Olima, W. and Kreibich, V. (eds) (2002) 'Urban Land Management in Africa', *Spring Research Series,* 40.

Rakodi, C. I., Kreibich, V. and Olima, W. (2002) 'Interactions between Formal and Informal Urban Land Management: Theoretical Issues and Practical Options', *Urban Land Management in Africa: Spring Research Series.*

Rarieya, M. and Fortun, K. (2010) 'Food Security and Climate Information, Kenyan Challenges', *Sustainability Science*, 5: 99–114.

9

A SPATIAL PLANNING PERSPECTIVE ON CLIMATE CHANGE, ASSET ADAPTATION AND FOOD SECURITY

The case of two South African cities

Willemien Faling

Introduction

Most studies on climate change in Africa are driven by the atmospheric sciences community and are disconnected from development-related issues. Thus, they remain inadequate to address the interconnected challenges facing the continent (Scholes *et al.*, 2008). If climate change and its effects are left unchecked, the plight of millions of poor households in Africa will only worsen in future. Moreover, should climate change go unabated, it could undermine or even reverse attempts toward achieving sustainable development (IPCC, 2007; World Bank, 2006).

There are strong links between climate change, asset adaptation and food security and the focus of this chapter is on how spatial planning at a city-wide level can reduce the consequences of climate change and contribute to asset adaptation and food security. The chapter describes the vulnerability of South African cities to climatic changes due to a combination of rapid, unplanned urbanisation, and spatial inequalities and inefficiencies. This is followed by a description of climate change risks for livelihoods, poverty, asset adaptation and food security. The second section discusses case studies of two local municipalities in South Africa illustrating the need for development plans that integrate climate change strategies. These cities, similar to others in developing countries, have to confront the dual challenge of protecting the natural environment, whilst pursuing economic growth in a sustainable manner in the face of multiple social, economic, political and environmental stresses occurring at various levels (Government of South Africa, Department of Science and Technology, 2007). The last section explains how spatial planning can intervene at a local level to address climate change, asset adaptation and food security, with the objective of building resilience.

Consequences of climate change for South African cities

Projected climatic changes over South Africa

The Intergovernmental Panel on Climate Change (IPCC) in its *Fourth Assessment Report* projects the following climate changes and variability for Africa: temperature increases, sea level rise, more frequent and severe weather events, flooding, droughts, tropical cyclones and heat waves – with consequences for human settlements, infrastructure, ecosystems, health, energy, housing, water and food security, migration, agriculture, tourism and biodiversity among others (Boko *et al.*, 2007).

In considering these issues, the IPCC expects the annual mean air temperature in Africa to increase between three and four degrees Celsius for the period 2088–2099 compared to 1980–1999 under the medium-high emissions scenario. Using regional climate models, Hewitson and Crane (2006) and Engelbrecht *et al.* (2009) project that South Africa will generally become drier, although summer rainfall will increase over the central interior, the Drakensberg Mountains and eastern parts of the country. A significant decrease in winter rainfall will be experienced in the south-western Cape, and significantly less summer rainfall in the Limpopo Province. The central interior of the country is the only region that is projected to become wetter in the climate scenarios (Engelbrecht *et al.*, 2009). The regional models furthermore suggest an increase in the frequency of heavy rainfall events in South Africa (Meadows, 2006).

Vulnerability of South African cities to climate changes

Not all cities and not all households are equally vulnerable to the impacts of climate change. Vulnerability refers to

> the degree to which a system (community) is susceptible to, or unable to cope with adverse effects of climate change, including climate variability and extremes. Vulnerability is a function of the character, magnitude, and rate of climate variation to which a system (community) is exposed, its sensitivity, and its adaptive capacity.
>
> (UNFCCC, 2010)

Vulnerability thus consists of bundles of natural, physical, economic, social, political, spatial, technical, cultural, motivational, ecological and institutional stresses that are unevenly distributed within society (UNISDR, 2009; Anderson and Woodrow, 1998).

Spatial inequalities and inefficiencies

Spatial inequalities, fragmentation and urban sprawl are characteristic products of apartheid spatial planning. However, in more recent times the need to house the urban poor at a very low cost and within a short time frame has led to low-density housing projects on the urban periphery – entrenching these spatial patterns. The majority of poor households are located furthest from socio-economic opportunities, denying the most vulnerable of the population equal access to employment opportunities, wealth creation and social infrastructure (Government of South Africa, The Presidency, 2006; Boraine *et al.*, 2006; du Plessis *et al.*, 2003). This sprawl and de-densification of cities have created capacity problems for network infrastructure and increased the cost of new service connections. It also means that mass-transit systems are not viable, placing huge transaction costs on the poor by them having to commute increasingly longer distances to and from work using mini-bus taxis (Behrens and Wilkinson, 2003; du Plessis *et al.*, 2003). Thus, poor households that are spatially marginalised have less income and time to invest in assets that could protect them from climate change and food insecurity.

Rapid, unplanned urbanisation

Urbanisation continues unabated in South Africa. Urbanisation in itself is not negative, for there is a strong correlation between urbanisation and economic growth, but the inadequacies in the response by governments to urbanisation increase the vulnerabilities of the poor. Political choices, and not a lack of resources, result in not everyone sharing in the benefits that urban areas have to offer (Satterthwaite *et al.*, 2010).

Due to urbanisation and smaller household formation, the demand for housing and services in South Africa is much greater than the supply by local governments (Boraine *et al.*, 2006). Consequently, informal settlements appear, often overnight, in high-risk zones susceptible to flash floods, landslides and/or sinkhole formation, this either being the only vacant land available, or close to employment opportunities and transportation routes. Informal settlements (unless upgraded) have no infrastructure or emergency service provision, and are constructed from poor building materials. This combination of high population densities, substandard housing and infrastructure, and projected climatic changes deepens vulnerability and puts low-income households at risk of loss of livelihoods, ill health, social tension, deepening poverty and the destruction of productive assets (Laukkonen *et al.*, 2009; Roy, 2009; World Bank, 2008; Parnell *et al.*, 2007; Bulkeley and Betsill, 2005; Annan, 1999).

Climate change risks for South African cities

Urban risk is a consequence of countless feedback loops and thresholds and competing ideas. A relatively minor catalyst can breach the critical threshold and initiate a series of knock-on events with repercussions throughout the urban system (Pelling, 2003). Climate change might be just such a catalyst. For some cities the impacts from climate change may be insignificant, while catastrophic for others, and outside their experience and ability to control. The poorest and most vulnerable communities are most likely to be the most affected (ALNAP and ProVention, 2009; Puppim de Oliveira, 2009).

Poverty, livelihoods and asset adaptation

Apartheid systematically and purposefully restricted the majority of South Africans from meaningfully participating in the economy. The assets of millions of people were directly and indirectly destroyed and access to skills and to self-employment was racially restricted. Partly as a result of this, pervasive poverty and unemployment are the foremost challenges facing the country (Government of South Africa, The Presidency, 2009). Poverty and vulnerability to climate change are closely linked with the most poor usually being amongst the most vulnerable. Parnell *et al.* (2007) describe a number of reasons why the poor are vulnerable: they lack skills and assets and therefore their livelihoods are at risk; cities in developing countries have limited safety nets such as welfare or health care systems; and many have informal or illegal residential status and cannot access welfare.

Households in South African cities have to contend with chronic or everyday risks as a function of their daily existence (Parnell *et al.*, 2007). Everyday risks lower people's threshold of resilience and pave the way for catastrophic events as they have very few resources to fall back upon. At the same time, everyday risks lower people's willingness to prepare for catastrophic events, as risk becomes an accepted part of life. This leads to the ratchet effect of vulnerability where each succeeding event reduces the resources of a household to resist and recover from the next shock (Wisner and Pelling, 2009; Pelling, 2003; Oelofse, 2002).

Many households depend heavily on the climate for their livelihoods, yet extreme weather conditions are common in South Africa, disrupting various socio-economic sectors. More frequent events caused by climate change are likely to deepen poverty and increase vulnerability, since injury, disability and loss of life directly affect the main asset of the poor: their labour (Scholes *et al.*, 2008). "Climate change will almost certainly make the process of eradicating poverty ... more difficult because of direct effects on poor people's livelihoods and the assets upon which they depend" (Laukkonen *et al.*, 2009).

Food insecurity

It is projected that climate change will result in overall reduced food production in South Africa (Benhin, 2006). South Africa is a semi-arid, water-stressed country. Climate change will exacerbate water scarcity due to a combination of increased demand, reduced groundwater recharge and deteriorating quality

(Meadows, 2006). Furthermore, changes in temperature and precipitation due to climate change, coupled with continued emissions of greenhouse gases, will bring changes in land suitability and crop yields. This will result in some cultivated areas becoming unsuitable for crops, and others requiring more irrigation. However, many farmers in South Africa cannot afford irrigation systems, thus when rainfall is late, early or low, it has wider consequences for national food security. Temperature increases will also enhance the ability of pest populations to survive the winter and attack crops in spring (Mannak, 2008; Schmidhuber and Francesco, 2007).

Urbanisation and population growth will further strain water sources and challenge food security as more land is needed for urban expansion, while the demand for food will increase. Food chains have complex linkages: the dependence on long international food supply chains, fuel and other goods makes populations vulnerable to rising food and fuel prices. Climate change-induced disasters also disrupt food demand and supplies, placing particularly low-income households at risk from food shortages or staple food price increases (Satterthwaite et al., 2010). Low-income urban households already struggle to meet their nutritional needs due to an inability to earn a decent income and the high price of food. Whereas households access food mainly through markets, subsistence farming, urban–rural linkages and sharing with other households, studies have revealed an increased dependence on market purchases among low-income communities, resulting in households spending increasingly more of their income on food (Baiphethi and Jacobs, 2009; Hendriks, 2005).

The next section considers the need for spatial planning interventions in two municipalities in South Africa, given environmental degradation and climatic changes.

The case of two South African cities

The Northern and Western Cape provinces in South Africa have been identified as two regions at risk from future climate variation and change (Midgley et al., 2005; Rutherford et al., 1999). Two municipalities in these provinces – George and //Khara Hais – were selected for a study commissioned by the South African National Disaster Management Centre in 2009. This section investigates how the two municipalities, faced with diverse but challenging climates, fared in anticipating and planning for climate change, food security and asset adaptation.

//Khara Hais Local Municipality

//Khara Hais is situated in the Siyanda District Municipality (Figure 9.1) in the Northern Cape Province of South Africa, a unique semi-desert area with hot average daytime temperatures and low precipitation. The municipal area includes the city of Upington, extensive stock farms and a narrow strip of intensive irrigation farming settlements about 15 to 20 kilometres apart on both sides of the Orange River. Agriculture (particularly dates, grapes and cattle), local commerce and tourism are the most significant economic sectors and depend heavily on the Orange River that runs through the municipality. The population is small, and only 25 per cent of the population is economically active, mostly in the agricultural sector. Other development constraints include poverty, poor skills, unemployment and HIV/AIDS (//Khara Hais Local Municipality, 2008, 2007; Siyanda District Municipality, 2008, 2007).

Climate change and environment degradation

//Khara Hais is periodically threatened by prolonged droughts. When it does rain, it results in flooding, erosion, instability in the vegetation and a decrease in biodiversity (Oosthuizen and John, 2005). It became evident from interviews with farmers, businesses and officials that the weather has become more erratic and the seasons have changed in nature. For example, summers have become even hotter and drier with high intensity rainfall. In addition, the water quality has systematically degraded over time because of growing agricultural and industrial

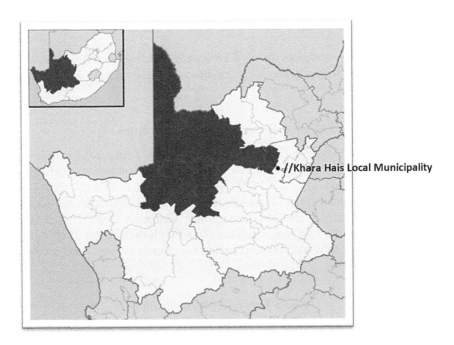

Figure 9.1 Siyanda District Municipality in the Northern Cape Province

activities upstream from //Khara Hais. Injudicious farming on floodplains, over-exploitation of groundwater and overgrazing causes brackish land, erosion, deterioration of the water quality, an increase in alien species, pests and weeds, and a decrease in biodiversity (van Niekerk *et al.*, 2009; Meyer, 2001). These changes in the climate and the environmental degradation have implications for food security (Figures 9.2–9.4).

Tourist activities furthermore cause land and water pollution, fires, destruction of the unique fauna and flora, damage to ecosystems, deterioration of gravel roads and erosion (//Khara Hais Local Municipality, 2008; Siyanda District Municipality, 2008).

Severe weather has a damaging impact on household assets. The residents of informal settlements and former black townships are the most vulnerable to flash floods, owing to gravel roads, substandard building material, poor construction methods and inadequate storm water provision (Figure 9.5). It is also feared that many people will flee farms and rural towns in the vicinity and migrate to Upington if water or employment opportunities become scarce. Climate migrants may seek employment, security of tenure, and access to basic municipal services, schools and clinics thus adding pressure to the already existing backlog on service provision (van Niekerk *et al.*, 2009).

Figure 9.2 Orange River at Augrabies, Northern Cape Province

Figure 9.3 Mr Dawid du Plessis stands in a dustbowl at a water valve almost covered in Kalahari sand, where his family had worked irrigated lands until the early 1970s

Figure 9.4 Damage caused by what locals describe as a "twister cyclone" that hit the farm Klipkolk in the Northern Cape

Figure 9.5 An informal settlement in Upington just before a summer storm erupts

Planning for climate change, food security and asset adaptation

An assessment of the strategic planning documentation of the local and district municipalities have revealed that, though cognisance is taken of environmental degradation and the concept of climate change, there is no climate change strategy for the district, nor any analysis of expected impacts of climate change on, for example, food security. Implicit in all development strategies is to provide poor communities with equitable access to assets such as housing and services, and enabling them to acquire assets such as education. Furthermore, in much of the strategic planning documentation such as the //Khara Hais *Integrated Development Plan* (//Khara Hais Local Municipality, 2007), *Spatial Development Framework* (//Khara Hais Local Municipality, 2008) and the Siyanda *Growth and Development Strategy* (Siyanda District Municipality, 2008) sustainability is encouraged for all future developments in the district, but only the //Khara Hais *Spatial Development Framework* attempts to propose specific interventions to promote sustainable development. One of these proposals is to allow for urban agriculture as a way to improve household food security. In the Siyanda *Growth and Development Strategy* feedback is given on existing community feeding programmes, but no strategies are proposed to deal with food security in an integrated way. Thus no connection is made in any of the documents between food security, asset adaptation and the impacts from climate change. Urban resilience, as a holistic, integrated, multidimensional concept, is not embedded in any of the strategies, while sustainable development mostly remains sophisticated rhetoric.

171

George Local Municipality

The George Local Municipality is situated in the Eden District in the Western Cape Province (Figure 9.6). It lies between the Outeniqua Mountains and the Indian Ocean on the famous Garden Route. The municipal area includes the City of George (including Pacaltsdorp and Thembalethu), the coastal towns of Wilderness, Harold's Bay, Victoria Bay and Kleinkrantz, productive land for agriculture and forestry, national parks, indigenous vegetation, and unspoilt coastline. The George economy is diversified and rooted in agriculture, manufacturing, tourism, trade and business, though all are strongly related to the natural resource endowment of the municipal area. The lowest-income groups in George reside furthest from job opportunities. Unemployment and poverty are also major socioeconomic challenges (George Local Municipality, 2007a, 2007b, 2008a; Eden District Municipality, 2006).

Climate change and environment degradation

Agriculture is a major land use in the municipal area, covering a large percentage of land. Commercial forests have been established by clearing the land of natural vegetation that had, in effect, protected the steep slopes of river gorges – one of the richest floras in the world (George Local Municipality, 2007b, 2008b). From interviews with residents, businesses, farmers and officials, their concern over the climate became clear. Longer periods of drought during winter (the rainy season) combined with bursts of torrential rainfall have been observed to cause "green droughts" (on the surface it looks green, but there is a general lack of water). Heavy downpours trigger flash floods and the run-off is channelled by the

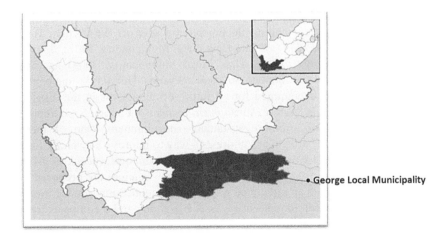

Figure 9.6 Eden District Municipality in the Western Cape Province

many ravines often causing landslides, eroding riverbanks, and damaging irrigation infrastructure (van Niekerk *et al.*, 2009). In addition, the natural vegetation,
forestry and agriculture are threatened by urban expansion, an increase in the
demand for water, the provision of land for small farmers and the development of
big golf estates (Eden District Municipality, 2008b; George Local Municipality,
2007b, 2008b).

Tourism has augmented the recreational activities on the estuaries and the
coastline, putting even more pressure on resources in the coastal zone. The many
residential developments along the coast, as well as the economic, industrial and
commercial activities have a destabilising impact on the environment; the coastal
towns and villages in the municipality are vulnerable to flash floods and sea level
rise. For example, in 2006, severe weather combined with spring tides caused
several roads and major bridges to collapse, dysfunctional municipal services,
rockslides in the Outeniqua Pass, houses in the coastal towns to be flooded and
sand dunes to be eroded from under beach houses (Figure 9.7). However, the most
affected people in George are poor people who settle in informal settlements on
floodplains or hillsides where they are vulnerable to flash floods and landslides
(Figure 9.8). Here their lives, livelihoods and assets are at risk (van Niekerk *et
al.*, 2009).

Figure 9.7 Dunes being eroded from under a beach house in Wilderness, George

Figure 9.8 A township built on a hillside in George

Planning for climate change, food security and asset adaptation

The Western Cape Province developed a comprehensive climate change strategy and action plan in 2008. This strategy still needs to be translated into local interventions. Climate change has been identified as a major threat in a few development planning strategies, and some mitigation and adaptation measures have been put forward in the Eden Disaster Management Plan (Eden District Municipality, 2008a) and *State of the Environment* (Eden District Municipality, 2008b). The latter report also acknowledges that food security and asset adaptation will be impacted by climatic changes, but no countermeasures have been proposed to deal with these challenges. The Eden *Growth and Development Strategy* (Eden District Municipality, 2007) identified a number of actions as part of a livelihood strategy to extend households' access to a portfolio of assets so as to reduce the poverty of communities. Startlingly, the George *Local Economic Development Strategy* (George Local Municipality, 2005) does not even acknowledge food security or asset adaptation. Sustainable development is, however, advocated and promoted in many documents such as the Eden *Growth and Development Strategy* (Eden District Municipality, 2007), *Integrated Development Plan* (Eden District Municipality, 2008a) and *Spatial Development Framework* (Eden District Municipality, 2003), as well as the George *Spatial Development Framework* (George Local Municipality, 2007b, 2008a, 2008b). Yet, it is not linked to climate change, food security or asset adaptation specifically. Though it is clear that climate change is a much bigger reality for George, a similar conclusion can be drawn as in the case of //Khara Hais. Asset adaptation and food security are barely addressed, and holistic, integrated, multidimensional measures to build resilient cities are not yet embedded in development strategies.

In light of the above case studies, the last section explores spatial planning interventions that could address climate change, food security and asset adaptation with the objective of building resilient cities.

Planning resilient cities

Spatial planning as a vehicle to plan resilient cities

At any given time, space embraces people's social, political, economic, environmental and cultural activities and the countless links between them. Spatial development frameworks have therefore become an important long-term, proactive planning instrument across the world (Claassen, 2009).

Spatial planning is the systematic preparation of spatial policies, of which the outcome is a spatial plan (Faludi, 2002). Spatial plans reintroduce the significance of space to public policy. It asks the "where?" of sector plans (Steenwegen, 2006). Spatial plans generally are long-term visions (usually 20 years) that shape future spatial development and infrastructure investment. They:

- are holistic
- provide spatial knowledge to decision makers
- proactively coordinate public- and private-sector investment
- engage communities
- protect resources, or allocate investment to achieve more balanced distribution of economic development
- contain uncontrolled, short-sighted market-driven development.

Most importantly spatial plans coordinate and integrate different socio-economic and environmental sectoral policies on vertical (same territory) and horizontal (between departments) levels ranging from economic development, transportation and environmental protection, to health, culture and language (Biesbroek *et al.*, 2009; Albrechts, 2006; Adams *et al.*, 2006; Alden, 2006; Kunzmann, 2006; Faludi, 2002).

For these reasons a spatial plan is a compelling vehicle to integrate climate change mitigation and adaptation, food security and asset adaptation measures with development strategies (Biesbroek *et al.*, 2009).

Climate change mitigation and adaptation

A resilient city indicates the capacity to successfully adapt to the impact of climate change and is the overarching goal achieved through mitigation and adaptation

(Hamin and Gurran, 2009). Mitigation refers to the reduction of greenhouse gas (GHG) emissions to counter global warming (UNISDR, 2009). Adaptation to climate change "entails taking the right measures to reduce the negative effects of climate change (or exploit the positive ones) by making the appropriate adjustments and changes" (UNFCCC, 2010).

Cities are one of the most important climate change battlefields: the manner in which developments are designed and planned will have a significant impact on future GHG emissions, as well as on settlements' ability to adapt to potential climate change (Roy, 2009; Bulkeley and Betsill, 2005). Likewise, mitigation and adaptation responses have a strong spatial dimension, synergies and trade-offs, hence spatial planning is called the "switchboard" for implementing mitigation and adaptation measures at local and regional levels (Biesbroek *et al.*, 2009). According to Blanco *et al.* (2009: 158) "adapting to climate change is at its core a call for planning" and adaptation is the "type of planning that fits naturally the agenda of urban and regional planning".

Asset adaptation

"Insecure land tenure in the city is arguably the most important single constraint shaping the willingness of individuals to invest scarce personal or communal resources in safety" (Wisner and Pelling, 2009). In the light of projected climatic changes, access to well-located land for the urban poor is crucial for sustainable economic growth, environmental protection, poverty reduction, social cohesion and political stability (Brown-Luthango, 2010). Proximity to social services, infrastructure and employment opportunities will greatly enhance households' resilience to climate change.

The urban land market will not necessarily provide for the poor to access land, therefore intervention in the market is required. In this regard an overall urban land reform strategy for South Africa is proposed by Brown-Luthango (2010), a strategy that identifies vacant/unused plots of land in the city that could be put to productive use. Municipalities will gain access to additional revenue from property tax, and the poor will gain secure rights to land and property as a means to access credit and to generate economic activity. Such a strategy has the potential to facilitate infill development, urban renewal and a more compact city (Brown-Luthango, 2010).

Food security

Spatial planning is seen as an instrument to ensure sustainable development by weighing short-term developmental challenges against long-term sustainability and making trade-offs that minimise conflict between these goals (Roy, 2009). Spatial plans can accommodate growing urban populations whilst also securing water and food by preventing the pollution of fresh water sources and the encroachment of cities on agricultural land. Thus, a land use decision is also a water use decision, and to plan for future food security requires integrated land use and water resource management (Gowing, 2003).

Urban agriculture is often practised by low-income households for subsistence or to augment their income. Increased natural production for consumption has the potential to improve food security in both rural and urban areas by increasing food supply and by reducing dependence on purchasing food (Baiphethi and Jacobs, 2009; Hendriks, 2005). Spatial development plans therefore ought to better protect productive agricultural land, as well as make provision for urban agriculture in appropriate parts of the city (Brown and Crawford, 2009; Boko *et al.*, 2007).

Spatial planning interventions

The nature and location of spatial planning interventions are often a cause for great debate. Questions that arise from this include: What types of interventions are effective in ensuring sustained livelihoods? What kinds of areas afford the vulnerable greater protection against the effects of climate change and meet their needs for food security and asset adaptation? Is it possible in all circumstances to adapt areas to climate change, or is resettlement the only alternative?

The *National Spatial Development Perspective* of South Africa offers some useful principles to guide regional spatial planning interventions. It proposes (1) interventions that promote inclusive and sustained economic growth as a precondition for other interventions; (2) basic service provision to all citizens, irrespective of where they reside; (3) fixed capital investment that focuses on localities of economic growth and/or economic potential; (4) in localities with low demonstrated economic potential, government spending should concentrate on human capital development rather than fixed infrastructure; and (5) that future settlements and economic developments should be channelled into activity corridors and nodes adjacent to or linked with main growth centres (Government of South Africa, The Presidency, 2006). On a local level it is generally recommended that compaction be increased, open spaces be managed better, energy sufficiency be improved, and the need to travel be reduced by creating more public transport infrastructure and integrating land use and transport planning (Bulkeley *et al.*, 2005). This section concentrates on city-wide interventions.

Urban transportation

Urban transportation is one of the biggest contributors to GHG emissions. The functional separation of land uses has increased journey distances and traffic volumes. This decentralisation and dispersion of land uses require an elaborate road network – which has become a bottomless pit of investment, and prevents clusters of high densities that can support public transportation from developing (Belzer and Autler, 2002; Newman and Kenworthy, 1996). The poor bear the brunt of the economic and social costs. Spatial planning can therefore have great mitigating impact in the long term by integrating land use and transport planning. The objectives should be to reduce the demand for private transportation, transport volumes and travel distances. This is done by optimising – often through densification – the spatial distribution and connectivity of urban activities to minimise the distances between land uses. Greater diversity of and accessibility to land uses in neighbourhoods designed for walking and cycling will result in lower automobile traffic volumes. Planning for adequate city-wide public transportation, while simultaneously slowing down or taxing automobiles and increasing the vehicle occupancy rates, will also reduce traffic volumes (Hamin and Gurran, 2009; Grazi and van den Bergh, 2008; Ruth and Rong, 2006). These options require new transport modes and infrastructure, which is an opportunity for adapting critical infrastructure to climatic changes such as severe weather and sea level rise (ALNAP and ProVention, 2009; Bart, 2009). The planning and implementation of appropriate infrastructure should be done thoroughly as transport infrastructure is particularly costly to install and complex to alter once in position (Kithiia and Dowling 2010; Coaffee, 2008).

Cities that have spatially integrated land use and transportation for the sake of climate change, and give priority to pedestrians and cyclists, will greatly benefit the livelihoods and asset adaptation of poorer households. A range of income levels will have more equal access to various land uses and opportunities (Rabinovitch, 1996). Injuries sustained in accidents and health effects from pollution will be reduced (Pelling and Wisner, 2009), and healthier lifestyles are encouraged through active travelling (Barton, 2009). Low-income households will spend less time travelling and less of their disposable income on transport; consequently they will have more time and capital available to invest in assets (Behrens and Wilkinson, 2003).

Urban containment, compaction and densification

Built-up areas worldwide will triple by 2030 if average densities continue at the current trend. Some of this growth is a result of urban population growth, but inefficient spatial planning policies are to be blamed for urban sprawl (World Bank, 2008). Urban sprawl increases journey distances and traffic volumes (Newman and Kenworthy, 1996). It thus disadvantages poor households as explained above and contributes to GHG emissions (Government of South Africa, Department of Housing, 2004). It takes more resources to adapt sprawled settlements to the impacts from climate change than compact cities. Urban sprawl furthermore encroaches on productive agricultural land, thereby threatening livelihoods and food security (Bart, 2009).

Limiting urban sprawl through strategies such as compaction, densification appropriate to a particular culture, urban growth edging, transit orientated development (TOD) and infill development may result in higher densities and a mix of land uses (Lau *et al.*, 2005). These strategies provide benefits for climate change mitigation and adaptation, food security and asset adaptation. This is because they promote greater interconnectivity between land uses; restructure a fragmented, inequitable and inefficient urban form; achieve social and economic diversity and vitality; protect natural and agricultural landscapes; promote optimal and efficient use of resources and infrastructure; reduce the cost of service delivery; allow for poor households to live closer to economic opportunities; intensify land uses; and reduce GHG emissions (Swilling *et al.*, 2008; Ruth and Rong, 2006; Jenks and Dempsey, 2005a; Banister, 2005; Watson *et al.*, 2004; Government of South Africa, Department of Housing, 2004).

Moderate densities on the other hand allow for ventilation between single units as well as for significant green spaces, and may be more effective under certain conditions (Hamin and Gurran, 2009).

Nodes and corridors

A polycentric spatial model clusters city features – particularly those that provide a service to the community – in strategic nodes and corridors. Public transit along these corridors connects the nodes to form a highly accessible, interconnected city. Dense, mixed land use nodes afford choice of lifestyle and location, encourage shared facilities and infrastructure, and prioritise the needs of pedestrians and cyclists (Jenks and Dempsey, 2005b). Thus, low-income households living in close proximity to nodes and public transportation networks have better access to economic opportunities, employment, wealth creation and social services than those households living on the periphery, and have more opportunities and resources available to invest in assets. They are also better able to withstand the effects of climate change, for by being close to nodes, they rely on already existing critical infrastructure such as storm water, sewage, energy, roads and emergency services. Adapting key urban activities to the impacts from climate change such as increased temperatures, different precipitation patterns and rising water levels is also more efficient when clustered than when dispersed (Swilling *et al.*, 2008; Ruth and Rong, 2006; Banister, 2005; Watson *et al.*, 2004).

Green space and urban agriculture

If not well planned, then high densities may result in a loss of permeable surfaces and tree cover that help reduce the need for air conditioning, threaten the carrying capacity of ecological systems, and increase the risk of urban flooding and heat island formation (Hamin and Gurran 2009; Laukkonen *et al.*, 2009). Urban parks, forests and greenery, connected via corridors to allow for animal species to migrate, should be maintained to cool cities and to sequester carbon. The green spaces and corridors should have multiple uses such as urban agriculture, recreation and leisure that can adapt to the impacts from climate change, for example serving as flood retention areas in the case of severe weather (Hamin and Gurran, 2009).

If implemented, the spatial interventions described above would not only have a significant impact on the environment when compared to developments in the 19th and 20th centuries in terms of reduced GHG emissions, but would also contribute to climate change adaptation and benefit low-income households significantly.

Conclusions

Poor urban households in South Africa are particularly vulnerable to the impacts of climate change and food scarcity due to the combination of structural poverty, substandard infrastructure and housing, and historical spatial planning entrenched by current spatial development trends. Increasingly, poor households are forced to live in spatially marginalised areas, aggravating their ability to adapt to the adverse effects of climate change. Spatial planning endeavours to dismantle these spatial distortions and implement interventions that are conducive to meeting the social, economic and environmental objectives of sustainable development. Spatial development frameworks do this by promoting integrated transport and land use planning; growth management strategies such as compaction, densification, urban growth edges, nodes and corridors and infill development; and appropriate higher densities, mixed land uses, and a network of green open spaces. These interventions have many social, economic and environmental benefits, such as allowing low-income households to live closer to economic opportunities, thereby saving time and resources to invest in assets, as well as protecting natural and agricultural landscapes.

The two case studies from George and //Khara Hais are probably representative of many cities in the developing world that do not specifically analyse and monitor hazard and vulnerability factors related to climate change, livelihoods or food security. These are some of the most underestimated issues in spatial planning and habitually left to the "environmental" or "social" people. Local municipalities are so overwhelmed with attempting to provide the basic needs of people and creating decent living environments for the poor, that it should not come as a surprise that climate change has remained a low priority on municipalities' agendas (Robberts, 2008). Given the significance of climate change and its consequences for food security and asset adaptation, sustainable development measures that specifically integrate climate change mitigation and adaptation measures are crucial to spatial planning. Furthermore, action plans must identify localities, allocate budgets and identify responsible people if these measures are to be successfully implemented.

References

Adams, N., Alden, J. and Harris, N. (2006) 'Introduction', in Adams, N., Alden, J. and Harris, N. (eds) *Regional Development and Spatial Planning in an Enlarged European Union*, Aldershot: Ashgate Publishing Ltd.

Albrechts, L. (2006) 'Shifts in strategic spatial planning? Some evidence from Europe and Australia', *Environment and Planning A*, 38: 1149–1170.

Alden, J. (2006) 'Regional development and spatial planning', in Adams, N., Alden, J. and Harris, N. (eds) *Regional Development and Spatial Planning in an Enlarged European Union*, Aldershot: Ashgate Publishing Ltd.

ALNAP and ProVention (2009) *Responding to Urban Disasters: Learning from Previous Relief and Recovery Operations*, London: Active Learning Network for Accountability and Performance.

Anderson, M., and Woodrow, P. (1998) *Rising from the Ashes: Development Strategies in Times of Disaster*, Boulder, CO: Lynne Rienner Publishers.

Annan, K. (1999) *Preventing War and Disaster: A Growing Global Challenge*, New York: United Nations.

Baiphethi, M. and Jacobs, P. (2009) 'The contribution of subsistence farming to food security in South Africa', *Agrekon*, 48, 4: 459–482.

Banister, D. (2005) *Unsustainable Transport: City Transport in the New Century*, New York: Taylor.

Bart, I. (2009) 'Urban sprawl and climate change: A statistical exploration of cause and effect', *Land Use Policy*, 27, 2: 283–292.

Barton, H. (2009) 'Land use planning and health and well-being', *Land Use Policy*, 26S: S115–S123.

Behrens, R. and Wilkinson, P. (2003) 'Housing and urban transport policy and planning in South African cities: A problematic relationship?', in Harrison, P., Huchzermeyer, M. and Mayekiso, M. (eds) *Confronting Fragmentation: Housing and Urban Development in a Democratising Society*, Cape Town: University of Cape Town Press.

Belzer, D. and Autler, G. (2002) 'Transit oriented development: Moving from rhetoric to reality', *Discussion Paper*, Brookings Institution Center on Urban and Metropolitan Policy and the Great American Station Foundation.

Benhin, J. (2006) 'Climate change and South African agriculture: impacts and adaptation options', *CEEPA Discussion Paper*, 21. Pretoria: Centre for Environmental Economics and Policy in Africa, University of Pretoria.

Biesbroek, G., Swart, R. and van der Knaap, W. (2009) 'The mitigation–adaptation dichotomy and the role of spatial planning', *Habitat International*, 33: 230–237.

Blanco, H., Alberti, M., Forsyth, A., Krizek, K., Rodríguez, D., Talen, E. and Ellis, C. (2009) 'Hot, congested, crowded and diverse: Emerging reseach agenda in planning', *Progress in Planning*, 71: 153–205.

Boko, M., Niang, I., Nyong, A., Vogel, C., Githeko, A., Medany, M., Osman-Elasha, B., Tabo, R. and Yanda, P. (2007) 'Africa', in Parry, O.C.M.L. (ed.) *Climate Change 2007: Impacts, Adaptation and Vulnerability. Contribution of Working Group II to the Fourth Assessment Report of the IPCC*, Cambridge: Cambridge University Press.

Boraine, A., Crankshaw, O., Engelbrecht, C., Gotz, G., Mbanga, S., Narsoo, M. and Parnell, S. (2006) 'The state of South African cities a decade after democracy', *Urban Studies*, 43, 2: 259–284.

Brown, O. and Crawford, A. (2009) 'Climate Change and Security in Africa', A Study for the Nordic–African Foreign Ministers Meeting. Winnipeg: International Institute for Sustainable Development.

Brown-Luthango, M. (2010) 'Access to land for the urban poor – policy proposals for South African cities', *Urban Forum*, 21: 123–138.

Bulkeley, H. and Betsill, M. (2005) *Cities and Climate Change: Urban Sustainability and Global Environmental Governance*, Oxford: Routledge.

Claassen, P. (2009) 'Spatial planning, with the Western Cape Province as a case study', in Strydom, H. and King, N. (eds) *Environmental Management in South Africa* (2nd edn), Cape Town: Juta.

Coaffee, J. (2008) 'Risk, resilience, and environmentally sustainable cities', *Energy Policy*, 36: 4633–4638.

du Plessis, C., Irurah, D.K. and Scholes, R. J. (2003) 'The built environment and climate change in South Africa', *Building Research and Information*, 31, 3–4: 240–256.

Eden District Municipality (2003) *Spatial Development Framework*, George: Eden District Municipality.

Eden District Municipality (2006) 'Local Economic Development', *Fact Sheet,* No. 1. George: Eden District Municipality.

Eden District Municipality (2007) *Growth and Development Strategy: Eden Local Economic Development Strategy*, George: Eden District Municipality.

Eden District Municipality (2008a) *Revised Integrated Development Plan: 2008/2009*, George: Eden District Municipality.

Eden District Municipality (2008b) *State of the Environment Report*, George: Eden District Municipality.

Engelbrecht, F. A., McGregor, J. and Engelbrecht, C. (2009) 'Dynamics of the Conformal-Cubic Atmospheric Model projected climate-change signal over southern Africa', *International Journal of Climatology*, 29: 1013–1033.

Faludi, A. (2002) *The European Spatial Development Perspective (ESDP)*, Cambridge: Lincoln Institute of Land Policy.

George Local Municipality (2005) *Placing the Economic Development of George in Context: Background document for the consultation process related to the LED-strategy development of George*, George: George Local Municipality.

George Local Municipality (2007a) *Integrated Development Plan: 2007–2011*, George: George Local Municipality.

George Local Municipality (2007b) *Spatial Development Framework Vol III: Urban Structure Framework*, George: George Local Municipality.

George Local Municipality (2008a) *Spatial Development Framework Vol I: Main Report*, George: George Local Municipality.

George Local Municipality (2008b) *Spatial Development Framework Vol II: Strategic Environmental Assessment*, George: George Local Municipality.

Government of South Africa, Department of Housing (2004) *Breaking New Ground: A Comprehensive Plan for the Development of Sustainable Human Settlements*, Republic of South Africa: Department of Housing.

Government of South Africa, Department of Science and Technology (2007) *South Africa's Climate Change Technology Needs Assessment: Synthesis Report*, Government of South Africa: Department of Science and Technology.

Government of South Africa, The Presidency (2006) *National Spatial Development Perspective. Republic of South Africa*, Pretoria: Government Printer.

Government of South Africa, The Presidency (2009) *Medium Term Strategic Framework: 2009–2014. Republic of South Africa*, Pretoria: Government Printer.

Gowing, J. (2003) 'Food security for sub-Saharan Africa: Does water scarcity limit the options?', *Land Use and Water Resources Research*, 3: 2.1–2.7.

Grazi, F. and van den Bergh, J. (2008) 'Spatial organization, transport, and climate change: Comparing instruments of spatial planning and policy', *Ecological Economics*, 67, 4: 630–639.

Hamin, E. and Gurran, N. (2009) 'Urban form and climate change: Balancing adaptation and mitigation in the U.S. and Australia', *Habitat International*, 33: 238–245.

Hendriks, S. (2005) 'The challenges facing empirical estimation of household food (in) security in South Africa', *Development Southern Africa*, 22, 1: 103–121.

Hewitson, B. and Crane, R. (2006) 'Consensus between GCM climate change projections with empirical downscaling: precipitation downscaling over South Africa', *International Journal of Climatology*, 26: 1315–1337.

IPCC (Intergovernmental Panel on Climate Change) (2007) *Climate Change 2007: Synthesis Report. Contribution of Working Groups I, II and III to the Fourth Assessment Report of the Intergovernmental Panel on Climate Change* (Core Writing Team, Pachauri, R.K and Reisinger, A. (eds)), Geneva: Intergovernmental Panel for Climate Change.

Jenks, M. and Dempsey, N. (2005a) 'The language and meaning of density', in Jenks, M. and Dempsey, N. (eds) *Future Forms and Design for Sustainable Cities*, Oxford: Architectural Press.

Jenks, M. and Dempsey, N. (2005b) 'Conclusion: Future forms for city living?', in Jenks, M. and Dempsey, N. (eds) *Future Forms and Design for Sustainable Cities*, Oxford: Architectural Press.

//Khara Hais Local Municipality (2007) *Five Year Integrated Development Plan (IDP): 2007–2012*, //Khara Hais Local Municipality.

//Khara Hais Local Municipality (2008) *Spatial Development Framework. Vol I–III*, //Khara Hais Local Municipality.

Kithiia, J. and Dowling, R. (2010) 'An integrated city-level planning process to address the impacts of climate change in Kenya: The case of Mombasa', *Cities*, 27, 6: 1–10.

Kunzmann, K. (2006) 'The Europeanization of spatial planning', in Adams, N., Alden, J. and Harris, N. (eds) *Regional Development and Spatial Planning in an Enlarged European Union*, Aldershot: Ashgate Publishing Ltd.

Lau, S., Wang, J., Giridharan, R. and Ganesan, S. (2005) 'High-density, high-rise and multiple and intensive land use in Hong Kong: A future city form for the new millennium', in Jenks, M. and Dempsey, N. (eds) *Future Forms and Design for Sustainable Cities*, Oxford: Architectural Press.

Laukkonen, J., Blanco, P., Lenhart, J., Keiner, M., Cavric, B. and Kinuthia-Njenga, C. (2009) 'Combining climate change adaptation and mitigation measures at the local level', *Habitat International*, 33: 287–292.

Mannak, C. (2008) 'How climate change threatens Africa's food security', *Mail and Guardian*, 25 July.

Meadows, M. E. (2006) 'Global change and Southern Africa', *Geographical Research*, 44, 2: 135–145.

Meyer, S. (2001) ''n Omgewingsentrum as omgewingsbestuursinisiatief vir die Noord-Kaap Provinsie', unpublished thesis, Randse Afrikaanse Universiteit, Johannesburg.

Midgley, G. C., Kgope, B., Morant, P., Theron, A., Scholes, R. and Forsyth, G. (2005) 'Status quo, vulnerability and adaptation assessment of the physical and socio-economic effects of climate change in the Western Cape', *CSIR Report no. ENV/-S-C 2005-073*, Stellenbosch: CSIR Environmentek.

Newman, P. and Kenworthy, J. (1996) 'The land use-transport connection: An overview', *Land Use Policy*, 13, 1: 1–22.

Oelofse, C. (2002) 'Dimensions of urban environmental risk', in Nomdo, C. and Coetzee, E. (eds) *Urban Vulnerability: Perspectives from Southern Africa*, Cape Town: Periperi Publications.

Oosthuizen, R. and John, J. (2005) *Northern Cape: State of the Environment Report – Atmosphere and Climatic Specialist Report*, Pretoria: CSIR.

Parnell, S., Simon, D. and Vogel, C. (2007) 'Global environmental change: Conceptualising the growing challenge for cities in poor countries', *Area*, 39, 2: 357–369.

Pelling, M. (2003) *The Vulnerability of Cities: Natural Disasters and Social Resilience*, London: Earthscan.

Pelling, M. and Wisner, B. (2009) 'Reducing urban disaster risk in Africa', in Pelling, M. and Wisner, B. (eds) *Disaster Risk Reduction: Cases from Urban Africa*, London: Earthscan.

Puppim de Oliveira, J. (2009) 'The implementation of climate change related policies at the sub-national level: An analysis of three countries', *Habitat International*, 33: 253–259.

Rabinovitch, J. (1996) 'Innovative land use and public transport policy: The case of Curitiba, Brazil', *Land Use Policy*, 13, 1: 51–67.

Robberts, D. (2008) 'Thinking globally, acting locally – institutionalizing climate change at the local government level in Durban, South Africa', *Environment and Urbanization*, 20, 2: 521–537.

Roy, M. (2009) 'Planning for sustainable urbanisation in fast growing cities: Mitigation and adaptation issues addressed in Dhaka, Bangladesh', *Habitat International*, 33: 276–286.

Ruth, M. and Rong, F. (2006) 'Research themes and challenges', in Ruth, M. (ed.) *Smart Growth and Climate Change: Regional Development, Infrastructure and Adaptation*, Cheltenham: Edward Elgar Publishing Ltd.

Rutherford, M., Midgley, G., Bond, W., Powrie, L., Roberts, R. and Allsopp, J. (1999) *South African Country Study on Climate Change: Plant Biodiversity, Vulnerability and Adaptation Assessment*, Cape Town: National Botanical Institute.

Satterthwaite, D., McGranahan, G. and Tacoli, C. (2010) 'Urbanization and its implications for food and farming', *Philosophical Transactions of the Royal Society B*, 365: 2809–2820.

Schmidhuber, J. and Francesco, N. (2007) 'Global food security under climate change', *Proceedings of the National Academy of Sciences*, 104, 50: 19703–19708.

Scholes, B., Ajavon, A.-L., Nyong, T., Tabo, R., Vogel, C. and Ansorge, I. (2008) *Global Environmental Change (including Climate Change and Adaptation) in Sub-Saharan Africa*, ICSU Regional Office for Africa.

Siyanda District Municipality (2007) *Five Year Integrated Development Plan (IDP): 2007/8–2011/12*, Siyanda District Municipality.

Siyanda District Municipality (2008) *Growth and Development Strategy*, Siyanda District Municipality.

Steenwegen, L. (2006) 'Sustainable development: Reality or myth?', in Adams, N., Alden, J. and Harris, N. (eds) *Regional Development and Spatial Planning in an Enlarged European Union*, Aldershot: Ashgate Publishing Ltd.

Swilling, M., de Wit, M. and Thompson-Smeddle, L. (2008) 'You the urban planner', in Zipplies, R. (ed.) *Bending the Curve: Your Guide to Tackling Climate Change in South Africa*. Cape Town: Africa Geographic.

UNFCCC (United Nations Framework Convention on Climate Change) (2010) 'Glossary of Climate Change Acronyms', http://unfccc.int/essential_background/glossary/items/3666.php (accessed 19 August 2010).

UNISDR (United Nations International Strategy for Disaster Reduction) (2009) 'Terminology on Disaster Risk Reduction', http://www.unisdr.org/eng/terminology/terminology-2009-eng.html (accessed 19 August 2010).

van Niekerk, D., Tempelhoff, J., Faling, C., Thomson, L., Jordaan, D., Coetsee, C. and Maartens, Y. (2009) 'The effects of climate change in two flood laden and drought stricken areas in South Africa: Responses to climate change – past, present and future', Report to the National Disaster Management Centre, Department of Cooperative Governance, Republic of South Africa.

Watson, D., Plattus, A. and Shibley, R. (2004) *Time-saver Standards for Urban Design*, Digitial Engineering Library, McGraw-Hill, http://accessengineeringlibrary.com (accessed 5 May 2008).

Western Cape Province (2008) *A Climate Change Strategy and Action Plan for the Western Cape*, Cape Town: Department of Environmental Affairs and Development Planning.

Wikipedia (2010a) Eden District Municipality, http://en.wikipedia.org/wiki/Eden_District_ Municipality (accessed 28 April 2010).

Wikipedia (2010b) Siyanda District Municipality, http://en.wikipedia.org/wiki/Siyanda_ District_Municipality (accessed 28 April 2010).

Wisner, B. and Pelling, M. (2009) 'Urbanization and disaster risk reduction in Africa', in Pelling, M. and Wisner, B. (eds) *Disaster Risk Reduction: Cases from Urban Africa*, London: Earthscan.

World Bank (2006) 'Natural disaster hotspots: Case studies', *Disaster Risk Management Series*, 6, Washington DC: The World Bank Hazard Management Unit.

World Bank (2008) *Climate Resilient Cities: A Primer on Reducing Vulnerabilities to Climate Change Impacts and Strengthening Disaster Risk Management in East Asian Cities*, Washington DC: World Bank.

10

CONSTRUCTING THE CLIMATE CHANGE–ASSET ADAPTATION–FOOD SECURITY NEXUS FOR PRO-POOR URBAN DEVELOPMENT

Bruce Frayne, Caroline Moser and Gina Ziervogel

Making the links between climate change, assets and food security

This book set out to explore the utility of a climate change–asset adaptation–food security nexus as a framework for pro-poor urban development. The contextual realities of humanity's collective urban future are that the cities of the global South will not only experience the greatest demographic growth, but that many of the world's poor will live in these cities. Also, climate science models predict that the largest impacts of climate change (and associated extreme weather events) will be in developing countries, with sub-Saharan Africa being the most affected. The urban poor – as we have argued – will carry a disproportionate burden of the costs associated with climate change. The case studies demonstrate that these dynamics between climate variability, assets and food security are indeed major challenges to the livelihoods of the urban poor in the so-called 'wealthy' and 'poor' countries in Southern Africa. In fact an important conclusion from the collection of case studies is that the poor face survival challenges that are similar across urban locations within the region (Figure 10.1).

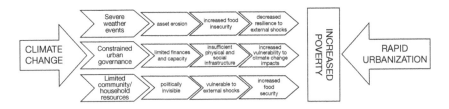

Figure 10.1 Development context of the 'nexus'

Given this context of climate change pressures and rapid urbanization, how then might we think about these compelling issues that link climate change, assets and food security and cities together and, in particular, how these emerging dynamics might affect the most vulnerable and least resilient – the urban poor? What the case studies show is that different actors in society experience the dynamics of this nexus differently, depending on their position and role within that society. Drawing on these different perspectives and experiences, this analysis therefore explores the potential outcomes of climate change and extreme weather events on both assets and food security (which are closely linked).

It is clear that knowledge of climate science at the urban level, and the accessibility of such information to the non-scientific community, will greatly enhance the critically important understanding of the impacts of climate projections on urban vulnerability to climate change. At the same time, such projections that link vulnerability associated with food security to other capital assets may facilitate more appropriate responses and recommendations for policy makers and planners. Using the empirical findings from the case studies and building on Ziervogel's (2009) work on climate and food security, Table 10.1 illustrates the impacts that climate change events are having within Southern African cities on the different capital assets of the urban poor.

These generalized climate change outcomes from the case studies on food security and assets suggest that there are multiple ways in which responses can be conceptualized within this climate change–asset adaptation–food security nexus. However, these are all new cutting edge issues; to date the tendency has been for researchers and planners either to work in 'isolation' on one of these critical climate change concerns, or to identify linkages between two of them, such as climate science and food security. Figure 10.2 describes the multifaceted nature of the links between climate change, poverty and food security, and provides a conceptual view of the emerging adaptation framework, while also identifying potential areas of need/action.

From the urban perspective, appropriate information on urban climate change risks is critical to the development of climate products (and policies) suited to different urban user needs. Part of the challenge here, and as discussed in the George and //Khara Hais (Faling) case studies, is to improve the science–policy–practice interface in order to make proper use of the increasingly relevant city-scale climate data and modelling that is being developed by researchers. This kind of data, combined with community and household level research can assist in understanding household asset adaptation to extreme weather events that are a consequence of climate change. Here the policy response would be to support, through an 'enabling environment', building long-term, multi-generational resilience, limiting damage and rebuilding and transforming the asset base of poor urban communities as illustrated in the cases of Mombasa, Lusaka and Harare (Omenya et al.; Simatele; Tawodzera). In this context, infrastructure development, including income support and social welfare, are important dimensions of an enabling environment; the case of Maputo demonstrates how poor levels of infrastructure combined with severe weather events erode the

Table 10.1 Climate change and its generalized impacts on food security and urban poor assets

Likely scenarios	Impacts on food security outcomes	Impacts on urban poor assets
Average temperature increase of 1°C by 2050	*Food availability* • Overall decrease in stability of food supply • Shorter shelf life for perishable products *Food accessibility* • Reduced availability leads to increased food prices making food less affordable *Food utilization* • Need to eat food sooner with shorter shelf life • Less cooked food required • Might require more fluid intake	*Human capital* • Changes in patterns of consumption • Increase in diseases related to shorter shelf life of food products • Increased on-site food production • Increase household spending on food *Financial capital* • Street vendors and home-based enterprises change perishable products they buy and sell • New investments by street vendors and home-based enterprises to protect perishable goods being sold and shelved • Increased price of perishable food *Physical capital* • Increased demand for water systems in human settlements *Social capital* • Increased pressure on social relations, patronage and reciprocity • Breakdown of social capital *Natural capital* • Staple crops may no longer grow • Crop type substitutions may rise • Possible improvement in crop growth and yield

Likely scenarios	Impacts on food security outcomes	Impacts on urban poor assets
Increased weather intensity and flooding	*Food availability* • Overall decrease in stability of food supply • Decrease in surplus production • Increase in food imports *Food accessibility* • Increase in food prices might make food less affordable • Food supply chains affected, with allocation problems *Food utilization* • Food safety problems due to emergency rations being used • Preferred foods not available • Frequent flooding resulting in people changing food types	*Human capital* • Rural–urban migrations • International migrations • Increased risk of riots and violence associated with access to affordable food in cities *Financial capital* • Street vendors and home-based enterprises change perishable products they buy and sell • Increased price of perishable food *Physical capital* • Increase demands in affordable and adequate land • Increased squatting in vulnerable and risk areas • Increase demand for physical collective assets (basic services and infrastructure) *Social capital* • Increased reliance on reciprocity (informal coping) between households • Health may be negatively affected (especially in cold weather) *Natural capital* • Increased soil erosion and need for fertilizers • Increased damage to crops and reductions in food production

Source: Adapted from Ziervogel, 2009 and Moser and Stein, 2011

Figure 10.2 Climate science–food security–asset adaptation framework

asset base of urban communities. Similarly, policy responses to the impacts of climate change on food security may include pro-poor urban design and planning (linked to physical and social infrastructure), local economic development, urban food production and regulatory frameworks. As vividly illustrated in the case of the Ithemba farmers in Cape Town (Haysom), even though the city is the only one in Africa to have an urban agricultural policy in place, competition between municipal sectors can threaten the food security and capacity to build long-term assets of entire communities. Moreover, the Cape Town food security case study (Battersby) makes it clear that the cross-scale linkages between different sectors in the food system are an important dimension to understanding climate related impacts on urban food security. The more general issue of migration as a result of climate change raised in the regional case study (Dodson) is also important and illustrates cross-linkages, in this case between geographically separate rural and urban sectors.

While this generalized adaptation framework is important as it brings together responses to impacts of climate change on the urban poor within the areas of climate science, asset adaption and food security, the case studies suggest that a programmatic focus on asset adaptation might be a more useful approach. As accumulating diversified assets is central to reducing vulnerability and improving resilience amongst the urban poor, placing asset adaptation at the centre of a framework shifts the emphasis away from climate change to pro-poor development. In so doing, constructing the climate change–asset adaptation–food security framework for pro-poor urban development would have two core objectives (as outlined in Chapter 1):

- At the analytical level, to understand the sources of *asset vulnerability* of poor households, businesses and community organizations in terms of the mechanisms through which variability associated with climate change impacts leads to the erosion of assets.
- At the operational level, to classify the types of *asset adaptation strategies* and sources of reliance that enable households and communities to protect themselves, or to recover, from the negative effects of severe weather associated with climate change.

The remaining analysis draws on the research and discussions in each of the case studies and highlights what we consider to be the most important interventions related to the three phases of the asset adaptation operational framework, prioritizing those focusing on local communities. Figure 10.3 illustrates the links between these three phases of the adaptation operational framework and the different actors in the system.

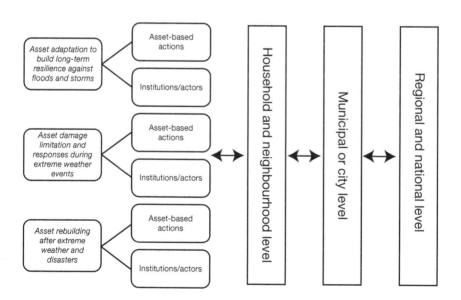

Figure 10.3 Adaptation operational framework phases and system actors

The adaptation operational framework, governance and community

Based on this framework (Figure 10.3), the tables and discussion that follow provide summaries of the three phases of the adaptation operational framework in relation to the system actors at the three scales at which they operate. In Table 10.2, the asset adaptation strategies identified are aimed at *building long-term resilience* against floods and storms. Long-term solutions not only require substantial short-term investment by cities in much needed physical infrastructure, including basic storm water systems and roads, but also preparedness strategies by households and communities at the local level. However, resource-constrained governments at all levels cannot address the current infrastructure backlog in many (if not all) of the cities in the case studies, let alone engage in the kind of proactive planning and capital investment that this analysis indicates is needed. Building intergenerational assets cannot be done unless resources flow into improvements in basic urban infrastructure, particularly as the urban poor often do not have the resources themselves to divert towards addressing their basic needs and, in so doing, building their resilience. Limited suitable land for urban development is a major constraint for the poor and, coupled with insecure tenure in many instances, poses insurmountable risks to extreme weather events. While the case studies show that bottom-up community strategies are widespread, they also point to the lack of government involvement and support in self-directed attempts to build resilience and long-term assets. The inability of municipal and regional/national governments to invest at the neighbourhood level may not be the result of an unwillingness to do so, but rather a combination of limited capacity and constrained resources. Getting access to and effectively using climate data at the city level is a major constraint facing cities in Southern Africa.

In Table 10.3, the framework focuses on responses by the various actors at *limiting asset damage* during extreme weather events. Together with properly developed and maintained infrastructure (as outlined in Table 10.2), early warning systems are one of the most effective ways of improving resilience to extreme weather events. These systems are not only technically capable of identifying risk events, but can (and must) also provide this information to residents in areas of impending storms, which gives them time to put into place bottom-up strategies that help reduce negative impacts. In the case of poor residential areas in the Southern African case studies examined, this simply does not happen. Even in some countries where good early warning systems are in place (for example, South Africa), the means of communicating information with poor communities is not readily available. Overcoming these kinds of constraints is not only a technical matter, but also requires significant cooperation between the household/neighbourhood, city and regional levels of governance. Furthermore, emergency preparedness and the capacity to respond to post-event situations are critical for limiting and/or restoring asset damage.

Table 10.2 Asset-based adaptation framework for long-term resilience against floods and storms

Asset-based actions	Institutions/actors
Household and neighbourhood level	
Households move to safer sites (erosion of financial/social capital)	Households, housing finance agencies
Households improve housing; risk reduction through community space management to install or keep clear drains	Households, community-based organization (CBOs), non-governmental organizations
Households protect productive assets	Households
Household property/possession insurance to protect financial capital	Insurance companies, non-governmental organizations, community-based micro-insurance
Community-based preparedness training including early-warning systems, safe sites and routes to protect human capital	non-governmental organizations, CBOs
Municipal or city level	
Local government provide or upgrade protective infrastructure and adjust official standards for building and land use	In partnership with CBOs and non-governmental organizations
Local government ensures appropriate infrastructure and storm water drains to cope with increased levels of rainfall	Government agencies
Local/city government support neighbourhood improvement actions including slum and squatter upgrading	Government agencies and households, CBOs, non-governmental organizations
City/municipal vulnerability analysis; land use planning to avoid risky sites; wetlands and floodplains retained	Government agencies working with non-governmental organizations and CBOs
Regional and national level	
Risk-reduction investments needed beyond city boundaries	Local and extra-local government
State framework to support the above	Regional and national government

Rebuilding assets after extreme weather and disasters is another important dimension of pro-poor development (Table 10.4). Disasters usually affect all of the five asset capitals, although often the most obvious – and often most significant – is physical capital. Housing amongst poor communities is often informally constructed and is particularly vulnerable to damage by extreme weather events and flooding. Yet faced with ongoing urbanization and pressures for even the most

Table 10.3 Asset damage limitation during severe weather

Asset-based actions	Institutions/actors
Household and neighbourhood level	
Community-based disaster preparedness training including early-warning systems, safe sites and routes	Community-based organizations (CBOs), non-governmental organizations, coordination with state agencies for early warning and responses
Households temporarily move away from high-risk sites or settlements	State provides transport to safe sites to those without access to private transport
Households prepare property to withstand event (e.g. stilts) or move productive assets	Households, CBOs, non-governmental organizations
Adopt cash-based social protection measures	Donors, non-governmental organizations
Reducing risks in affected areas (e.g. draining flooded areas, clearing roads); recovering assets	Government (mainly agencies responsible for disaster response), perhaps international agencies
Municipal or city level	
Preparation of safe spaces with services to which people can move temporarily and organizing corridors for mass evacuation	Government, non-governmental organizations, CBOs. Police and civil defence clear main routes to enable fast evacuation and also to prepare for the distribution of relief aid
Rapid repairs to key infrastructure and services such as health care, safe water provision	Utilities, disaster-response agencies
Human capital and social protection of displaced people, especially for elderly and children	Government ministries of health/education/welfare, non-governmental organizations
Protection of physical capital to prevent looting and further erosion of assets	Police and security services
Regional and national level	
Flood management upstream	Private and state-owned flood management
Disaster early-warning system	State at national and regional level

basic of social services, governments in Southern African cities are hard-pressed to respond positively to post-disaster reconstruction in ways that build the assets of the urban poor. Often the poor are simply left to cope as best they can, relying on NGOs and community-based organizations (CBOs) where resources may be available. Rebuilding in ways that improve assets while minimizing future disasters by reconstruction activities that combine long-term resilience and asset damage limitation strategies must be understood, planned and implemented vertically by and through all levels of governance, including neighbourhoods.

Table 10.4 Asset rebuilding and transformation after severe weather

Asset-based actions	Institutions/actors
Household and neighbourhood level	
Displaced households seeking land rights and titles associated with political capital; rebuilding physical capital	Households, government agencies, non-governmental organizations
Rebuilding houses, homes and physical capital with community involvement that can also rebuild social capital	Households, non-governmental organizations, community-based organizations (CBOs), government
Rebuild productive capital relating to income-generating activities	Relatives sending remittances, financial service institutions
Rebuild neighbourhood infrastructure such as transport links, and water and sanitation infrastructure	Households, CBOs and government
Securing provision of infrastructure to enhance well-being for affected and host populations where relocation has been necessary	Affected and host households, local government, non-governmental organizations
Municipal or city level	
Building/rebuilding infrastructure (to more resilient standards)	Government agencies , CBOs, non-governmental organizations
Rebuilding of systems of safety and security in communities	Police and security systems
Building/rebuilding livelihoods and productive capital	Government working with households
Regional and national level	
Rebuilding productive capital of region	Financial services and banks
Regional reconstruction of natural and physical capital – such as water systems	Contributions of state/provincial governments and national governments to this reconstruction

This framework stresses urban infrastructure as key to asset protection and accumulation across generations, and that this needs to occur within properly resourced municipal/city and regional/national governments. This is no different from other contexts where infrastructure is considered a foundation of development. For example, the C40 Clinton Climate Initiative focuses on infrastructure, with communities 'embedded' in this approach. Here the strategy deals with infrastructure from a climate change perspective on a sector by sector basis, and includes buildings, energy, lighting, ports, renewables, transport, waste and water.

In addition to physical infrastructure, we also argue that in the context of urban poverty and limited resources that characterizes the cities and towns of Southern Africa, social infrastructure must also be directly addressed. While addressing physical infrastructure is a critical mitigation strategy that may have positive spin-offs for the urban poor, building and protecting valuable social assets amongst low-income communities must be centre-stage of any climate change action plan in the context of developing countries. Cities in Southern Africa will not achieve mitigation targets nor will they effectively build human resilience unless the poor themselves are the focus of such strategies. Of the cities participating in the C40 Clinton Climate Initiative, 29 have climate action plans whose targets are all expressed in terms of reductions in emissions (C40, 2011). While reducing emissions is important with long-term benefits that will accrue to the poorer sectors of urban society, these plans generally do nothing to directly address the livelihood needs of the urban poor (who are the most vulnerable and least resilient). The case studies in this book make it clear that pro-poor approaches to addressing climate change must be central to addressing poverty and urban development in Southern Africa; it is not enough to achieve reductions in emissions alone. Climate action plans must be comprehensive and provide a vital opportunity to marry the macro efforts at slowing climate change and the micro efforts of so many urban communities and households to earn a decent living under difficult conditions.

Conclusions

The real challenge that this book raises is for urban governments to bring together these efforts that are at vastly different temporal and geographic scales, and to think creatively about how to use climate change mitigation and adaptation actions to reduce community and household vulnerability and promote asset accumulation and wealth generation for the urban poor, who are the majority in Southern African cities. To do this, the urban poor will need to find their voice in the politics of the city. For the poor to find their voice, the city will have to listen more closely to what they have to say. It is here, at this junction of top-down and bottom-up needs that researchers can play a variety of critical roles. Climate science modellers must continue to strive to make their work relevant to the city scale; social scientists must work to bridge the gap between the language of climate science and city officials and community organizations who need to access and understand this knowledge; and action researchers must work to identify the needs of all actors in the system, and to bring those findings to the policy arena. This climate change–asset adaptation–food security nexus therefore provides a framework that is useful in achieving the dual aims of society of addressing climate change and poverty in Southern Africa (and potentially in other regions too). The framework developed in this book is therefore a start, and we are eager to see how this approach is taken forward and developed further by researchers and urban managers as the dynamics of the climate change–assets–food security nexus unfold.

References

C40 (2011) *C40 cities climate leadership group*, http://www.c40cities.org/ (accessed April 2011).

Moser, C. O. N. and Stein, A. (2011) 'The importance of assets in current development debates: Millennium Development Goals, social protection and climate change', *Global Urban Research Centre Working Paper*, 7. Global Urban Research Centre, Manchester: University of Manchester.

Ziervogel, G. (2009) 'Climate Change and Food Security in the Western Cape', unpublished paper.

INDEX

For Product Safety Concerns and Information please contact our EU
representative GPSR@taylorandfrancis.com Taylor & Francis Verlag GmbH,
Kaufingerstraße 24, 80331 München, Germany

Printed and bound by CPI Group (UK) Ltd, Croydon, CR0 4YY
08/05/2025
01864325-0001